JAMES FORSYTH

JAMES FORSYTH

---- ✶ ----

THREE PLAYS

THE OTHER HEART
HÉLOÏSE & ADELAISE

With an Introduction by
TYRONE GUTHRIE

HEINEMANN

MELBOURNE LONDON TORONTO

William Heinemann Ltd

99 Great Russell Street, London, W.C.1

★

Published 1956

★

Copyright, James Forsyth

344703

822
FOR

Printed in Great Britain by
J. and J. Gray, Edinburgh

CONTENTS

v

ILLUSTRATIONS

PREFACE

BECAUSE I believe that these plays lend meaning to one another I am particularly glad to have them appear together in print. In fact, with the editing of the plays, this belief has grown. And with the fun of contriving a " crest " for this book emerged a rather serious contention: that all three may well be in pursuit of one concept of human dignity.

That is why " Cappa, Cuculla, Corona " is set down as an apt sign for this book. The Cap scholastic, which has affinities with the Fool's cap, holds the laurel wreath of glossy ambition and is a driving force in *The Other Heart*; the Cowl ascetic, which looks not unlike the chivalric helm, holds the thorny crown of a higher aspiration and leads the way in *Héloïse*; and the Crown proper which rises from and is above both, holds the holly wreath of a natural Majesty, and haunts *Adelaise*. The hope is that this concept of human dignity is a little raised by the love in the plays to measure up with a not unpassionate notion of more than temporal Majesty.

In respect of these three plays I owe a special debt of gratitude to the British Broadcasting Corporation in general and to those members of the Corporation in particular who were responsible for taking the unusual step of having radio versions of all three performed within one week (Third Programme, August 1951.) Especially am I indebted in this to E. J. King Bull, who with a deep understanding of their intention, produced all three plays. And to all those in the theatre who had to put up with this dramatist in the writing of and in the thrashing out of the final form of these plays, may I renew my sincere thanks. The birth of plays is quite a business, during and after which gratitude is seldom justly dispensed.

In particular, may I say how grateful I am to Tyrone Guthrie for his many encouragements over many years and his unremitting faith in the outcome of my work; and to Michael Powell for his courageous launching of *Héloïse*.

Anstye, Sussex, *April* 1956.   J. F.

ix

INTRODUCTION

By Tyrone Guthrie

THE way of the playwright whose aim is more than entertainment is not an easy one. Inevitably if he has anything serious to say his work will be considered " difficult ". Managements will wag admonitory fingers, scratch dubious heads, draw in long sibilant breaths and say that The Public will never, never swallow stuff like this; and Managements will be right—*for a time*. But public opinion has a way of catching up with works of art; yesterday's avant-garde becomes tomorrow's rearguard.

The work of James Forsyth has now been avant-garde for fifteen years. That is nothing in the theatre. The theatre-going public still regards Ibsen and Tchehov as moderns. The cinema-going public, if we are to believe our eyes, still regards Homer and the Author of the Book of Genesis as moderns; naughty, saucy, wicked things. The most successful plays, not only in our theatre but the world over, derive technically from Ibsen and Tchehov, but the quintessence of Ibsenism has been heavily diluted with draughts of popular journalism, and then laced with nips of Freud.

To be successful, which in the theatre is synonymous with being popular, a work of art must deal with familiar characters, expressing familiar ideas in a familiar convention. That is why successful plays are very rarely good ones; and why good plays are very rarely successful—*at first*.

James Forsyth's plays are to my mind good plays. That they have not met yet with much success in our theatre is not at all surprising, though it must often have been distressing for the author not to have eaten, and to have felt that his sweetness was comparatively wasted on the relatively desert air.

Why do I admire them?

Are they in any conventional sense tidily constructed? No. In my opinion they do not always tell their stories very well; and

xi

the theme, the philosophy which the story exemplifies, is something I find strangely elusive. But the characters he has conceived are, to me, realised with quite extraordinary intensity and depth.

I think one of the tests of a character in a novel or a play is this: is it static, or does it develop? Great characters are wrought upon, we see them change under the pressure of events. During the course of *Vanity Fair* we learn more and more of Becky Sharp, we both like and dislike her more. Amelia Sedley, on the other hand, remains as she was in the beginning, is now and ever shall be, a bore.

From this test Forsyth's characters emerge with high honours. Abelard and Héloïse, especially in my opinion Abelard, are conceived with extraordinary nobility and force. Their faults are stated as well as their virtues; these are not just a romantic hero and heroine, though they are persons of heroic stature. The interest is to see what the play's events do to them, what they turn into. This, I suggest, is the main interest of all these three plays. They are less concerned with What Happened, than with the Effect of Happenings upon the Protagonists. That is why it does not matter too much that the happenings are sometimes neither vividly nor clearly related.

There is another element which gives these plays remarkable power: their " atmosphere ". The environment of the characters is evoked in a manner which continually reminds us of Shakespeare. They live in a world which is so vividly imagined that every picture, every sound, suggested by the verse to the mind's eye and ear, fits like a piece of an elaborate, magnificent jigsaw puzzle, into a single composite pattern. This pattern, for all its complexity, has an extraordinary unity. Each of the three plays has its own distinct, powerful and interesting atmosphere.

I would instance particularly the long sequence of images which evoke the South West Wind at the beginning of the Third Act of *The Other Heart;* or the vision which Adelaise describes to Friar Peter.

This very power of evocation presents, however, problems of production which have stood in the way of the plays' success. As a producer I am continuously perplexed about how these plays are to be presented in visual terms. With their frequent changes of locality, most of them impossible to realise in naturalistic terms, it is out of all question to use straightforward, representational scenery and effects. Yet a highly simplified, stylised pictorial statement just looks arty and poverty-stricken, unless it is achieved with the economy of genius, the sort of genius expressed in Picasso's setting of the ballet *Tricorne*. I am sure that my own confusion about this matter is no more than a question of date. One belongs to an epoch of mise-en-scène, which, while consciously and intellectually rejecting naturalism, still clings to familiar techniques. For another generation the problem very well may not exist.

I appreciate, in fact, that problems no less hard, which absolutely defy solution in literal, naturalistic terms, pervade the plays of Shakespeare—the storm in *King Lear* for example. But even in Shakespeare they are a formidable barrier to stage production and have caused many otherwise reasonable people to believe that Shakespeare can be better appreciated in the study than on the stage.

A playwright, whose work has yet to win critical and public acclaim, who comes at an epoch when the theatre is still dominated by naturalism which never plagued the First Elizabethans, may well find that the imaginative and technical effort which his work demands of his collaborators in the theatre, is something sadly daunting to the less adventurous.

James Forsyth has, through the auspices of The Old Vic, been able to equip himself for his task by serving a practical apprenticeship in most branches of his craft; and, more fortunate than most " difficult " playwrights, has had a good deal of work produced. The fact that, till now, he has had no great share of critical acclaim, nor any great fortune from " royalties ", does not in the least shake my belief in his quality, nor my confidence that eventually his work will be fully appreciated. Meantime, however, it is pleasant to welcome the appearance of these three plays in print. Not only are they now accessible to those who prefer their plays " in the study "; they are available in a form more durable, and somehow more important, more intimative of immortality than typescript.

Lincolns Inn, *March* 1956.

xiii

THE OTHER HEART

CHARACTERS

CATHERINE DE VAUSSELLES	A widow and gentlewoman of Paris.
MARTHE	Her companion housekeeper.
FAT MARGOT	A woman of the streets of Paris.
FRANÇOIS VILLON	A student of the University of Paris.
WILLIAM VILLON	Guardian of François—an old cleric of St. Benoit, Paris.
PHILLIPE SERMOISE	A priest and friend of Catherine.
CASIN RENÉ DE MONTIGNY " THE SPANIEL " " THE WOLF "	Friends and accomplices of François.
NOAH	A fur merchant and friend of Catherine and of William.
GEMINI	A jailer of Meung-sur-Loire.

1ST CARPENTER
2ND CARPENTER
SERGEANT OF THE PARIS GUARD
1ST GUARD
2ND GUARD
WATCHMAN
CITIZENS AND GUARDS

The action of the play takes place:—before a door in the yard of St. Benoit; before a window in the house of Catherine de Vauselles Paris; by a whipping post; in a cell of a prison at Meung; by a gibbet in Malay-le-Roi.

The play is intended to have two intervals falling after the curtain to Act I and after the curtain to Act II. And the playing time is approximately 2 hours 15 minutes.

The Other Heart was first produced at The Old Vic Theatre, London, on 15th April 1952, and subsequently at His Majesty's Theatre, Johannesburg, July 1952.

It was presented by The Old Vic Theatre Company with the following cast:

CATHERINE DE VAUSSELLES	Irene Worth
MARTHE	Marie Ney
FAT MARGOT	Sheila Ballantine
FRANÇOIS VILLON	Alan Badel
WILLIAM VILLON	Paul Rogers
PHILLIPE SERMOISE	John Horsley
CASIN	Douglas Campbell
RENÉ	Douglas Wilmer
" THE SPANIEL "	Kenneth Griffith
" THE WOLF "	Daniel Thorndike
NOAH	Anthony van Bridge
GEMINI	Rupert Davies
1ST CARPENTER	Rupert Davies
2ND CARPENTER	James Ottaway
WATCHMAN	Richard Davies

CITIZENS AND GUARDS:—Sarn Adeane, Jennifer Bourke, Sonia Graham, Margaret Lane, Joan Plowright, Roger Cage, Rex Robinson, John Walker.

The play directed by Michael Langham

Scenery and Costumes by Hutchinson Scott

Music specially written by John Buckland

4

ACT I

SCENE I

Paris, approximately 1455—Summer evening outside a house with a red door in the yard of St. Benoit.

There is a bench in the yard, and the gate which encloses the yard can be seen. Before the rise of curtain the Deep Bell of the Sorbonne tolls.

On the rise of curtain WILLIAM VILLON *and* PHILLIPE SERMOISE *come in by the gate.*

TWO OF THE GUARD ROYAL *follow them and remain by the gate.*

SERMOISE *and* WILLIAM *proceed towards the door in a rather strained silence.*

(SERMOISE *is a heavy, unctuous sort of clerk with a precise manner covering a violent nature.*)

(WILLIAM VILLON *is an ageing cleric with a benign and intelligent concern for all.*)

WILLIAM: Well, here we are! It was good of you to escort me home—so handsomely (*Nodding to indicate* GUARDS.) and to have shared the " grave risks " we should have run—according to you.

SERMOISE: I assure you, Master Villon, that the risks were not imaginary; nor the Guards unnecessary.

WILLIAM: And I assure you, Monsieur Sermoise, that I have known Paris a great deal longer than you.

SERMOISE: And I am not convinced that that is the best of briefs for impartial judgement on this seething city. (*Dismissing the subject on his own terms.*)

WILLIAM *shrugs and searches for his door-key.*

But you seem to have found a peaceful backwater of Paris? Yes (*Looking round.*)—it must be pleasant to officiate within University.

WILLIAM: Yes—(*Peering short-sightedly at him.*) I dare say that life must seem rather more grim when viewed from the walls of The Chatelet.

SERMOISE: The Bishop's Prison is where I examine.

WILLIAM: Examine? Yes—the Law is a stern vocation, I know. Some other night we must talk away the contents of a bottle of Burgundy. I am trying very hard to make my nephew François take an interest in the Law. (*Again peering at him.*) That would seem to amuse you?

SERMOISE: Hasn't the Law rather taken an interest in him?

WILLIAM: Oh, that? What student has not crossed swords with the Law at some time or another, eh? Just spirit, just spirit.

> *There is the sound, in the distance, of a bell tolled in alarm, to which* SERMOISE *immediately reacts.*

What is it?

SERMOISE (*curtly*): The Alarm Bell of—(*Stopping and pointing.*) What direction is that?

WILLIAM: Mont St. Geneviève.

SERMOISE: Then I have cause to thank God that I brought the guards. I have to go up there (*and then obviously to make an impression socially*) to escort Madame de Vauselles down to the Provost's Torchlight Reception.

WILLIAM (*troubled*): Madame Catherine de Vausselles?

SERMOISE: I daren't disappoint the Provost. He cultivates her. She cultivates me.

WILLIAM: Did you say Madame *Catherine* de Vausselles?

SERMOISE: I did. (*Suspiciously.*) Why?

WILLIAM: A remarkable creature—apparently.

SERMOISE: In what respect?

WILLIAM: Oh—nothing. (*Moving to the red door.*)

SERMOISE (*persisting*): Why did you make that remark?

WILLIAM: I have a slight antipathy, Monsieur Sermoise, to being " examined " on my own doorstep.

SERMOISE: Why did you refer to her as " remarkable "?

WILLIAM: Oh, because of certain evidence. Yes—I found on my François' floor, up there, a poem about this lady.

SERMOISE: A poem? (*Sharply.*) By him? About Madame Catherine?

WILLIAM: To be accurate—two: both highly *remarkable*. Oh, François is above reproach, I am sure. He writes personal poems about everybody. As yet I have still to find the one about me. It will be scurrilous. What did you say?

> *A hubbub of voices is heard in the distance.*

SERMOISE: That is rioting. Which means, Master Villon, your university students again. Well, I hope that your François is not out of doors. For the time for tolerance is gone! (*Moving off.*) Goodnight!

WILLIAM (*calling after him*): If my François is still out of doors he has very good reason to be! He is celebrating his capping today, (*proudly*) as Master of Arts!

SERMOISE (*turning at gate*): And your young Masters of Arts are mostly, Monsieur, veterans of vice! Yes—and the brains of the underworld.

WILLIAM: Oh, you exaggerate.

SERMOISE: I do not! I happen to know that this city is seething in a tide of vice which war has promoted and which now your tolerance fosters! There remains one way—the rod! the rack! the gallows tree! For I tell you, old fool, there comes a time when to forgive your young criminal is to commit every crime you give him the liberty to commit! Come! (*to* GUARDS) Mont St. Geneviève.

> *As* SERMOISE *sweeps out in temper,* WILLIAM *turns away, talking, as one used to his own company:*

WILLIAM: What an unpleasant fellow! (*Moving to door.*) I do believe that our Monsieur Sermoise loves Punishment more than Correction and perhaps Crime more than Criminal Law. Well, no doubt he was exasperated in me —that I showed no criminal tendencies whatsover.

(*Putting key in lock, and with a hint of anxiety.*) I wonder if
François is perhaps in?

> *He opens the door.*

François! (*Calling.*)

> Old WILLIAM VILLON *goes in, calling.*

François! François! . . .

> *As the door is closed behind him there comes Drunken
> Singing off, and approaching:*

CASIN AND " THE SPANIEL " (*off*):

> " *God help both Popes and Paris too*;
>   Till King with the Great Schism cope;
>   Till Dauphin dangles from a rope:
>   Till every parish has its pope—
>   For surely two popes is too few—
>   *God help both Popes and Paris too*; . . ."

> FRANÇOIS *enters, " chaired " between his singing companions,*
> CASIN *and* " THE SPANIEL ".

> CASIN *sings with gusto.* " THE SPANIEL " *sings with reluct-
> ance. And* FRANÇOIS *is blissfully beyond utterance.*

CASIN AND SPANIEL (*advancing step by step with their human burden*):

> " Till the tail-less wolf is dead; . . .
>   Till Paris sleeps at peace in bed; . . .
>   Till stomachs swell with more than bread; . . ."

CASIN: " Till I! . . ." (*Sustained.*)

SPANIEL: " Till I! . . ." (*Sustained with above.*)

FRANÇOIS (*to their surprise—though weakly*):
>   " Till I! . . ."

CASIN AND SPANIEL: "Till we! . . . (*Advancing precariously to bench.*)

CASIN: Can dump this piece of po–et–ree! Rest!

> *They collapse on the bench.*

> *And as they collect themselves the alarm bell again sounds
> and* SPANIEL *gets excited.*

What is it now, Spaniel?

SPANIEL: The bell! (*Shouting in his ear.*) The bell!

> *The alarm bell stops.*

8

I've been trying to tell you all the way down, that *that* is the Alarm Bell.

CASIN: And what if it is, my Spaniel, eh? What if it is! Isn't your nose wet and aren't we all in good condition, eh? And hasn't the Faculty's poet here excelled himself? Eh, François?

FRANÇOIS (*solemnly and to nothing in particular*): No.

SPANIEL: Oh, I wish you gentlemen hadn't celebrated so well. You don't seem to realise what you've done.

CASIN: We have, my good dog, improved the world with wine. And it's a miserable world of miserable people, and needs improvement, eh François?

FRANÇOIS (*solemnly*): No.

CASIN: Again " No ". For the last two streets all he could say to anything was " Yes " or " No ". Now " Yes " has dropped out of his vocabulary, and to all the miserable world may say all our François can say is—(*mimicking him*)—" No ". Isn't that so, François?

FRANÇOIS (*thickly*): No.

CASIN: The scholar with the one-word vocabulary. But up! Master of Arts! You take his prosaic feet. I'll take his poetic head. And we'll dump him on his academic door-step.

They lift FRANÇOIS.

Bring out your bodies! Oh! It's a miserable world, Spaniel—so let's make the misery agony, and sing.

" Till I! . . ."

As they carry FRANÇOIS *with more care than co-ordination towards the red door..*

I said, sing!

CASIN (*miserably*): " Till I . . ."

FRANÇOIS (*faintly*): " Till I . . ."

9

CASIN: " Till we . . ." (*And after a deep breath, rattling it off.*)
    " Outsmart the Swiss, outdrink the Dutch,
      Outgorge the German, outwit the Irish,
      Outshout the Scot, outcount the Jew;
      Till! . . . (*Sustained.*) . . .

CASIN AND SPANIEL:

    " We have rid French France of all
      that's foreign, fat, short, thin and tall;
      and England sinks with all her crew
      under the Atlantic blue! . . .
      Till I! . . ."

SPANIEL: " Till I! . . ." (*Vilely out of tune.*)

CASIN: Till *you*; . . . can sing a damn sight nearer true! . . .

    Alarm bell of district nearer.

BOTH (*versus bell*): " *God help both Popes and Paris too*; "

CASIN: Hup!

    They sling FRANÇOIS *on to the doorstep of the red door, and
    the bell stops. Silence but for a groan from the inert* FRANÇOIS

There! Let him lie. He's pickled. He'll keep. And may
the wolves within the walls not snatch him up—for the
poor beasts would die of indigestion.

SPANIEL: His cap.

    SPANIEL *retrieves the cap from where it had fallen.*

CASIN: Ha, good dog. (*Taking cap.*) Cappa academica!

    CASIN *stands ceremoniously above the bemused* FRANÇOIS *and
    holds his cap out over drooping head:*

Here, I re-present to you this glorious piece of millinery,
presented to you, this miserable day, by the greybeards
of the faculty, in the miserable University of *glorious*
Paris!

    He lets the cap drop abruptly on FRANÇOIS, *who raises his
    head.*

FRANÇOIS: What? Where?

CASIN: Doorstep—threshold of sobriety—about to knock.

> *But, as he is about to knock,* FRANÇOIS *is surprisingly roused into action, and clutches at him to drag him away from the knocker.*

FRANÇOIS: No, no!

CASIN: Oh, but, yes, yes. (*Struggling to hold him.*) Spaniel, hold him!

FRANÇOIS: No! (*Struggling free, and staggering away.*) I will not walk through that blood-red door. (*Subsiding in a heap.*)

CASIN: Evidently. So you've got to be *put* through it. Spaniel, retrieve!

> *They both get him on his feet and face him with the door again.*

SPANIEL: Home, Master François. The alarm has gone. The Guard is called out. It's not safe out here. Go in, please.

FRANÇOIS: No.

CASIN: Are you sober enough to know where you are? It's the yard of St. Benoit—the old red door—of your old ruddy uncle. Get in! (*Forcing him towards the door.*)

> *During this struggle between the conscious and the unconscious,* RENÉ DE MONTIGNY—*the flashy young blade of the fraternity runs in. He is followed by a loping poacher called "* THE WOLF".
>
> *The latter carries an Inn Sign, and as* FRANÇOIS *wrests himself free of the other two his progress is suddenly arrested by this sign with its image of a leopard.*

FRANÇOIS: No; I . . . Oh (*Seeing the sign*). . . . Leopard?

RENÉ: Yes. Friend of yours?

WOLF: You've done it. (*Growling at* FRANÇOIS.) Look—(*Drawing finger down edge of board.*) blood.

RENÉ: Yes, my little Francois, you've done it now.

FRANÇOIS: But, René—what have I done? (*Perplexed.*)

RENÉ (*taking charge of the situation*): Wolf!—stand guard and give
us the sign if the riot begins to swing this way. I would
have our tavern poet here comprehend the corporeal link
between Inspiration and the Law. Hold that up! (*Trans-
ferring the heavy inn sign from the hulking* WOLF *to the little*
SPANIEL.)

WOLF: I don't like the sound of what's going on up there.

RENÉ: As long as it is north of the Rue St. Jacques. (*Sharply.*)
Do as you're told, animal!

WOLF: I don't like it.

> *Growling,* THE WOLF *slouches over to the gate.*

CASIN: What the devil's he done?

RENÉ: Oh, you've done it too.

SPANIEL (*scared*): Have I done it too, Master René?

RENÉ: No, my good dog. You shall have a bone: probably one
of theirs. Hold up the sign!

CASIN: Why, what have we done?

RENÉ (" *taking the bench* " *on the bench*): Did not this poet, in the
first place, conceive the inspirational shape of this inspired
evening?

CASIN: He did.

RENÉ: Did not *he* have the original idea that we should unhitch
every inn sign upon the Mont St. Geneviève—and put
them up for mock trial—" The Jackass ", " The Three-
Legged Donkey ", " The Lion ", " The Lamb " and then
this—" The Leopard "?—No?

SPANIEL: He did, you know.

RENÉ: And did he not preside—cap and all—over the so-called
" court " in the upper room of " The Three Beds "?

CASIN: He did, m'lud. (*Deciding it is all a joke.*)

RENÉ: And was it not *he*—Master Villon, Master of All Arts—
who passed judgment on " The Leopard " here?—" for
the crime of being spotted with the small-pox, when he

obviously had it in him to be emblazoned with the Great Pox "? And did not then *he* commit this poor beast to be, " cast into outer darkness "?

CASIN AND SPANIEL: He did.

RENÉ: *And*—when it was cast out through that upper window and hurtled into the murky night did not *we* hear from the street below a plaintive and quite unrehearsed cry of remarkable anguish?

SPANIEL: *I* did.

RENÉ:—fell slap on the ear of an unfortunately attentive Town Guard.

SPANIEL: Oh dear! (*Scared—as ever.*)

RENÉ: Plaintiff will appear less one ear.

CASIN: Oh, naughtly little François! To lose the ear of the Law— on such a weighty matter too! (*Handling inn sign.*)

RENÉ: And is it not so, that the hand which launched this beast upon that murderous, nocturnal parabola . . . was . . .?

SPANIEL: Yours. (*To* CASIN, *as he leaves the sign in his hands.*)

CASIN: Oh. (*Daunted.*)

> *Alarm bell of St. Benoit itself.*

WOLF (*at gate*): Gardez Loup!!

RENÉ: Here comes the holocaust! After me!

> SPANIEL *needs no invitation and darts off ahead of everybody.*

WOLF: Run! They're by the Mathurins and rolling this way!

CASIN: Spaniel, come—(*Sees he is gone.*) Gone! René! What do we do with the evidence? (*Holding up inn sign.*)

RENÉ: Run and drop it in the Seine.

CASIN (*about to go*): But our little François?

RENÉ: Let him lie! He doesn't know what he's done. Innocence survives! He'll survive! Come!

> RENÉ, CASIN *and* THE WOLF *run out.*
>
> *As the sound of the riot grows* FRANÇOIS *rises unsteadily to his feet, and surveys his cap, ruefully.*

> SPANIEL *and* THE REST *dash back and out the other way,*
> *spinning* FRANÇOIS *in passing. And, as he is doing miracles*
> *to retain his balance after this, a crowd is heard passing in the*
> *street and a* SERGEANT *and* TWO OF THE TOWN GUARD
> *dash in.*

1ST GUARD: That's one of them! Look!—his cap!

2ND GUARD: Now my Master of murky Arts!

> *As they advance on him.*

FRANÇOIS: No. (*Fearfully.*) No.

> *They seize him.*

SERGEANT: Hold the little devil still!

2ND GUARD: Will we take him to the Chatelet, Sergeant?

SERGEANT: No. The prisons are already too full of Masters of
Arts tonight. No. I'll give him a lesson here and now
the University left out of his curriculum.

> *They beat* FRANÇOIS *mercilessly.*

FRANÇOIS: No! It's a mistake! I'll go through the door. Oh!
I didn't mean—Ah!

> FRANÇOIS *is thrown down and kicked aside.*

SERGEANT: And let that be a lesson to you! (*Standing over him
in anger.*) So far tonight there's been two guards killed—
killed!—two! And if I could have my way with you young
gentlemen of University, I'd crucify a whole class of you!

(*To* GUARDS.) Come on!

> *Sounds of crowd off.*

1ST GUARD: There they go again!

> THE SERGEANT *and* THE GUARDS *go.*
> *And as the sound of the riot dies away, a suddenly sobered*
> FRANÇOIS *raises himself up.*

FRANÇOIS: Oh. (*Groaning.*) To this the Hundred Years of War
was Peace. Oh, Fortune . . . there's logic in this somewhere. But why pick on me? (*Looking in hostility at the*
cap.)

RENÉ *runs back in, breathless, as* FRANÇOIS *casts his cap from him, and it lands up in* RENÉ'S *hands.*

RENÉ: Oh. (*Getting breath.*) The whole town is in full cry after the whole Gown. But I hope they drop the chase soon. I'm overdue to a lady. (*Dusting himself.*)

FRANÇOIS: Ah, René, how I envy you your natural gallantry. I could be gallant too (*dreamily*)—by book. Yet with this warm night and the cold moon's light I might—I might get a long way to blinding one woman's judgement with words, till she overlooked the look of me and saw what struggles in my eye; for it's all clear, there.

RENÉ: What? (*His attention being on the world of action and the state of the riot.*) Yes—all's clear. Chaos has moved round the corner. It will always be there. But I must restore the ruins of a promising night. So!——

Plumping François' cap on FRANÇOIS' *head.*

Carry your dusty laurels home. And may the academic cap never quite fit. (*With a sort of protective affection.*) Get in where it's safe, brother poet.

RENE *brusquely bangs the knocker.*

FRANÇOIS: No! (*springing towards the door in alarm*).

RENÉ: What on——!

FRANÇOIS: Sh! . . .

FRANÇOIS *listens apprehensively at keyhole.*

(*Turning in relief from door.*) Thank God he's divinely deaf.

RENÉ: What on earth is the matter with you?

FRANÇOIS: I stand at the cross-roads of life, René. And I am *terrified* to go that way—through that red door.

RENÉ: You?—(*laughing*)—terrified?

FRANÇOIS (*nods*): For, sitting waiting behind that red door, is all of Moses and the Law brought up to date and simplified to one person.

RENÉ: Old William? Huh! *He's* not going to worry about to-night's escapade, even if it gets the length of the Bishop's prison. He's simply going to be overjoyed that you have your cap.

FRANÇOIS: Yes—my cap. And this " triumph " will only spur him on to spur me on to more distinguished laurels. Ugh! You've no conception of that tender tyranny. Ambition, in him, knows no bounds—in me. Master of Arts. Then, Master of Law, Master of Theology, Master of Medicine, and I shouldn't be surprised if we are not, before we're through, Master of the King's Music, too! . . . Me!

RENÉ: Not *you*. (*Laughing.*) For tonight you have put a stop to all study. They'll close University over this riot.

FRANÇOIS: Worse and worse. Then he'll make me become a scrivener's scribbler, right away.

RENÉ: *Make* you? Where's your resistance, man?

FRANÇOIS: Doesn't apply—you don't understand. Once I get myself through that red door I shall come face to face with the most persuasive greybeard gentleness in all Paris. My more than father—Would to God he were less! For when he opens his mouth I just stand and stare, and, no matter what he asks me to do, I answer very dutifully, " I will. Yes, I will ". And I know I shan't. And I know I owe him everything too.

RENÉ: Nonsense, to that! You owe him only the use of his name and the misuse—if you ask me—of your gift for low life and high poetry. To bed, François! For you are on the backwash of barrelled burgundy and liable to love your despondency. I have better company—a certain pneumatic poetic female: Fat Margot.

FRANÇOIS: I had better company still—(*dreamily*) in mind.

RENÉ: Oho? (*Interested.*)

FRANÇOIS: But—to bed.

RENÉ: But if——

FRANÇOIS: No. I can't risk his plans, and his plans are me. He sees how the King is now trying to bring the whole of the war-torn kingdom under one Law—He sees vocations for law makers—hence he sees me—a brilliant lawyer. Me! But, I ask you, *me*! (*excitably*).

RENÉ: All right! All right!

FRANÇOIS: But it's laughable!

RENÉ: Then why not laugh?

FRANÇOIS: At *him*?

RENÉ: Look, Francois. (*With finality.*) See this? (*Holding up cap.*) Sell it for cash. Yes, and spend the cash soon. The old King needs no lawyers now. He needs a priest. As for his son—he'll be King of Chaos. Make hay while you can. For were it Moses himself behind that Red Door—and your hand were the Almighty One that had engraved the Law on the tablets of stone—there wouldn't be even enough time to climb Moses' mountain. And if posterity is worrying him, then let him puff his way up the Mount, and scratch his old initials upon the adamantine posterior of the Devil Stone. It may last. You won't. Nor will I. But if I end up on a gibbet, François, my boy, at least I'll end satisfied. I'll die with the salt smack of life on my lips. And no bitter taste. So!—to Hell with Old William *and* Ambition too. I'm for Fat Margot and the zoo of entire sensations. The Provost's polite society will have to do without Montigny. For the moon's up. Sweet dreams.

FRANÇOIS: No. (*Decisively.*) I'm going in there. And I shall come out again. I shall have it out with him for once and all. His world's the dream world—not yours nor mine. I shall go in there and I shall say, " Uncle William, you are the soul of dead chivalry, defunct generosity and ancient gentility. But, good as you have undoubtedly been to this fatherless piece of Fortune "—me—" it does not give you the right to say. . . ." (*Stopping short as he sees* WILLIAM.)

> *The door has opened and* OLD WILLIAM *comes out and stands there.*

WILLIAM: Ah, Master de Montigny!

RENÉ (*to self*): Moses, in moonlight! (*To* WILLIAM.) Good evening, Master Villon.

WILLIAM: Ah, but we have *two Master* Villons now, haven't we, François?

FRANÇOIS: Yes. (*As he puts the cap behind him to hide its state.*)

WILLIAM: And he has done good work eh, Master René? To get his cap so soon?

RENÉ: Oh, he's done better work since. Haven't you, François?

WILLIAM: What did you say? Better? Oh, yes. We shall go from strength to strength now, shan't we, François?

RENÉ: Shan't we, François?

FRANÇOIS: Yes.

WILLIAM: Well, I take it that you have had quite a night?

RENÉ: Oh, we have. Haven't we, François?

FRANÇOIS: Yes.

WILLIAM: What it is to be young!—and at the crossroads of life! But we must all sleep sometime. Thank you for escorting our scholar home. Goodnight, Master de Montigny. (*Pointedly dismissing him.*)

RENÉ: Goodnight, Master Villon—(*with a flourish to* WILLIAM)— primus.

WILLIAM: My greetings to your father.

RENÉ: Goodnight, Master Villon (*with a flourish to* FRANÇOIS)— secundus.

> RENÉ *goes and* FRANÇOIS *and* WILLIAM *are left alone.* FRANÇOIS, *immobile and avoiding* WILLIAM's *gentle eyes.*

WILLIAM: You might have said goodnight to your friend. Not that I approve of him as a friend. But a little courtesy—a little chivalry—. What is it, François? You haven't lost your cap, have you?

FRANÇOIS: No. (*Producing it.*)

WILLIAM: This afternoon, I was so proud of you. But it is late now, eh? François, you are not ill?

FRANÇOIS: No.

WILLIAM: You haven't got into any serious trouble, have you?

FRANÇOIS: No.

WILLIAM: Well, aren't you going to come in?

FRANÇOIS: No.

WILLIAM (*searching for a reason*): François, you're dreaming again.

FRANÇOIS: No! (*Loudly and looking at him in the face for the first. time.*) I do not dream. I see . . . and what I see is real, is true.

WILLIAM (*puzzled*): What's true?

FRANÇOIS: The . . . the world.

WILLIAM: Yes, of course our world is true. (*Humouring him.*)

FRANÇOIS: Not *our* world. Mine!—the world *I* see.

WILLIAM: Ha, you bad boy! You've had too much wine.

FRANÇOIS: I am deadly sober. And I am not " bad ". I'm wicked. (*Intensely.*) Positively wicked!

WILLIAM (*worried*): François, I don't understand this. . . .

FRANÇOIS: No, (*quickly*) and never will.

WILLIAM: François. (*Slowly.*) This is no way to talk to *me*. I am tired. I have waited up some time. And I have allowed you, for this special night, every sort of liberty. And now you (*at a loss*) . . . I am offended. Oh, but you do not know what you say. It is the fumes of hypocrene, eh? Come— my wicked one! (*Putting his arm round* FRANÇOIS' *shoulders and guiding him towards door.*)

FRANÇOIS (*weakening, then shaking himself free*): No! I have reached a conclusion.

WILLIAM: Will you stop this nonsense and come in! I cannot stand here all night arguing. (*Testily.*) Are you coming in.

FRANÇOIS: No.

WILLIAM (*nonplussed*): And what do you propose to do at this hour?

FRANÇOIS: Live my life at any hour. I have lived yours hour by hour, day by day—up till now.

WILLIAM: I . . . I . . . just cannot understand you at all.

FRANÇOIS: Will you remember that, dear Uncle? (*Almost tenderly.*) Will you?

WILLIAM: Remember what?

FRANÇOIS: That you *cannot* understand me?—Please?

WILLIAM: François, I don't know quite what you are trying to say. But before you say anything more hurtful, will you remember this; that nobody will understand you; that nobody understands me; that nobody understands anybody in the way you think.

FRANÇOIS: That's not true.

WILLIAM: Oh, but it is. And remember this. That I love you. Yes, love you—and that, my boy, is more than understanding. You will find that out. But go wherever you would go tonight. Do whatever you would do. I will not stop you. I can't. You can. And God will, certainly. God forgive you! Take the key!

> *He almost throws the key at* FRANÇOIS' *feet and, going in, slams the door.*

> FRANÇOIS *looks at the key lying at his feet.*

FRANÇOIS (*with a sort of quiet amazement*): I've done it.

> RENÉ, *who has obviously been eavesdropping, slips back in.*

RENÉ: Bravo, François! Now, come.

FRANÇOIS: No. (*Still facing the door.*) I am going alone. My life is my own. But——

> FRANÇOIS *proceeds deliberately towards the red door and places the cap on the knocker.*

This, Old William, belongs to you far more than it does to me.

> *Leaving the cap hanging on the knocker he turns towards the gate, brushing past* RENÉ.

RENÉ: Hey! Where are you off to?

FRANÇOIS: I wonder. (*Stopping and looking at gate.*) Yes—I wonder. I am free. The moon is rising over Paris now, as it has risen year after year, within its lunar constancy;

thousands of people turn in towards sleep,
in the expectation of a morning they'll know.
For the world presumes the world will be so;
but I . . . wonder.

      FRANÇOIS *slips out into the night.*

RENÉ: Oh. (*Putting his hands up in mock prayer.*) From worse
than the leopard, Lord!—preserve.

      RENÉ *hears the door opening behind him and runs out. Then
as curtain begins to fall,* OLD WILLIAM *peers out at the
empty yard.*

WILLIAM: François?

      He turns to see the cap hanging in front of his face as . . .

THE CURTAIN FALLS

SCENE II

*A room in the House of Catherine de Vausselles. The same night—
later.*

Before rise of curtain there are sounds of riot in the streets.

On rise of curtain MARTHE *comes in and, crossing, looks down and out
of the window. She seems concerned at what she sees.*

CATHERINE *comes in, coming up from the street.*

MARTHE: Did they draw your carriage right up the hill?

CATHERINE: Yes. (*Laughing breathlessly.*) Lord knows what the
madcaps will think of next.

MARTHE: But you are back early, surely? (*Assisting* CATHERINE
off with cloak.) What happened, Madame Catherine?

CATHERINE: Later. I'm too breathless to explain. And Monsieur
Sermoise is coming upstairs. He has even less breath
than I, but he is full of explanations. Ask him.

      PHILLIPE SERMOISE *comes in, and stands panting from
exertion.*

21

SERMOISE: Devils! They don't deserve protection of Church. Devils! And I mean devils. I mean Hell's agents. I do!

As CATHERINE, *still laughing, takes off her hood.*

Oh, you may laugh at me, Madame Catherine, but I have seen how these gifted young devils may grow, till in the dungeons of the Chatelet they are hoary satans. And as for that young devil! Madame Catherine you should have let me lay hands upon him there and then and——. (*Gasping for breath.*)

CATHERINE: Gently, gently, my dear Monsieur Sermoise. If your concern is really for me—here I am, home, safe and sound. I hope I still have a carriage horse; but it's my only serious concern.

MARTHE: Yes, madame, I saw the horse arrive.

SERMOISE: And with that devil of the devils on it's back!

CATHERINE: Which devil now? You have populated Paris to-night with legions of devils. They are only amused and amusing students.

SERMOISE: That is not true! (*Violently.*) There are two forces drive us, Catherine. (*Hysterically.*) Two! Evil and Good. And it is not the force of Good which drives these creatures to destruction, pillage, and . . . rape . . . yes . . . and . . .

CATHERINE: . . . Very well! (*Impatiently.*) very well!

SERMOISE: And that devil on the horse's back was him.

CATHERINE: Oh! Really! It was? Well, there's no harm done.

SERMOISE: No harm! (*Gasping.*) Is it harmless to insult you in company with his ribald verses and then . . . (*choking*).

CATHERINE: Marthe, wine for Monsieur Sermoise. (*As* MARTHE *gets wine.*) You must not get so agitated about this.

SERMOISE: But am I to take no action against him?

CATHERINE: No, Phillipe. That is up to me—if I choose.

SERMOISE (*distraught*): Catherine, you cannot approve of this—this——

CATHERINE:—Scamp—not devil. He has wit. I approve of that. (*As wine arrives by* MARTHE's *hand.*) Drink.

SERMOISE: But, Catherine, he is a common clerk, a nobody, an adopted pauper . . . and you . . . you . . . everyone knows how the Provost himself . . . worships you, and I . . .

CATHERINE (*curtly*): Drink!

SERMOISE: If his mind is as vulgar as his verses, then . . .

CATHERINE: Drink!

SERMOISE (*drinking*): To your beauty and to . . . your beauty!
(*He drinks his glass in one gulp.*)

MARTHE (*with wine bottle*): Will Monsieur Sermoise have more of the . . .

CATHERINE (*shortly*): No.

Crowd cheering off.

MARTHE: Your carriage has now been unhitched of ten two-legged donkeys.

SERMOISE: I shall raise the Royal Guard and clear them all back into their colleges. Oh!

As there is a knocking on the street door below.

That is the street door—isn't it?

CATHERINE: It is all right. It is a strong door.

SERMOISE (*to* MARTHE): Let no one in. No one!

CATHERINE: Let Monsieur Sermoise out. You can go through the garden. (*To* SERMOISE.) Wouldn't that perhaps be wiser?

SERMOISE: Yes, I suppose so. (*Uncertainly.*) Yes. But, Catherine, you were deeply insulted.

CATHERINE: Yes, I was insulted. Now, goodnight.

SERMOISE: But how can I let it go unpunished?

CATHERINE: You must find a way. Goodnight . . . Phillipe.

SERMOISE: Goodnight . . . Catherine. (*Kissing her hand.*)

Further knocking on the door below.

CATHERINE: And, Marthe dear, (*as they go*) on your way back do see who it is at the street door.

23

SERMOISE: But—(*Turning in amazement.*)—you know who it is. Catherine—Catherine, disrespect of womanhood is the very seed of the chaos they sow. I will not allow you to demean yourself by——

CATHERINE (*interrupting angrily*): How dare you!

SERMOISE: No!—(*Losing control.*)—I *will not* stand aside and see your beauty debased just because you refuse to see that Hell-pit itself can gape at your feet, that our world's in eruption! That not all the wealth that the worldly Provost can lavish on you can protect you as I can. But . . .

> *As he sees her scorn and realises how far he has gone.*

I . . . (*abjectly*) . . . I love you. (*Turning away.*) Goodnight . . . Catherine.

CATHERINE: Good*bye* . . . Monsieur Sermoise.

> *He turns at the finality of her words.*

MARTHE (*gently*): Come along, Monsieur. (*And as they go.*) Be careful. The stairs are steep.

> SERMOISE *and* MARTHE *continue out and* CATHERINE *deals with her feelings by removing her outer garments, letting down her hair and shaking herself free of this disturbing part of the evening.*
>
> *Through this the knocking persists below then stops; to be followed by the slamming of the street door.*
>
> MARTHE *presently comes back in.*

MARTHE: It was a young man—a scholar, at the door. He said he expected you expected him. (*Going to assist* CATHERINE *in her preparations for bed.*) So I boxed his ears and sent him packing.

CATHERINE: Oh! He had a sensitive ear, too. Ah, well! Fortune may make something yet of a boxed ear. Did you see our explosive priest on his way?

MARTHE: Yes. I made *him* climb the garden wall.

CATHERINE: Marthe!

MARTHE: I couldn't reduce the injury to his dignity; so I tried to reduce the dignity—which is sound nursing. But I wonder, madame, if that man will not haunt our back door like a hungry wolf.

CATHERINE: Oh, he's up, he's down. But, Marthe dear one, I have had such a complicated evening.

MARTHE: I can believe it, Madame. Let me—

As she helps CATHERINE *into disrobing gown.*

CATHERINE: Ah, Marthe, I don't deserve having you—*and* endowed widowhood. Do I?

MARTHE (*simply*): No. Now what brought you back so soon?

CATHERINE: Madame the Provost's intellectual evening collapsed completely.

MARTHE: Oh. Why?

CATHERINE: Because of a certain young man.

MARTHE: I see. And Monsieur Sermoise and he crossed swords? —intellectually.

CATHERINE: Oh, no. I doubt if he noticed Phillipe at all. His eyes were entirely for me.

MARTHE: Yes, Madame. Keep still. But that priest worries me. For, in his way, he loves you. And that's pitiable as well as dangerous.

CATHERINE: Dangerous? Nonsense!

MARTHE: Oh, he is a very impulsive, very violent man; and entirely jealous.

CATHERINE: I'll let my priest go. I promise. I do. Oh, but isn't it nice to be free yourself and have men tie themselves to you?—like puppets on strings.

It has become obvious that CATHERINE *is a little too well wined and dined.*

But I'll let them all go. Except—perhaps one—or two— —or . . . (*sighing*) . . . Ah, Marthe, at my time of life there is a typical danger, isn't there: one agitates the autumn leaves by a last grand nostalgic sigh towards summer. Mm?

MARTHE: I don't consider you typical, Madame. No—nor summer over—with this heat.

CATHERINE (*laughing*): Marthe, within five years let's marry again —someone comfortable—someone eminently sane who does not try to check up on my soul every time I happen to catch his eye; someone you approve of this time: Noah the Furrier!

MARTHE: If Monsieur Noah approves of you; which he wouldn't if he heard you now.

CATHERINE: At any rate, someone very different from the five young men one might enjoy in the interim, mm? (*Wickedly*) *Might*, mark you! My sins are still speculative.

MARTHE: Yes, Madame. (*A little weary.*) Your hair, now.

> *As* MARTHE *does her hair.*

CATHERINE: Am I cynical?—and cruel?

MARTHE: Not cynical.

CATHERINE: Have men not given me cause to be cruel? But I forget that Romance is preserved for you in a dead lover. Marthe, how did your scholar die?

MARTHE: Dreadfully naturally. By not eating enough to live.

CATHERINE: Was he so poor?

MARTHE: Paris was poor—to the point of famine; and he was good—to the point of self-sacrifice. I was away.

CATHERINE: He must have loved you very deeply. I would . . . I mean, Romance must have great possibility still, or I'd not be so bitter—would I?

MARTHE: Mm. (*Mouth full of pins.*)

CATHERINE: I'll not be cruel to one man for five years. Will that do?

MARTHE: Five minutes of thinking so, and I may have enough peace to finish your hair.

> CATHERINE *sits in over-exemplary silence.*

There was a young man . . .?

CATHERINE: There *is* a young man. Do you know old William Villon, who officiates at St. Benoit—a dear old man— well, he has a son—at least a sort of adopted one. Madame de Loré, the Provost's wife, says he has genius—as a poet.

MARTHE: Oh. Oh, yes.

>MARTHE *produces from her bosom a piece of paper folded into the shape of a " dove."*

This further piece of poetry flew up and in the window, just after you'd gone. So it's he.

CATHERINE: Yes. (*Taking the dove.*) He told me to burn this and commended me, for reality, to his tavern ballads.

>CATHERINE *opens and reads the poem:*

CATHERINE: " Two we were, yet had one heart . . ."

MARTHE (*continuing, by heart*):

>" It died in her dying; so must I—"

CATHERINE:" like some stone angel—always fly,
>transfixed forever by Love's art. . . ."

MARTHE: " in Death."

It could be of his Mother, but don't you think that you should start off with someone less sensitive; and lead up to poets?

CATHERINE: Oh, I can assure you he's not all sensitivity. You should have seen him, Marthe. He drifted into the Provost's affair like a ghostly scarecrow on the move across the fields of Elysium. Naturally, Madame asked him to read something of his own writing. So—(*She laughs.*) I don't think our Master Villon will be invited to the Provost's parlour again.

MARTHE: Oh?

CATHERINE: You see, Madame de Loré loves Chivalry—(*mocking*) and the poetry of Alan Chartier.
For instance she refers to me
as La Belle Dame Sans Merci.

MARTHE: Mm!

CATHERINE: Women, to Madame, are the reason why men defeat dragons.
>It's rather a strain.
So I don't think I will be invited again
to Madame's parlour. I giggled.

MARTHE: Oh.
At Master Villon?

CATHERINE: At what he read.
For, when he was asked to read,
he slowly pulled out a crumpled screed
from his worn pouch. It seemed to me
that wine and ink in equal degree
had gone into its composition, *and*
it was to me.
As he read it there was a hush.
I blushed. Yes, I did. I *did* blush.

MARTHE (*teasing*): Of course, Madame.

CATHERINE: Even you
would have blushed if you'd heard that poem through.
It was rather broad.

MARTHE (*smiling*): And about you.

CATHERINE: Not " *about* " me, *to* me.
It was about women generally.

MARTHE: Then no wonder, Madame, it was broad.

CATHERINE: And witty, and somehow so sad too,
that no one knew quite how to respond.
There was silence.
           Then Philipe blew up, begged to withdraw; withdrew me; plumped me in my carriage and drove me away. And do you know, we hadn't crossed the Island before Master Villon attended by a whole flock of Gown had managed to subdue the Guards of the Town, unhitched the horse and—well, here I am. You said the horse *was* in?

MARTHE: Yes. Perhaps it was as well that I boxed his ears. That's your hair in order. Shall I close the shutters on the night air?

CATHERINE: No (*drowsily*). It's a warm night—and there's a dream in my head.

MARTHE: Mm. (*Sniffs.*) It's a damp night—and there's a hot brick in your bed.

      MARTHE *turns to go.*

      CATHERINE *laughs and* MARTHE *turns.*

28

CATHERINE: There was one verse I recall in the poem down
there:
> " It is not their pure minds, nor their pure hearts,
>   but the authority in their other parts,
>   enslaves us so . . ."

Of course, he'd had some wine.

MARTHE: I hope for his sake, and yours—and mine
that Master Villon had had lots of wine.
I'll see to the morning things below. Goodnight,
Madame. God rest you!

CATHERINE: Goodnight! I had some wine too.

MARTHE: I was aware, Madame. (*Going.*) I was aware.

> MARTHE *goes out and down and* CATHERINE, *left to herself,
> reads again the contents of the paper " dove ", with some
> seriousness.*
>
> *As she is folding it again, thoughtfully,* FRANÇOIS *climbs
> stealthily in by the window, and stands just inside, unseen by her.
> In the distance the Great Bell of Sorbonne sounds and* CATHER-
> INE *looks up:*

CATHERINE: Oh! (*Seeing him and catching her breath.*) Master
Villon . . . what do you want?

FRANÇOIS (*with almost whispered restraint*): Oh, madame, the question must not be so crude, or the answer will seem so.

CATHERINE: What do you mean?

FRANÇOIS: Oh, madame, please! (*Coming further in.*) It may take
seasons to explain why budding keeps rotation with the
spring and when the leaves fall. . . .

CATHERINE (*interrupting*): . . . Master Villon . . . (*Loudly.*) How
dare you come in at my window!

FRANÇOIS: Because, madame, I dare not batter down your door.

CATHERINE: Do not trifle with me; (*Rising.*)

FRANÇOIS: Trifle! Madame, trifle! What a word for this!

CATHERINE: For this! For what! Answer me. Why are you
here?

FRANÇOIS (*looking at her silently for a moment*): Because . . . I cannot keep you out of my mind: and as like attracts like, the image I have here is drawn towards the original there, and despair is diminished in the process. *And* . . . Madame . . . I cannot keep you out of my mind.

CATHERINE (*a little pleased*): I see. And how long have I been lodged there?

FRANÇOIS: In my mind? Oh, ever since the world began.

CATHERINE: Yes, quite; but more precisely.

FRANÇOIS: Oh . . . since . . . Tuesday week.

CATHERINE: Then perhaps by tomorrow . . .

FRANÇOIS (*quickly*): . . . Tomorrow? By dawn I do not expect to have a mind of my own; so the problem, you see, might solve itself overnight.

CATHERINE: Now you make me angry!

FRANÇOIS: Thank God for that! For anger's nearer this passion than pride.

CATHERINE: Did you say " passion "? (*Amazed and amused.*)

FRANÇOIS: I meant passion for Life; not passion for . . . well, (*Coming further into room.*) what can I say?

CATHERINE: Not another word. And not another step! Stand where you are. You pester me with verses for a week. You insult me in company. You mob my carriage; and now you break into my house and standing there, you talk of passion!

FRANÇOIS: Madame, I am ashamed . . . to talk of passion . . . standing here. But I had not meant to stand here for so long. On the introduction of passion I had hoped to be . . . at least away from the window.

CATHERINE (*unable to prevent herself laughing*): You must go.

FRANÇOIS: Catherine—(*With a sudden desperate seriousness.*)
  Mary and all the angels brought me here,
  out of despair of the world and wonder at you;
  for all of Fortune and the laws of chance
  had brought me to that point where I might come

and climb the drain-pipe to this upper room,
in hopes of . . . hope.
I would laugh myself back down that drainpipe again,
if something had not happened to make it seem
my hopes were this height—were here when I came in.

CATHERINE: Something happened?

She turns to avoid his eyes.

Why—what do you mean?

FRANÇOIS: Tonight you looked into my eyes.

CATHERINE: Your clothes were hardly worth the looking at; if I
looked at all, why not look at your eyes?

FRANÇOIS: Not *at*, but *into* my eyes. (*She turns.*)
And the eye is the seeing thing. But when eyes meet,
and vision searches vision's origin,
the process then is not the process of sight.
For then we make that dark tunnel in which may meet
the undefended selves who in the light
would die—of exposure.
                    But—(*turning away*)
it's a double process and I can only see
from this one end. And it is probable I
go too fast too far; and all alone.
I am impatient, Madame, and I lack chivalry.

CATHERINE: You do.

FRANÇOIS: I was born nearer the earth, Madame, than you—
where men and women unfortunately do not grow by acts
of calculated chivalry. No! And now I come and go and
come and go between the whole of heaven and earth while
you—or my Lord or Madame the Provost walk between,
and do not know the heights or depths or who lives at
them. Earth's most glorious thing is a worm inspired;
as heaven's must surely be the lusty angel singing doubt-
fully. But I cannot fight for ground and dream of the sky.
I must be there. The torture is half-way. I'll burrow back
in moleskin. Yes—I must go. (*Moving towards window.*)
This night was special, but I begin to see I am too innocent.

CATHERINE: You! (*Laughing.*) Innocent!

FRANÇOIS: Oh, I have picked locks, cut purses and made one
woman cry with the poor man's pleasure. *But*, intrinsically
I maintain I am innocent. For, I trust today and hope for
tomorrow's wonder. Beauty I trust—and women in
beauty too. But the cold is the cold. Perhaps there has
to be more loveliness than this. There's a wonder. Adieu.
(*Putting leg over sill.*)

CATHERINE: Master François—

> *He stops, expectantly.*

—I am not satisfied with the reasons you give—for this.

FRANÇOIS: Come to that—I am never satisfied with reason. So—
if you ask me rightly—I'll give you reason and more.

CATHERINE: Was it (*casually*) some college wager brought you
here?

FRANÇOIS: Oh no, Madame——drink. And, secondly, a horse.
But in the beginning the driving idea was mine—so my
heart harnessed them: the horse—and the wine.

CATHERINE: But you said this night was " special " for you?

FRANÇOIS: Yes. Tomorrow I must choose a vocation. And, Oh!
the idea of choosing a vocation today?—
It's like ordering a statue for a possible niche
on the façade of a cathedral yet to be built
in a city which has perpetually been
rocked with earthquakes.
                    I'd rather cling
to the rocking earth and know the feel
of life as it is awesome, deep and real,
and damn vocation!
                    Oh Madame de Vausselles,
I wish I might lie long in bed with you
and tell you about the world. I do. I mean lie.
And I mean the world unworldly.

CATHERINE: Really! (*Gasping.*)
Are you never afraid of the liberties you take?

FRANÇOIS: No.
For they're all lovely and isn't Love the key
to Heaven and isn't Heaven the goal

appointed by The Lord, implemented by all
The Saints, The Church, the . . . (*Stopping.*)
Why?

Why do you look afraid?—of me?

CATHERINE: Doesn't blasphemy even frighten you?

FRANÇOIS: Was this blasphemy? Oh. (*Sighing.*)
There's a heart to all our hearts which when it beats
is inclined to make me, Madame, go
beyond Bell, Book and The Law,
towards outrageous truths.
Pax.

CATHERINE: What heart is this?

FRANÇOIS (*childishly solemn*): One does not know.
But sometimes, when all things grow still
because there's harmony—I feel it flow.
God's blood!—I hear it beat. I know—
Oh, conceit of conceits!—it seems I know
the heart of Creation.

> *Suddenly embarrassed by this confession*

And now, Madame,

I have a head, which beats louder than any heart I know.
Excuse me for this—(*Moving off.*)—
a seriousness crept in; I'll creep out.

CATHERINE: François?—

> FRANÇOIS, *turns at his name on her lips, for the first time.*

FRANÇOIS: Catherine?—

> *They face each other across the room.*

CATHERINE: Would you care for wine?

FRANÇOIS: Yes—(*simply*)—please.

> *She laughs and turns to collect and pour the wine.*

CATHERINE: Are you *entirely* insincere?

FRANÇOIS: No, no—not I! I am a poet. I see reality on the far
side of sincerity. Yet let the occasion, not the poet, talk
now.

> *As he accepts the glass of wine from her hand, and they drift
> towards the open window.*

33

CATHERINE: To——

FRANÇOIS: Hush! To Time. Let Time speak.

                                   See—
      Through the rooftops towards Notre Dame
      a mist is rising up and drowsing in
      the calm, silver elbow of the Seine.
      At a hundred open windows young girls dream—
      beyond the book of Romance and The Law—
      of armoured lovers, while their elbows grow
      cold to the cold window-sills.
      Is this not, Catherine, peace?
      Is this not Time stood still?
      To Peace: that silent, timeless tick of Time.

         He drinks. She does not.

CATHERINE: You frighten me.

FRANÇOIS: It is not me that now is frightening you.
      It's the arrest of time, by peace, in you.

CATHERINE: Peace has always frightened me.

FRANÇOIS (*putting his glass away*): But now—
      might I not say something perfectly true
      which could take your fear of Peace away?

CATHERINE: Don't—(*tremulously*). Don't, François, take my fear
                                   away,
      without complete conviction—will you?

FRANÇOIS: No.

CATHERINE: Oh, how can you be so sure?
                          Say it, François.
      And may God destroy you!—if it is not true.

FRANÇOIS: I love you.
               I love you, Catherine, in a way——
      that I wish I'd never used the words till now.
      I love you against all reason, against my will;
      against my limitations and my fears;
      against the total wisdom of the years
      of all the cynical world; against the Law!

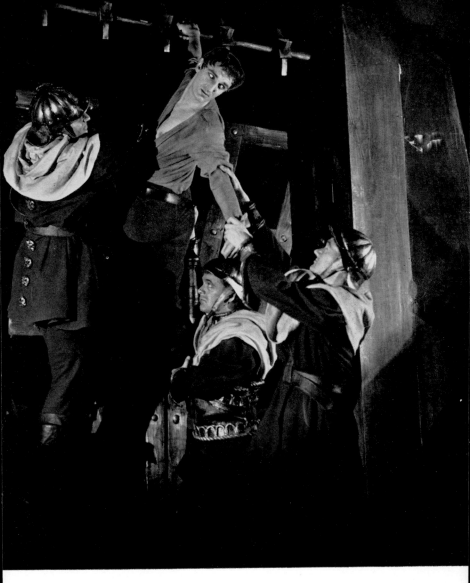

THE ARREST OF FRANÇOIS

Act II, Scene III

ALAN BADEL AS
FRANÇOIS
AND
IRENE WORTH AS
CATHERINE DE
VAUSELLES

PAUL ROGERS AS
OLD WILLIAM VILLON
AND
ALAN BADEL AS
FRANÇOIS

against all power—except this wonder now;
which sweeps us on.

She turns away.

                  Mark you,
I do not talk of lust, which, as we know,
is contrary to no man's will.
I talk—

CATHERINE: —of passion?—passion still?

FRANÇOIS: No.
If ever the word did ever apply,
I talk of Love.

She faces him in wonder and doubt.

CATHERINE: What should I say?

FRANÇOIS: Your part is passive silence, but you could cry;
which is permitted and not uncustomary—
so other poets say. (*Smiling, in passion.*)

She stares at him, in longing and doubt.

Shall we go where we lose the moon and gain privacy?
or down into your walled garden where we may
have sweet mock-orange and the sanctuary
of scented shadows? Or—Catherine—
where sleep may follow loving to its dream
with not an alteration but that sigh
when the tide of sleep comes creeping up the thigh
towards the heart?

Still she stares at him, and he continues, now laughing in passion.

Or half-way down the stair!—
If I can hold you close where I'll not share
you even with the moon.

CATHERINE: I think that you *do* love me: me—I mean me.

FRANÇOIS: Is that so strange?

CATHERINE: Would it seem strange to you
that I am a stranger to love—I mean love?

FRANÇOIS: And I
that stranger too.

CATHERINE: But you seem so . . . familiar . . . with everything.

FRANÇOIS: I am the familiar of Fortune. She does with me
    what she wills, but I begin to see
    she will be wonderful.
                      Catherine——

> *As they embrace the Scene Curtain falls slowly and music,
> developing to the tavern music of the next scene, covers the
> scene-change.*

SCENE III

*Outside the House of the Red Door—In the yard of St. Benoit—later
the same night—full moonlight,*

Before rise of curtain music and singing from a tavern is heard off.

On rise of curtain SERMOISE, *in a black cloak, comes through the gate
and goes toward the red door. He looks up at the window above and
backs away drunkenly.*

Curfew bells begin to ring.

There is the sound of approaching voices and SERMOISE *backs into the
shadows.*

2ND GUARD (*off and calling*): Cover your fires! Cover your fires!

> *A group of tavern customers, including* RENÉ, FAT MARGOT,
> THE WOLF *and* SPANIEL *are herded in by the* 2ND GUARD,
> *who is shepherding them through the gate before closing it.*

(*Ringing handbell and calling.*) Cover your fires! Get along.
Gates closing. Guard your gates! Cover your fires!
Guard your gates!

> RENÉ *and* MARGOT *slip aside into the shadows so that when
> the* GUARD *chains up the gate they are left on the inside.*
> *Curfew bells stop.*

2ND GUARD: Cover your fires! (*He moves off along street, calling
and ringing.*) Cover your fires! . . . cover your fires! . . .

> RENÉ *leads* FAT MARGOT *into the open.*

RENÉ There! (*conducting her to the bench*). Take your wonderful weight off your amazing feet and set your astounding bulk-beauty at rest, on that strong bench (*with a flourish*).

  MARGOT *giggles, and complies.*

And, Madame (*reclining on bench*), let me cushion my head on your ample bosom; and try to assess your pneumatic beauty—rising and falling. *Must* you breathe?

  MARGOT *giggles his head off her bosom into her lap.*

Now I can't see a thing beyond your—double chin. But I sense the moon, and the rise and fall is smooth.

MARGOT: Lord, how you do go on! (*Laughing as she looks down on him.*) But, Master René, don't you want to come back to the house?

RENÉ: Patience, Margot! Here we have interim peace—and extra-mural poetry (*Glancing up to where he considers François asleep by now.*)—and there's rhythm in your breathing. So, heave away, my mattress!

  MARGOT *laughs her high-pitched, bawdy laugh.*

Dear Will of Occam! (*Sniffing.*) *What* is that perfume you have soaked yourself in?

MARGOT: I don't know its name, but it does fetch, doesn't it?

RENÉ: Then let's call it "Fetch-and-Carry". For fetch it may, but carry it certainly does. Whew! Let me up for air.

MARGOT: Lord, how you do go on! (*laughing her laugh*).

RENÉ: For godsake, Margot, be silent! So long as you are silent you are, for me, miraculous womanhood. So . . . Sh! And let the moon comment.

  For one moon-gazing moment MARGOT *suppresses her laughter, then it breaks out again.*

MARGOT: You *do* go on! (*laughing*).

RENÉ: Oh! (*rising*). If there is no other way to keep that red mouth within the sphere of silence, then . . .

  Kissing her lengthily, and relapsing on to her bosom.

Mmah! . . . I feel like a night hawk, obsessed by some lunatic purity to embrace a cloud.

MARGOT: *Me*—a cloud?

RENÉ: No—a haystack. Sh!

> *Kissing her before she can get further than:*

MARGOT: Lor, how you. . . .

RENÉ: Ah! (*Sighing and lying back.*) Thank God the moon cannot speak, or right in the face of some lover's sweet dream she'd probably say, in a vulgar squeak, " Lor, how you do go on!" Margot!—look up at the moon; let it look at you; and let me embrace you—all that I can—*and*, for the sake of a great illusion, be silent.

> MARGOT'S *laugh again.*

Oh! . . .

> RENÉ *throws himself upon her and kisses her into complete silence when* FRANÇOIS *suddenly appears at the top of the gate and jumps down into the yard.*

MARGOT: Ah! . . . (*screaming out before* RENÉ *can get a hand over her mouth*).

RENÉ: François! Where did you drop from, in Heaven's name?

FRANÇOIS (*moving like a sleepwalker*): Heaven, René.

MARGOT: Nearly scared the——

RENÉ: Sh! Look.

> FRANÇOIS *wanders about as if he were the inhabitant of another world. They watch him.*

What do you make of that, haystack?

MARGOT: Perhaps he's in love (*giggling*).

RENÉ: Sh! It could be the combination of moon and academic elation. Any moment now and poetry could burst forth from him. Sh! He's muttering in metric despair.

MARGOT: Maybe he's drunk. In *what* despair?

RENÉ: He is about to become coherent. Sh!

FRANÇOIS: René—

RENÉ: Ye-es, François? (*coaxingly*).

FRANÇOIS: I love her.

MARGOT: See! (*Going into a triumphant laugh.*)

RENÉ: Quiet! Love who, François?

FRANÇOIS: " François " (*saying it as* CATHERINE *said his name*).

MARGOT: Himself! Ha!

RENÉ: Shut up (*to* MARGOT). Who? (*to* FRANÇOIS).

FRANÇOIS: Catherine. Catherine de Vausselles.

RENÉ: Catherine de?—Oh! (*groaning*). . . . Poor old cockle. *Poor little* François!

FRANÇOIS (*simply*): Why?

RENÉ: Love? You've given *her* the gift of Love? Well, you'll never get it back again. Love! That crystal of a creature cannot love—at least not anyone but Catherine de V. Now, Margot here—Margot can love. She has the warmth and the accommodation too. But Catherine . . . No. My haystack to your iceberg any day. It needs a certain relaxation to life, François, to let the milk and honey flow. No, no, since ever I knew her that Catherine has made a good thing of playing fast with many and loose with none. She just hasn't the heart to love anybody!

FRANÇOIS (*quietly and calmly*): She loves *me*.

RENÉ: Though, Margot, between you and me—*What did you say?* (*to* FRANÇOIS.) Do you mean she . . .

    FRANÇOIS *nods.*

Well! A conquest for our François! A conquest! (*Seizing* FRANÇOIS *by the arm.*) Make room on the reprobates bench. Move up, haystack!

    FRANÇOIS *is reluctantly made to sit, squeezed between the two.*

FRANÇOIS: No, René (*deadly serious*), not a conquest. I love her. But, René, it is a dreadful thing, really to love a woman. For where can it ever end?

    MARGOT *giggles.*

RENÉ: Quiet, you! Oh, no doubt the good Lord will find some way to bring it to a conclusion, François.

    MARGOT's *bawdy laugh makes* FRANÇOIS *get up.*

Now don't shatter my little poet's dream. Look. He's at it again (*as* FRANÇOIS *drifts dreamily about*). I'd give a lot to recapture that lost state of bliss. There's no reality

worth that illusion. Ah, let's borrow some purity of the
whitewashing moon and compromise with a kiss.

> *As* RENÉ *embraces* MARGOT, FRANÇOIS *continues to dream
> and talks to them as if they were listening:*

FRANÇOIS: The world is not evil and good.
> The world is all good, unassorted in
> its states of Love. The Devil too
> is god of the Dark tormented through
> being in the sphere of Light.
> > There is no sin—
> except chaos.

> SERMOISE *edges out of the shadows at his back.*

> Heaven seems almost unnecessary;
> if here and now all hearts as one
> can beat to the true creative time of——

> *He comes face to face with* SERMOISE.

> Who are you?

> RENÉ *jumps up in surprise and reaches for his dagger. And
> they all wait for comment or movement from the threatening,
> drunken, bulk of* SERMOISE.

(*Frightened.*) What do you want?

SERMOISE (*thickly*): Justice.

RENÉ: Who is it, François?

FRANÇOIS (*truthfully*): I don't know. I don't.

SERMOISE: Oh, yes, you do. And he knows why I'd cut out his
filthy tongue.

MARGOT: He's got a knife! Come on, Master René (*pulling at his
sleeve*). Come on!

> RENÉ *cautiously addresses* SERMOISE.

RENÉ: What do you want?

SERMOISE: Ask him. He knows.

FRANÇOIS (*really frightened*): Go away! You don't know me at all!

SERMOISE: Oh, yes, I do—Master François Villon (*advancing upon*
FRANÇOIS).

> MARGOT *falls back but* RENÉ *stands firm.*

MARGOT: Master René, are you coming with me?

RENÉ: Now look here, priest—

SERMOISE (*turning on* RENÉ): Don't *you* get involved in this. For I know you too—and your record. I have some authority at the Chatelet, Monsieur de Montigny.

> RENÉ *wavers.*

MARGOT: By the cellars.

FRANÇOIS: René!—(*Calling in despair to him from the far side of* SERMOISE.)

RENÉ: Who is it? Who is he?

MARGOT: I'm going.

RENÉ: François, for the last time, *who is it?*

FRANÇOIS: I... (*troubled*) ... I don't know.

> SERMOISE *just laughs, but* RENÉ *is shaken by the hesitation of* FRANÇOIS *who has " seen that face somewhere before ".*

RENÉ: All right. He's yours. (RENÉ *turns to go.*)

FRANÇOIS: But René, he's wrong! It's a mistake! I've done nothing *wrong!*

RENÉ: Look, cockle. Whoever goes to Hell honestly is a friend of mine, but if he's slithering in, pleading innocence, then—Let go! (*as* FRANÇOIS *runs to him and grabs him*).

FRANÇOIS: But René.

> RENÉ *sends* FRANÇOIS *reeling and slips out with* FAT MARGOT *and as* SERMOISE *steps aside to block his escape,* FRANÇOIS *finds that he himself is in possession of* RENÉ'S *dagger.*

SERMOISE: I heard what you said in the garden.

FRANÇOIS: I have never seen you before.

SERMOISE: But I have seen you. And I have heard you—you!—

> FRANÇOIS *evades* SERMOISE, *who at every turn bars his way with his black bulk.*

I am not clever. I am not witty, Master Villon. But I have strength. I have strength. So—you will never again be able to soil any woman's immortal soul with that vile tongue.

> *As he corners* FRANÇOIS, *and advances.*

FRANÇOIS: Don't touch me! (*Putting his hand on his dagger.*) Don't touch me. . . .

> SERMOISE *advances.*

SERMOISE: You turned her away from me towards the pit of Hell. and now . . .

FRANÇOIS: . . . Don't! (*panicking, as* SERMOISE *is almost on him*). Don't!

> SERMOISE *springs on* FRANÇOIS *and lets out a shriek as he staggers away and falls.* FRANÇOIS *is seen holding a dagger.*

Oh . . . Oh . . .

> *He stares at the dying* SERMOISE, *slowly crosses himself and backs in a daze towards the Red Door. As he goes towards it, the Red Door opens.* FRANÇOIS *whips round in fright and drops the dagger at his feet.* OLD WILLIAM VILLON *stands in the doorway.*

WILLIAM: François! I heard a cry. Who cried out? I . . .

> OLD WILLIAM *sees the dagger. The* GUARD (*off*), *calling and approaching in the silence.*

2ND GUARD: Cover your fires! Cover your fires!

> OLD WILLIAM *sees the body of* SERMOISE.

WILLIAM (*in appalled whisper*): François!

FRANÇOIS (*in feverish whisper*): He tried to kill me. I don't know who he is. Unless he's the Devil. You couldn't hang for killing the Devil, could you?

2ND GUARD (*nearer*): Cover your fires!

WILLIAM: Oh, François!

FRANÇOIS (*trembling*): Uncle William, I was just coming home. And . . .

2ND GUARD (*appearing outside by the gate*): Cover your fires!

> *Both stand petrified. But the* GUARD *continues past the gate, calling:*

CURTAIN FALLING

(*Going.*) Cover your fires! Cover your fires! . . .

CURTAIN

ACT II

Catherine's room, several months later.

Before rise of curtain there is the sound of a lute being plucked.

On rise of curtain, CATHERINE *is discovered, fingering a lute. A fire burns in the brazier.*

MARTHE *sits in the window, sewing.*

CATHERINE *is saying over the words of a song, against the music:*

CATHERINE: " My love in his madness is a man;
      my love in mildness is a child . . ."

    Stopping to consult music.

MARTHE: It's snowing again.

CATHERINE: " Against his frenzy I am strong;
      It is his mildness does me wrong;
      For how can I be reconciled
      To being mastered by a child? "

    Marthe (*frowning*), this song that you gave me . . .

MARTHE: Well? Do you not like it?

CATHERINE: I love the melody. The words . . .

MARTHE: It always reminds me of winter now—the melody.

CATHERINE: Of some special winter—when somebody died? (*Playing lute.*)

MARTHE: When somebody died.

    CATHERINE *stops playing and listens. There is a knocking on the street door.*

CATHERINE: Who can that be?

MARTHE: Well, who do you think? (*Rising.*) No one else comes to visit us now, but our dear fur merchant.

CATHERINE: Noah?—of course.

> MARTHE *goes. And, as* CATHERINE *sits alone, she sings the song completely.*

> " My love in his madness is a man;
> My love in mildness is a child.
> Against his frenzy I am strong;
> It is his mildness does me wrong.
> For how can I be reconciled
> To being mastered by a child? "

As she is completing the last phrase of this song, old WILLIAM VILLON *comes in with* MARTHE. *He signs to her not to interrupt, and* CATHERINE *continues singing without turning to see who it is. The song ends.*

Well—(*setting lute aside*). How is the furrier's trade, Noah? Are skins——

She stops as she sees OLD WILLIAM *standing there. She signs to* MARTHE *to withdraw.*

WILLIAM: Madame de Vausselles, (*diffidently*) I have spent the day hoping it would not be necessary to come here. Oh, only to avoid pain. In fact, that is why I have not come here before. During all these months—these difficult months, when François has been—so I believe—out of Paris and in hiding—I have kept away. But today I come —and guiltily. For, you see, I come quite selfishly to protect someone dear to me—Oh not, of course, to protect him from you; but from himself. It may be that I shall seem insensitive to your feelings in this, but, Madame, I am not come here to cast judgements on ways of life; I am simply come to save one life from what may be dreadful consequences. I only confuse you, I see. (*He stops, perplexed.*)

CATHERINE: Master Villon, till I know what you intend I can only fear that . . .

WILLIAM (*quickly interrupting her*): Oh, Madame, I hope you will see that I intend no harm to you. During all the inquiry, I went out of my way to avoid involving you.

CATHERINE: Really? (*Not facing him.*) I do not see that I could have been involved.

WILLIAM: Are you quite sure, Madame? For you see, François has been seen in Paris, and—

CATHERINE: Oh! (*hiding her agitation quickly*).

WILLIAM: Yes, he's here. Somehow, he must have been informed that I had obtained the King's pardon for him. I have searched for him all day. I dare say he wants to avoid me. For I have to stand completely responsible to the Law for his good conduct. And that, as you can see, creates obligations. It is for me to see that he does not slip back. *He must not slip back!* Madame, on the least default, the pardon could be annulled and they could then . . . hang him, summarily. I have cause to believe that he will come here! that, Madame, he may be here now . . .?

CATHERINE: I can assure you, Master William, that he is not here —nor has been since . . . since the death of Monsieur Sermoise.

WILLIAM: I must be glad. Fortune anticipates one so, and I work against time. But I know he will come here. And in his strange state . . . well . . . I fear he may have changed. In his despair and loneliness may not he have been forced to keep the company of thieves and worse? He may have joined the League of Beggars? Yes. Anything may have happened to him. He was never unimpressionable. So, Madame de Vausselles, whatever François may do now or say, try not to believe him. He does not lie, but in his love of life he may sometimes not see the difference between right and wrong; and then we—we forget the old truths. You are older than he, and . . . no . . . I can see I shall merely succeed in offending you. It's difficult for me.

CATHERINE (*nervously*): I cannot see that it comes within your authority to advise me on my conduct, not even if it be towards . . . him whom you represent. But, whatever has been (*with a sort of defiance*), I can assure you now that I wish nothing further to do with him.

WILLIAM: Oh! (*Involuntarily shocked.*) Eh, yes. Yes . . . that is best. Of course, it will be hard for him to have you seem so . . . indifferent. But, oh, do not think I do not agree . . . only . . . I fear a little what he may do if . . . You will—if possible—won't you, be gentle with him. Yes . . . I see . . . it is difficult . . . anyway . . . perhaps he will not come. Perhaps I am just an over-fond old man; but, Madame, if you only knew François as I do . . . how lovable he is . . . but . . . perhaps I should go. God's will be done. Yet we are accessory. No, I shall let myself out. (*Turning away.*) I should not have come. (*Going.*) I should not have come.

WILLIAM *goes.*

CATHERINE *absently fingers the lute to the tune of "My Love in his Madness is a Man".*

MARTHE *comes back in.*

MARTHE: Has he gone, Madame? Why didn't you call me? I should have helped him out.
Door slammed below.

CATHERINE (*fingering lute*): His "charge" is back in Paris.

MARTHE: Oh. Master François? But surely that is risking arrest?

CATHERINE: No. (*Rising and laying aside the lute.*) He has been given his pardon. But now, on the slightest lapse, he could be hanged—summarily. Marthe, if he comes here what shall I do?

MARTHE: Surely that depends on you—and your intentions?

CATHERINE: I'll not see him. The past is the past.

MARTHE: And if he comes to the door, I am to send him away?

CATHERINE: If he comes to the door. (*Ruefully.*) It is I should be in prison if he is free—to be safe.

MARTHE: Must we be safe?

CATHERINE: You don't understand him. I do. And I wish I did not. Send him away? Turn back the West wind.

MARTHE: He may not come at all.

46

CATHERINE: If he is in Paris he will come here. That I know. And the folly will repeat itself.

MARTHE: Folly?

CATHERINE: Marthe, he made a sort of image of me: some Belle Dame I could never be. And yet I did believe in her—while he was here. For, Marthe, he has a sort of aura within which you become divested of reality. It is rather like being bewitched. No, it is true! And you are laughing at me.

MARTHE: No, Madame (*sadly*), no.

CATHERINE: Yet I wish you would. I wish I might laugh. How could such a dangerous creature have become such a part of my life? He comes from the gutter, and yet—and yet I know that if ever he comes here again, the same tragi-comedy will begin—the same passion for life be turned towards me and I be tempted to take, to assume, the stature he falsely gives me. Marthe—

MARTHE: Madame—calm! You will marry Monsieur Noah—in good time. He is quite certain to ask you again. He is late. (*Looking down through the window.*) Oh!

CATHERINE: What is it? What did you see?

MARTHE: For the moment I thought it was him—over by the whipping post in the snow.

CATHERINE: Noah?

MARTHE: No.

CATHERINE: Not François? Where? (*Joining her at the window.*)

MARTHE: Whoever it was, he is gone now; beyond the garden wall.

CATHERINE: Marthe, I'm frightened. Look. There is one of the Guard Royal, standing over under the sign of the Lamb. Run and call him in. Don't argue. Run!

MARTHE: The Guard, Madame? (*Incredulously.*)

CATHERINE: Yes—the Guard. No one yet knows why he killed Phillipe Sermoise—not really. He may even kill me. Run and fetch the Guard—quickly—he's moving.

MARTHE: But what can I say?

CATHERINE: Anything that gets him here. Use the Provost's name. I need protection. It's his duty.

As MARTHE *goes there is a knocking at the door.*

CATHERINE *listens, then is going apprehensively into bedroom when* NOAH *comes in.* (*He is a middle-aged man with a natural gentility.*)

Noah—thank God! (*Going to him.*)

NOAH: Madame Catherine! (*Greeting her.*) No sooner had I knocked at your door than your Marthe flew out and I was pushed in. (*Genially.*) I would feel privileged by this privacy but that I suspect I owe it to some emergency.

CATHERINE: Dear Noah, you do. Sit. You look tired. But why did you wait till now to call?

NOAH: I spent the night in exemplary service to the citizens of Paris; voluntary watch duty. I spent most of the day regretting it (*wearily*). It was a bitter night. Snow fell.

CATHERINE (*hiding her own urgency*): Then may I offer you some of this ... " warmth " ... (*fetching wine*) before we talk of our " emergency ".

NOAH: A gracious thought, Catherine. I heard the wolves in the night. They say the old King is dying.

CATHERINE: Wolves? Yes. (*Nervously making conversation.*) A woman is reported to have seen a wolf carrying a child through the Porte St. Jacques in broad daylight. (*She hands glass of wine to him and goes to the window.*)

NOAH (*sipping*): Wait till today noon and that woman's neighbour will tell her neighbour, in all holy sincerity, that there were *three* wolves, and *six* children were carried away. In fact, it's only a matter of time before the whole of Paris is wolfed in one day by one original gossip. (*Noticing that she pays no attention.*) Are you ... expecting someone?

CATHERINE: Yes (*turning from window*). I am afraid I will have to extend your term of voluntary guard duty. I need a protector, Noah.

NOAH: Madame (*rising*), I hope fashions have not altered so far that you are trying to propose to me?

CATHERINE: Dear Noah. (*Smiling.*) No. I want your protection against one person; a former acquaintance of yours.

NOAH: Oh? (*encouraging her*).

CATHERINE: François Villon.

NOAH: Oh. (*Finishes his glass to hide his own fears.*) But surely now he is . . .

CATHERINE (*quickly, nervously*): . . . He is in Paris again. And they say he's grown dangerous, and I have every reason to believe that he is on his way here. He will insist on seeing me. I will not see him. And yet I have no hope that he'll go away. You see, he is . . . infatuated with me. (*With forced lightness.*)

NOAH (*with sad humour*): I find it difficult to stay away for a similar cause. Oh, in a milder case. But this Villon is young and it seems to me more gifted with spirit than common sense, and I am sure, not as dangerous as you make out. If you forbid him your door, will it not make him the more infatuated?

CATHERINE: No. I'm sorry, Noah. I cannot see him.

NOAH: But what have you to fear, Catherine?

Sound of door closed below.

Catherine, you haven't answered me.

Sound of steps on stairs.

MARTHE *comes in with* 1ST GUARD *who salutes* CATHERINE.

MARTHE: The Guard, Madame.

GUARD: I understand, Madame, that you have the Provost's authority for taking me off my present duty.

CATHERINE: Well—yes. Though the situation is different now. (*Looking to* NOAH.)

GUARD: I assume that you've not brought me here for nothing.

CATHERINE: It is only that I am the subject of persecution from a certain student of the university.

GUARD: And the student's name?

NOAH: Catherine, if you . . .

CATHERINE: I'd rather not give his name just now.

GUARD: Why?

CATHERINE: In case what I fear does not transpire.

GUARD (*a bit exasperated*): And what *do* you fear?

CATHERINE: I simply believe that he is on his way here. And that he may try to force an entry.

GUARD: Let him try (*boastfully, tapping his truncheon*). If he attempts to force an entry I shall use the full authority granted to me in this present emergency; of dealing " immediately and summarily " with culprits of the University.

> *There is a knocking at the street door. They all look at one another.*

I'll see to him. (*Turning to go.*)

CATHERINE: Wait! (*restraining* GUARD.) Marthe, look out of the window. (*Calling to her.*) Carefully!

MARTHE (*looking*): Yes, Madame. It is. At least I think so. . . . There's frost on the glass.

> NOAH *joins her at the window.*

NOAH (*looking*): No. Oh yes, it is. (*Finally.*) It is, Catherine.

GUARD: All right!

CATHERINE: Go to the door, Marthe. Take the Guard with you. But (*to the* GUARD) I wish you to take no action unless he tries to force his way in or to use violence. And even then, I only wish protection. I make no charge. Is that clear?

GUARD: Yes, Madame (*Resenting all this restriction.*) But . . .?

CATHERINE: Marthe, tell him I am not in . . . no. Tell him I am here, but that on no account will I see him. It must be final. Go now.

GUARD: Very well.

> *The* GUARD *and* MARTHE *go.*

NOAH: Well, we must hope that he accepts her word for it, and goes peaceably. For it would be a tragic thing to put him on the wrong side of the law now. (*Restlessly*) How I hate the strutting brutality of these Royal Guards. Catherine

"Master Villon . . . How dare you come in at my window."

ACT I, SCENE II

"I'll come back. And then God help you, Catherine."

ACT II, SCENE I

Photographs of 'The Other Heart' by John Vickers

(*with some courage*) before anything happens, I'd like to know . . . is this . . . well, is this a question . . . of . . . love?

Sound of the door closed below. CATHERINE *turns and waits.*

Catherine, can't you answer me?

MARTHE *comes back in alone. She looks disturbed and at a loss.*

CATHERINE: Well?

MARTHE: I told him.

CATHERINE: And did he go?

MARTHE: He stood there . . . looking. (*Distressed.*) So I closed the door.

CATHERINE: And he said nothing? (*On edge.*) What's the matter with you, Marthe?

MARTHE: He reminded me of someone. He just looked at me so; and stood there. I don't think he believed what I told him. It was beginning to snow and . . .

NOAH: But he didn't go away?

MARTHE: I don't know, Master Noah. He just stood there looking at me. Snowflakes were beginning to drift inside. So I closed the door. I left the Guard standing inside the door.

CATHERINE: See what he is doing now, Marthe.

MARTHE: You mean . . . François?

CATHERINE: Well, who else? (*In nervous anger as* MARTHE *moves to stair.*) No, no!—by the window.

MARTHE *goes to the window.*

MARTHE: Oh! ! (*Starting back.*) He's standing looking up at the window.

CATHERINE (*in a quite irrational state by now*): Close the shutters.

MARTHE: But, Madame, if I . . .

CATHERINE (*violently*): . . . Close them!

MARTHE *closes the shutters and, of course, shuts the light out too.*

Oh! (*Realising what she has in fact done.*) No!—don't open them again. Light the candles.

MARTHE: I'll have to go below to fetch a light, Madame.

CATHERINE: Then go quickly. And be careful of the stairs!

> MARTHE *gropes for the exit and goes.*

NOAH (*in near darkness*): Catherine, (*Incredulously.*) this is more than strange.

> *Sounds of lute being plucked by* CATHERINE.

It is fantastic.

CATHERINE: There are passions in life, Noah my dear, more fantastical than you may know. Help me—to protect myself.

NOAH: From yourself, Catherine?

CATHERINE: Yes, and from him, and his fantasy—for he is as catching as the plague.

NOAH: But if your fear of him is so deep?

CATHERINE: I'll not be dragged down! Nor will I be responsible for his destruction! Understand?

> *As* MARTHE *hurries in with taper and sets it to the candles.*

NOAH: No, Catherine, I *cannot* understand. How a woman of your strength of character can be carried away by . . .

CATHERINE: Ah! ! . . .

> CATHERINE *cries out like an animal. For the light reveals* FRANÇOIS *standing in the room.*
>
> *There is a silence as* CATHERINE *and* FRANÇOIS *gaze at each other.*

FRANÇOIS (*simply, tensely*): Why is it so dark in here?

> *No one answers.*

Catherine. (*Simply, like a shocked child.*) That woman said you would not see me. Was that true? Was it true?

> *She does not answer.*

NOAH: Master François, I think that . . .

FRANÇOIS (*persistently*): Was it true?

> *His eyes never leave* CATHERINE *for a moment. He looks, hunted, and heedless of anything but her.*

CATHERINE: Yes.

FRANÇOIS: Why? (*With frightening lack of emotion.*) Why would you not see me? Why?

CATHERINE: Because . . . (*With a superficial defiance.*) I consider I have nothing further to say to you.

FRANÇOIS: To say? You consider? (*With the same frightful absence of emotion.*) Nothing further—to say?

NOAH (*trying gently to break the tension*): Master François, don't you think that, placed as you are with regard to the Law, it would be wisest for you to go?

FRANÇOIS (*his eyes still mercilessly on* CATHERINE): Is the reason for wanting to keep me out this gentle gentleman here?

CATHERINE (*desperately*): Master Noah is about to marry me!

NOAH: Catherine! (*Amazed.*)

FRANÇOIS: Why? (*Insistently, flatly.*) Master Noah seems to want to know, too. Why?

NOAH: Master Villon, I consider . . .

FRANÇOIS (*turning on him suddenly*): Consider, sir, the disadvantage you see me in! And remember that all that brought me here is of fatal gravity to me. Would it not be less than kind to allow me a last word in privacy with Madame de Vausselles?

NOAH (*after an awkward pause*): Catherine, I think I might wait below—within call? Unless you wish it otherwise?

> *As* CATHERINE *makes no answer* NOAH *goes.*

MARTHE: Madame, shall I stay?

> *As* CATHERINE *makes no reply* MARTHE *goes.*

> *Again* CATHERINE'S *fingers play nervously with the lute. He looks at her—tense, suppressed, lost.*

FRANÇOIS: Tell me I'm asleep and this is a dream.
For I walk through a nightmare city, Catherine,
whose every childhood shadow I should know;
and yet from every corner and every door
shadows fall I had not seen before,
and from their cloak of darkness figures spring
whose faces, strangely, are familiar.

(*Like a lost child.*)

I am linked with a past I did not know I shared,
where stalks every creature I have feared,
labelled, Evil.
          And it all began with you—
and in such goodness. Why?
Do you know why?

CATHERINE: Must you pretend to childish innocence now?

FRANÇOIS: Pretend? (*At a loss.*) Why is our world of light so
dark today? Why are you so false?

CATHERINE: I am not false. But once *you* falsified me and my
world, to make me seem the woman you loved.

FRANÇOIS (*incredulous*): Seem? Then it seems so again.
Seem! (*All the pent-up emotion pouring out.*)
It seemed as if *you* loved me—and more!
It seemed as if this house, this room, this floor,
had drifted level with heaven and all we'd to do
was walk the way of trust towards that shore,
where the great waves come and curl and beat and go,
in tide with all that makes God's goodness flow
towards this world of—

CATHERINE:—No! (*Stopping him.*) Not again! You build your
own intoxication with words; you sweep sense off its feet
to what you know is a calculated end.

FRANÇOIS: Oh! (*as from a blow*) Call me ugly, call me mad; call me
crude, dishonest; but never dare to call me *calculating*. I
made no plan. I laid no siege to you. The walls to that
white citadel gave way to inner pressures, inner treachery—
if there was treason. Catherine, look at me. Look at me
and deny, if you can, that you *did* love me—Love!

CATHERINE: You mustn't cry out. They will hear you below and . . . Oh God, why did you have to come back? It was done.

FRANÇOIS: I came to see, and to touch, and to know that at least *you* were not of this nightmare now. Who sent that black devil to attack me? Who?

CATHERINE: No one sent him.

FRANÇOIS: Not you?

CATHERINE: How could you think so?

FRANÇOIS: What dare I not think now? Then what fiendishness goaded him on? Why should he try to kill me? Why?

CATHERINE (*wearily*): Because you are what you are; and he was jealous.

FRANÇOIS: Jealous? Why?

CATHERINE: Because . . . he loved me.

FRANÇOIS: " Loved "—Does the word apply?

CATHERINE: There are, I think, ways in which the word applies that you, François, may not ever know. (*Angered.*) He died believing he was protecting me.

FRANÇOIS: From what? From me? He was evil, and you know it. You know what he tried to destroy in destroying me. You know! And yet in this weird complacency you seem not to care! Catherine—

> *She turns from him.*

do you *want* to destroy me?

CATHERINE: You must go. I consider this has come to an end; for if ever this infatuation was love, it is not love now. And I despise what it is! And I shall despise you.

FRANÇOIS (*desperately*): Is this true? In your heart of hearts, Catherine, is this true?

CATHERINE: My heart is not involved—(*Avoiding his eyes.*) The truth is clear. This is no longer Love—if ever it was.

> *He looks at her, and at her hands, nervously clutching and unclutching.*

FRANÇOIS: You lie badly, Madame, with your hands. Oh God,
how it hurts. But there is a heart beyond these hurtful
ones—a heart to the human wonder which is not
so human as it's heavenly. I thought
it beat in us. I thought God's love came in.
Call this blasphemy, call this sweet lust a sin,
and accept to take away God's gift to man—
of adoration.
                    I adored you. Yes—*adored*.

CATHERINE: François, François you are not of this world.

FRANÇOIS (*ruefully*): Was that not disproved beyond all doubt—
upon this earth and on your sweet body too?

CATHERINE: You must be mad!

FRANÇOIS: The madness is you. For what madness to send me
away from you now. I love you. I love you! Life has no
meaning without you. It's true! Tell me to my face that
you don't love me. Then, I'll go. Catherine, turn. Turn,
Catherine! Or, by heaven I'll burn all shadows from us
both—and fire the house!

As he reaches for the candlestick CATHERINE *turns.*

CATHERINE: No! No, François, I cannot love you now.

FRANÇOIS: There is no can or will—*Do* you love me?

CATHERINE (*almost inaudibly*): No.

FRANÇOIS: Oh . . . (*Shaking his head.*) Catherine! Catherine de
                                    Vausselles,
it was love I saw; and the other heart beat here.
Remain the liar for reasons I may not know;
and for reasons you may not admit because you
are afraid of Life where life is new,
and old as creation. (*Gazing at her.*)
                    There goes the fear now—
behind those lashes, beneath that troubled brow,
and to the heart. I can do nothing now.
My world is upside down. I ascend from above.
I laugh in tears. My fears I terrify.
    (*Moving to door and turning at exit.*)

This is the death of a beauty greater than you;
and—oh—looking at you now, my love,
how beautiful that makes it. It was in the air.
It was my very atmosphere. I'll die.

CATHERINE: Oh, François, I could not help this. Help me now
    to——

FRANÇOIS (*turning on her*): No!—by God. I'll let you drop
    away.
    And I think you'll drop to the foot of the pit of Hell.
    For it seems, my love, it *seems* to me
    that you have both the scale and capacity
    for utter damnation. It should not be!

(*Breaking down.*)

God should not allow the cruelty
of one-sided adoration! Oh! . . .

    FRANÇOIS *buries his head in his hands.* CATHERINE *goes to
    him.*

CATHERINE: I did not choose this, François.
                    François—you know,
    how at Pentecost they let the white doves go
    inside the sacristy in Notre Dame?
    One of these doves would always come here,
    and strut on that windowsill, out in the sun;
    but it never came in. For it was afraid—
    not of me, but of the room:
    of the atmosphere in which I was at home.
    And there is something about you, François, which I
    must look upon with fear.
    I have wings, but I am afraid to fly
    in certain atmospheres. I'd rather die.

FRANÇOIS: There is something about me? (*Raising his head.*)
    Something . . . evil?

CATHERINE: Not evil.

FRANÇOIS: Ugly?

CATHERINE: No. Something simply disastrous for me—fatal.

57

FRANÇOIS: We all must die. But, Oh, would to God that I
          had Fortune's eyesight and might rise so high
          as to see the earth-plan of my life. For I *do*
          anticipate disaster. (*Turning back to her.*)
                              But why?—Why
          should you sense this danger in me,
          unless you are part of the answer? Why?
          Oh, Catherine might not this be
          the end for which we had to meet?
          I dare not let you go—not now.
          I do not hold the authority
          to let you go.

CATHERINE: But you must. You must!

FRANÇOIS: No!
          It's an offence to reality! What can be your fear?
          Can you be afraid of anything more
          than of the disaster which is bound to ensue
          if you deny this dependence?—this bond to me.
          Catherine!

          CATHERINE *breaks away from him.*

CATHERINE (*hysterically*): I am not bound to you, nor to anyone!
          I must be free of you! I will be free!!

FRANÇOIS (*loudly*): *This is no answer!!*

CATHERINE: You mustn't cry out so!

FRANÇOIS (*seizing her*): Not *me*! It is life at its very source which
          cries out now. There must be more reason for throwing
          life away! Why? (*Shouting.*) Why? Why?

CATHERINE: Go! Go!

FRANÇOIS (*drawing his dagger on himself*): *I will have an answer*—or
          I will die now. I'll not live without an answer!

CATHERINE: But there is no answer other than *you*—what you are!
          (*Then seeing dagger.*) François! No! Help! (*She struggles
          with him.*) Help! Noah! Noah!

          NOAH, *the* GUARD *and* MARTHE *rush in.*

          Take him away! Take him away! (*Sobbing.*)
          FRANÇOIS *is overpowered and held by the* GUARD.

58

FRANÇOIS: So, (*Accusingly at* CATHERINE.) I was not to succeed. Take me away from her.

GUARD: We'll whip some respect into you.

FRANÇOIS: Catherine. Ah! (*As* GUARD *tightens his grip.*)

CATHERINE: No! Let him go. I make no charge. I make no charge. I only wanted protection.

GUARD: That's what you're getting. (*Tightening the grip on his arms.*)

NOAH: Stop that! (*Furiously.*) If he's to be punished, it will be according to the Law and not according to your appetite!

GUARD: But he's used violence, hasn't he? He's attacked her.

CATHERINE: No, he didn't.

MARTHE: Then, Madame, what do you wish to happen?

CATHERINE: I only want him to go free. But he must promise to leave me and go away. (*Looking at* FRANÇOIS.) He must promise never to come back.

> FRANÇOIS, *looking her in the face, shakes his head.*

FRANÇOIS: I'll come back. And then God help you, Catherine. (GUARD *starts to drag him out.*) For this fear will stay when all your beauty has gone by the way, and then—God help you!!

> *The* GUARD *hustles* FRANÇOIS *out.*

MARTHE: Oh, Monsieur Noah . . . !

NOAH: It's out of our hands now, see to your mistress. (*Turning to go.*)

> NOAH *goes.*

MARTHE: She needs no help. I'll see you out.

> MARTHE *goes while* CATHERINE *recovers herself. After a time* MARTHE *returns.*

Master Noah has asked me to say that he will not return till you send for him, but, Madame, why? . . .

CATHERINE: There are loves, Marthe, which to us must be intolerable burdens. I know what I can bear.

MARTHE: And he?

CATHERINE: Let in the light.

> MARTHE *opens the shutters to let in light. But the sound of the crowd is let in too.*

CATHERINE (*with her back to the window*): Marthe, what do you see?

MARTHE: What you would expect. But I think you have forgotten what it may cost him when the Guard discover who he is: not just that whipping post, but that great, gaunt, leafless tree, over on Monfaucon. God forgive you.

> MARTHE, *turning from the window, goes out.* CATHERINE *does not see her go.*

CATHERINE: But, Marthe, I tried. I tried to send him away. I didn't *want* him to suffer. But . . . Oh, close the shutters.

> *Sound of whipping rises from outside.*

Close the shutters! (*Turning to find her gone.*) Marthe!

> *The sound grows outside and* CATHERINE *fearfully shuts her ears to the sound and stumbles blindly towards her room.*
>
> *As the Scene Curtain falls—the sound of the crowd outside grows; and covers the scene-change. . . .*

SCENE II

A Whipping Post near Catherine's House, on the Mont St. Geneviève—Sunset of the same day.

On rise of curtain the tail end of a crowd is moving off, to leave FRANÇOIS, *chained to the post, head down.*

FRANÇOIS'S *shirt is thrown at him by the* GUARD, *who now goes.*

NOAH *comes forward and silently and solemnly picks up the shirt and puts it over* FRANÇOIS'S *back. But when he shakes it off,* NOAH *stands, irresolute and unhappy.*

1ST MAN (*as crowd go*): But what did he do?

2ND MAN: You can flog as many scapegoats as you like, it won't help.

1ST MAN (*persisting*): What did *he* do?

2ND MAN: But there's got to be some justice somewhere, eh?

1ST WOMAN: And who wants Justice? What we want is being safe in our beds of a night.

1ST MAN: What did he do?

1ST WOMAN: Broke into that house over there, and went for the lady.

1ST MAN: But *what did he do*?

2ND MAN: " Breaking and entry "—I suppose.

1ST MAN: Oh. Of the lady? Ha!

> CROWD *go, laughing.*

> FRANÇOIS *painfully raises his head, to find only one* DUMB BEGGAR *and* NOAH *left.*

NOAH: I'll try to let your uncle know, before the Guard discover your identity. And I should like you to believe that I had no part in this.

> FRANÇOIS *just gives him a withering stare.* NOAH *turns and goes, unhappily.*

FRANÇOIS: Oh, Fortune! (*Groaning.*) Hello, brother dog (*To the* DUMB BEGGAR.) Whipping today. Oh—women should not be understood but overcome. (*As the* BEGGAR *stares at him.*) Go away!

> The DUMB BEGGAR *snatches up* FRANÇOIS's *fallen shirt and hobbles off.* FRANÇOIS *twists painfully to look up and off.*

God!—and the candles still burn in the room. Yes, burn. Burn! And, Catherine—I'll come again. But this time I'll come not asking why? We'll not be so intense and true, but more expeditious. Noah? Bah! I'll come with money, position and power. And, Madame, I'll not be denied my hour—if it takes a lifetime. (*Looking off and down.*) Power?—I do have a sort of power.
Position—I have the gifts for it—
But . . . Money? It saves such sweat and time:
and I have none. Yet down there—
within the wedge of my view—

  hundreds of money chests must lie
  entirely idle. St. Severin has *two*
  coffers whose contents one might collect
  for a worse cause than this crusade
  against La Belle Dame's travesty
  of chastity in retrospect. But—(*Listening.*)
  Oh, pray God they've not found out my real name.
  Oh, God, don't set me aswing in the wind
  over there on Monfaucon! I don't want to die.
  I don't want to die.

   WOLF *slinks in alone. He turns and gives a low whistle.*

   SPANIEL *comes in at speed. A further whistle.*

   FRANÇOIS *whistles the same call.*

   THE WOLF *and* SPANIEL *stop—frozen to the spot—*CASIN
   comes in.

FRANÇOIS (*calling, quietly*): Casin!

   CASIN *too, " freezes ".*

WOLF: I don't like this.

SPANIEL: Let's run.

CASIN: Sh!

FRANÇOIS: Casin!

   CASIN *comes gingerly forward.*

  Ah! . . . Thank God it's you, Casin.

CASIN: Villon! By all that's wonderful in a miserable world!
  Welcome back to Paris. (*Bowing.*)

FRANÇOIS (*wryly*): Thank you. The country was so boring—so
  green, you know.

CASIN: Really! And how were the women?

FRANÇOIS: Not so green.

CASIN: Ha! It's Villon! (*To others.*) Oho, you've not taken long
  to get back into harness. (*Examining chains, etc.*)

WOLF (*lugubriously*): What's he doing up there?

FRANÇOIS: Admiring the sunset. What do you think? Get me
  out of this ironmongery.

CASIN: But what got you married to the " Wooden Widow " ?

SPANIEL: And what got you the lattice work on your back? (*As they gather round him.*)

FRANÇOIS: I broke into a woman's house in search of bliss. She took exception to the ecstasies. So did the Law. Can you pick these cockles? (*Indicating locks.*)

SPANIEL (*flatly*): No.

WOLF (*impatiently*): Come on. The dish'll get cold.

FRANÇOIS: What dish? Get me out of this, Casin.

WOLF: That rat Tabary won't wait.

SPANIEL: No, he won't. And then there'll be no watchdog this side of " the grief ".

FRANÇOIS: Casin? Are you doing some " coin-collecting " to-night? Could I come in on it? Could I?

WOLF: Come on! (*to* CASIN)

SPANIEL: Casin!

CASIN: Now what's the hurry?

WOLF: I'll tell you what's the hurry.

CASIN: Oh no, you won't. That's the trouble with you.

SPANIEL: But, Casin—

CASIN: And with you too! You rush at things. It won't do. You must court corruption casually—like a lady of leisure. It's the courtship that makes it all worth while. What's the good of a life of crime, eh?—if you don't enjoy it? (*Sitting calmly at foot of whipping-post, yet all the while examining locks and chains.*) So, you want to join us?

WOLF: Oh, I don't like this!

CASIN: Stop pawing me, Spaniel (*Slapping him down.*)

WOLF: There's a job to be done and—

CASIN: And you want to rush away and go and get it over, eh?

WOLF: Yes, I do!

CASIN: That's what makes the morbid world so miserable! You rush at things. Let the Law rush to conclusions. You and I must dally, deviously, or we may be brought to a conclusion—like you know who. He rushed.

FRANÇOIS: For God's sake, Casin. The guards will come back.

WOLF: But Tabary won't wait! He'll have run away by the time we get there.

CASIN: So one rat's gone!

SPANIEL: And how can we manage . . .?

CASIN: So we lose Tabary. But François here considers that he has a case for some " cockle-picking ". Now, François, do you think you're fit to climb? You were a drainpipe expert in your day.

SPANIEL: Oh, come on, we can't wait.

FRANÇOIS: Casin, if you drop these chains from me, I could fly— not climb.

CASIN: So you would rush too? Tut, tut!

WOLF: Are we to be here all night?

CASIN (*decisively*): Spaniel. Get busy with your " nightingale ".

WOLF: But they'll close the gates?

SPANIEL: And the Guard know Villon now.

CASIN: Keep watch (*to* WOLF). Spaniel! Do you hear, dog!

WOLF: I don't like this.

CASIN: Keep watch, I said! (*drawing dagger*). We're one short already, aren't we?

> WOLF *lopes off to keep watch.*

> Spaniel! Pick these " whelks ".

SPANIEL: I didn't bring my tools for this. (*Hesitantly bringing his tools from an inner pocket.*)

CASIN: Then give them to me! (*Snatching them.*) And keep watch too, or I'll pick your cockles.

> SPANIEL *scuttles off into the shadows.* CASIN *sets to work to free* FRANÇOIS.

FRANÇOIS: You're snatching me from the " leafless tree ".

CASIN: I'm not doing it for your health. I need your cat's eyes. Start thinking now of the ground plan of the College of Navarre.

FRANÇOIS: Yes, I know it. What do I do? I need a big " helping." Is it a big " dish "?

CASIN: Not " broad beans "—a basinful. C. of N.—sacristy coffers. (FRANÇOIS *gasps*.) Remember? We did the survey when we had René

FRANÇOIS: What can I hope for? Because it's all-or-nothing for me now—with the long drop just ahead. What share do I collect?

CASIN: René's share—second to mine. But don't breathe a word to the animals. (*Indicating* WOLF *and* SPANIEL.)

FRANÇOIS: No. But what's happened to René?

CASIN: Nothing that nature didn't predict.

> *A whistle and* WOLF *comes in.*

WOLF: A cloak coming up the hill . . . Quick!

FRANÇOIS: Don't leave me, Casin. Finish this! (*He is still held by one ankle.*) Casin!

WOLF: Didn't I tell you . . . (*exit*).

CASIN: Damn! I'll be back. Wolf! Wolf! (*Exit.*) Wolf!. . .

> *Enter* OLD WILLIAM, *panting from having climbed the hill.*

FRANÇOIS: Oh God! (*Hiding his head and arranging things to make it seem that he is still fully chained to the post.*)

WILLIAM (*advancing*): Oh François, François! Master Noah told me. Oh God forgive you!—I could not believe it.

FRANÇOIS: Uncle William, please leave me—leave me alone.

WILLIAM: But I can't leave you here in the cold—It may snow again.

FRANÇOIS: Please leave me. It's all I deserve.

WILLIAM: Yes, yes, but think where this is leading you. Think of your friend Montigny.

FRANÇOIS: Why?

WILLIAM: Think, François. Think! Think where this is leading you!

FRANÇOIS: Why? What's happened to René?

WILLIAM: Hanged, François. Yes—on the great high gibbet on Monfaucon—he's over there now, (*pointing*) swinging in the cruel wind; and the crows about him.

FRANÇOIS: Hanged? René? (*Appalled.*)

WILLIAM: The Church, and even his great family, were quite powerless against the Law. And I cannot always protect you, you know.

FRANÇOIS: René, hanged?

WILLIAM: I must get you home. I *must* get you home.

FRANÇOIS: René?

WILLIAM: Chains? Oh, it is not legal that a student should be so punished by the Civil Power. It's not right. I'll see the Chancellor. But the Provost must not know. François, I *will* get you free. I will get you free tonight. I will go to the Chancellor now. But they are getting weary of me. I cannot go on. I cannot always save you. I am breaking the law. I feel it.

FRANÇOIS: Hanged?

WILLIAM: François, if this happens again, there will be nothing I can do to save you from the rack! From worse—

FRANÇOIS: René (*In tears.*)

WILLIAM: Don't cry, François. But this is the very last time— do you hear me?

FRANÇOIS: I am cold.

WILLIAM: Oh, your poor back. (*Putting his own cloak over* FRANÇOIS.)

FRANÇOIS: Ah! (*As cloak hurts.*) Why must you be so kind to me? Leave me! It only makes me hate myself.

WILLIAM: No, no! You must not hate yourself. I'll go now. I won't be long. But—Oh, yes, it will take time. My legs —my legs. I have to stop so often. But (*moving off*) I shall hurry.

FRANÇOIS: René!

WILLIAM (*as he goes*): Don't despair, François. One must never despair. René de Montigny was evil. But you—you are different . . . quite different.

> WILLIAM *hobbles off down the hill.*

FRANÇOIS: That's not true! René was fine, generous and gallant!
> CASIN *nips back in and continues work on the locks without comment.*

Casin—is it true? Is René . . . hanged?

CASIN: Yes—bloody fool! They pumped him full of water till he confessed. You know, " The Question ". Come on. (*Standing up and putting tools away.*) What's the matter. You can't change your mind now!

FRANÇOIS: He'll come back.

CASIN: René? What the—

FRANÇOIS: Old William—he'll come back. It will kill him if he finds me gone and—(*Looking off and up.*)

CASIN: If you let me down in this, damn you!—

FRANÇOIS: I shan't. She had the windows open this way—to gloat.

CASIN: Are you coming or are you not coming? François!

FRANÇOIS: Yes—I'm coming.

> CASIN *goes, with* FRANÇOIS *following.*

CASIN (*off*): Spaniel! (*Calling as he goes.*) Wolf! Wolf! Wolf!
> *As the moon comes through,* CATHERINE *slowly comes in, and finds the post empty.* MARTHE *follows with a lantern.*

MARTHE: Madame, Madame. You should not have come from the house like this. It is out of your hands now. Leave him in peace. Monsieur Noah went to . . .

CATHERINE: Yes, he's gone. (MARTHE *moves forward and examines the chains.*) What did Noah say?

MARTHE: He went to fetch Master William Villon.

CATHERINE: What did he say—about me?

MARTHE: About you, Madame? (*Looking up.*) Noah?

CATHERINE: Yes, what did he say?

MARTHE: About you—do you really want to know?

CATHERINE (*after a long pause*): No. (*Desolately.*) He's even robbed me of Noah. (*Moving to go.*)

MARTHE: He? But do you understand what *you* have done?

CATHERINE: Better than you. (*As she goes.*) Better than anyone. He is free.

> CATHERINE *goes and* MARTHE *follows, and the scene changes.*

SCENE III

The Yard of St. Benoit — Later the same night.

Before rise of curtain the deep Bell of Sorbonne sounds.

On rise of curtain, NOAH *comes out through the open Red Door, obviously looking for somebody.*

OLD WILLIAM *lets himself into the yard by the gate and drags his feet towards the door; till he sees* NOAH.

NOAH: I waited on. I thought I might have a word with him. Where is he?

WILLIAM: I do not know. (*Bitterly.*) The Law can take its course now. In fact, I shall insist upon it. The locks of the chains were picked. He was gone. He has deceived me and despised my love. I'll not be despised. (*Weeping.*) I'll not be despised.

NOAH (*assisting him*): Come inside. I'll stay the night with you. Come now.

WILLIAM: Bolt and bar the door.

> WILLIAM *goes in.*

NOAH: But, if he should come . . .

68

WILLIAM (*off, and almost shouting*): Bolt and bar the door!

> NOAH *goes in, closing the door. The bolts are slid-to.*

> *After a moment a small sack, which jangles, is chucked into the yard and* FRANÇOIS *follows it, over the gate, and picks it up.*

FRANÇOIS: Now, Catherine! I can buy up the whole Royal Guard—and enter by the front door, with a golden key.

> *As he picks up the sack there is an " owl hoot" and* CASIN *comes to the far side of the gate.*

CASIN (*through bars, whispered*): They've scented something.

FRANÇOIS: Are you sure?

CASIN: Let's get out of here with this. (*Indicating his " loot ".*)

FRANÇOIS: Out?

CASIN: Yes, out of Paris.

FRANÇOIS: Out of Paris?

CASIN: Why not? There's a place near Montpipeau where we can live for years on this. It's a miserable world anyway. But there is a woman at Montpipeau not entirely miserable.

FRANÇOIS: I cannot leave Paris now! No, they can't possibly have found out yet. You've made a mistake. Oh!

> *Alarm Bell off.*

CASIN: All right. Your risk—not mine. If you change your mind make for Orleans. Ask at the Three-Legged Miller for me. Here come the two-legged bloodhounds! Adieu!

> CASIN *goes.*

> FRANÇOIS *hurries to the door and knocks quietly but insistently He knocks again. The Alarm Bell stops.*

WILLIAM'S VOICE: Who is there?

FRANÇOIS: François. Uncle William! Uncle William! I have come back. Please let me come in. (*No response.*) Uncle William!

WILLIAM (*off*): Go away. I cannot do anything more for you! You are not above the Law! Go! For pity's sake, go away, François! Leave Paris! Leave this country—this world! Go!

> FRANÇOIS *stands back aghast.*

FRANÇOIS: But Uncle William, Uncle William!

> *Alarm Bell again and shouts off.*

> FRANÇOIS *jumps back into the shadow as a* SERGEANT *of the Guard unlocks the gate and comes in leaving a Guard at the gate. He crosses straight to the door.*

> *Bell stops.*

> SERGEANT *knocks sharply at the door.*

WILLIAM (*inside*): O, François!

> WILLIAM *re-opens the door.*

(*Coming out.*) O, François, what am I to do with you? *He sees the Guard.*

SERGEANT: The church of the College of Navarre has been ransacked. Yes. Name of Villon?

WILLIAM (*stunned*): Yes.

SERGEANT: Then I believe you stand responsible for your son, François.

WILLIAM: Not my son—but—François. Oh François——

SERGEANT: Is he in the house? I said, Is he in the house?

WILLIAM (*to self*): " Cursed is he that shall be hanged . . ."

SERGEANT: What did you say?

WILLIAM: The Word of God . . . Deuteronomy. " Cursed is he that shall be . . ." . . .Aah!

> *As beyond the Guard he sees* FRANÇOIS *huddled against the wall, the old man gasps and collapses.*

NOAH (*off*): Master William? (*Coming out.*) Is it him? Is it . . . Oh! (*As he sees the Guard.*)

SERGEANT: He's just fainted, sir.

NOAH: Help me carry him in. It is a bitter night, and he is old.

THE SERGEANT *and* NOAH *carry* WILLIAM *in.*

Slowly, FRANÇOIS *comes out of hiding and, as he turns to go through the gate left open by the Guard, the* IST GUARD *springs out of the shadows and bears him down.*

FRANÇOIS: Ah!! . . .

GUARD: Got you!

THE ACT CURTAIN FALLS

ACT III

SCENE I

A Dungeon Cell, of the Bishop's Prison at Meung, near Orleans—some years later.

Before rise of curtain, the Sound of the Wind.
The deep Bell of Sorbonne strikes once and as the curtain is rising—
FRANÇOIS'S *voice cries out of the dark.*

FRANÇOIS: No!!

> *Another stroke of the bell.*

No!!

> *Another stroke of the bell.*

No!!
No! (*mounting*) No!! No!! Aaaaaah!!! (*Screaming.*)

> *In the dim light one can pick out the figure of a man huddled on the floor, ragged, and writhing in his sleep. He lies still against a grating in the wall. It is* FRANÇOIS.

> *The Bell strikes several strokes, and* A VOICE (*like that of* SERMOISE) *speaks.*

VOICE OF EXAMINER: Stop!

> *The Bell stops.*

Take the water away! Take the funnel from his mouth! Raise his head! Raise it up! Up! Now, answer me. Are you of the League of Beggars?

FRANÇOIS (*in sleep, fearfully*): Yes.

VOICE: Additional to the crimes in Paris—for which you have yet to pay in full—are you guilty of stealing a silver chalice from the Church of the Virgin, at Baccon?

72

FRANÇOIS: Yes!

VOICE: And of three crowns from the offertory?

FRANÇOIS: Yes!

VOICE: And of three crosses from a hill?

FRANÇOIS: Yes!

Increasing of tempo of question and answer.

VOICE: Of a golden throne?

FRANÇOIS: Yes!

VOICE: A crown of thorns?

FRANÇOIS: Yes!

VOICE: A virgin's child?

FRANÇOIS: Yes! Yes!

VOICE: The Glory of Man?

FRANÇOIS: Yes, yes, yes!! (*Almost shouting.*)

VOICE: Why? Why?

FRANÇOIS (*crying out in despair*): I don't know! I don't know!

VOICE (*coldly and calmly*): Does the prisoner know *anything*? Again! Is this the Bishop's Prison at Meung, in the province of Orleans?

FRANÇOIS: Yes!

VOICE: Are you François Villon?

FRANÇOIS: Yes!

VOICE: Alias Montcorbier? Alias Mouton?

FRANÇOIS: Yes!

VOICE: And the Pope—the Pope of Avignon?

FRANÇOIS: Yes! Yes! !

VOICE: And the Devil?—the Devil in Hell?

FRANÇOIS: YES! YES!

VOICE: (*coldly*): The prisoner's a fool! Take him straight to the gallows!

FRANÇOIS: No! No! I only do what I have to do. You wanted me to say " Yes ". You made me! Bishop of Thibaud! You . . . you are hanging yourself.

VOICE: Take him away!

FRANÇOIS: You cannot do this to me! I have poetry—I have beauty inside me! It *will* not hang! It belongs to the earth!

VOICE: Then get off the earth, my beauty! Up the ladder. Up!

FRANÇOIS: No.

VOICE: Up!

FRANÇOIS: No.

VOICE: Up!

FRANÇOIS: No.

VOICE: Now; (*As final command.*) *Take the ladder away!*

FRANÇOIS (*screaming out*): Aaaaaaaaah!

> *There is a sudden shaft of light from above as a trap in the roof of the dungeon is opened. The head of* GEMINI, *the jailer, appears.*

GEMINI: What's up, down there? Are the rats at you? Hey! Villon! Hullo! (*To self.*) Either that was his last scream or he's at his nightmares again. Hullo, down there! Are you asleep or dead! or both? I'll tickle him up.

> *A rope is let down on the figure of* FRANÇOIS, *who lies in a pool of light from above.*

Hey! François, m'old fish; Hey! Nothing biting. Villon! Mouton! Montcorbier! (*Banging him with rope.*)

> FRANÇOIS *sits up.*

FRANÇOIS: No! (*Seeing rope as noose.*) Oh! Where am I? (*Looking up.*) Who is that? (*Clutching rope's end.*)

GEMINI (*mockingly*): Did you ring, monsieur? It's your old nurse, Jailem Gemini, and you're still snugly tucked away in the prison of the Bloody Bishop of Meung, province of Orleanais. Would you like an account of local customs

74

too, and a short history of the long river Loire? Eh?
What do you want? Remember you're not in Paris now.
And, by the way, lucky for you! There's plague swept
Paris.

FRANÇOIS: What's the Plague to this? (*Brokenly.*) Oh, Gemini,
for pity's sake, get me a cell above the ground. That big
rat doesn't run away any more when I kick at him.
(*Beyond tears.*) He's had half of one of my toes.

GEMINI: *Half* your toe? What are you trying to do?—*starve* the
poor brute? Ha! Ha!

> *He begins drawing up the rope and* FRANÇOIS *grabs at it and
> is hauled off the ground.*

FRANÇOIS: Take me out of here.

GEMINI: Get off that rope! Get off that rope!

> *By vigorous shaking he dislodges the weak* FRANÇOIS *on to the
> floor and pulls the rope up.*

(*Hauling up.*) Ungrateful! Aren't you? After me lodging
you in the one and only underground cell with an air-
shaft that reaches the sky! You can put your ear to the
grating and listen all day long to the sound of the birds.
If that isn't catering for the poet in you, what is? (*Leaning
down.*) Have you been listening today? Did you hear
something special, François? We're hanging today! You
can hear the crowd roar in the village square now. Don't
you go gnawing your heart away and worrying your self
sick about this damp cell. We're hanging today. And you
are on the hangman's list! Ha!

FRANÇOIS: They musn't hang me! I've got to get back to Paris.
It's important! They can't hang me!

GEMINI: O, I don't think they'll find it impossible. But listen—
(*confidentially*)—you've still got a chance. The new King
got to Orleans yesterday, and he is going on towards
Bordeaux. Now, he'll either go through Clery, across
the river, or come this way, through our own village—
Meung.

FRANÇOIS: The new King?

GEMINI: Yes. He entered Paris ten days ago *and wherever he passes* *the prisoners go free; in a General Amnestry!*

FRANÇOIS: Free. Prisoners go free?

GEMINI: And if the Bishop only knew for certain that the King was going to pass through Meung here, he'd bundle you into barges and row you all across the river to Clery. Then, when the King had gone through, he'd ferry you all back over again—and hang you at leisure. *But*—he's not certain, see. And, as I say, you're on the list and we're hanging today! So don't you be mean to that big black rat. Why shouldn't he, rather than a crow, have the second helping of your toe! Ha! (*Chuckling.*)

> The trap door is slammed down again and FRANÇOIS *gropes* *about in the dim light.*

FRANÇOIS: Oh, God, send the King this way! God send the King this way! God send the—(*Stopping and listening.*) Sh! Silence! (*Beating the ground with his fist.*) Silence in the rat kingdom! . . .

> He drags himself to the grating and listens.

No. (*Rolling away.*)
Only the dear fiends roaring again,
at the sight of the next poor fool to swing.
Yet—(*Listening again.*)—God! what this place has done
for my ears! Now that my eyes have nothing to do,
it's a wonder that my ears don't grow to twice their
size. Sh! (*Looking to trap door.*)
There's tramping all over the prison now.
The Bishop's boys will drag me up.
I'll see my country once more—and go.
I'll see the green world. It should be?—Oh,
Mary Mother, it should be Spring.
What a hellish inconsiderate thing!—
—to hang a poet in the Spring! Sh!

> (*Listening, at grating.*)

Oh heart stop beating. Hush, heart!
No—it is not the voice of the crowd,

but the moan of the wind. (*Reflectively*.)
                    The wind . . .
and when it whistles so
the South-West wind is blowing through
Orleanais towards the North—
towards my Forbidden City. But, Oh!—
if I were freed I would return;
despite the two-legged wolves that wait,
I'd return to Paris and I'd make her pay;
I'd take her merciless body and . . . Oh! (*Coughing painfully*.)
God forgive me these unfounded lusts!
for there's not a muscle in me now
will serve its normal function. Oh . . .
But *if* I were free—(*Lying back*.)
free as the wind! I see it run;
ahead of the clouds and under the sun
and away from where the great Loire lies,
under the tossing willow trees,
and feels the black feet of the swan
strain to keep his dignity
unruffled.
                    From every exposed tree
on every hill of France will fall
the weak twig; flags will fray.
And—the wind insisting—all life will be
of the one mood. People will say,
" It is wild ". And the " it " will be
partly human.
                    Farthest away,
the mood of the wind will make a red door
slam-to in the yard of St. Benoit,
and old William will sit and stare.
In his short-sighted, silent world
he will not hear the wind whine,
but a door will open and no one come in;
and so he'll conclude from the draught on his knee
that it is the West Wind returning—not me.
And up on the Mont St. Geneviève
a woman will decide to wear

a kerchief over her red hair;
while walking the garden in search of a flower
to confirm Spring.

(*Sitting up fearfully.*)

Over my head again! Nearer. Oh—
What a pity! What a pity to die so!
My God! Why at least could it not be
on Montfaucon where swinging I'd die
with Paris printed in my eye and—(*On his knees.*)
They are stopped above me now.

Catherine! !

I see your true face now!

(*In a tirade of mounting agony.*)

You are that great Eastern deity,
carved in stone, whom travellers say
stares and stares at infinity
while on her lap some human dies,
emitting all his pigmy cries
to appease a wrath which never shows
upon that face but when the wind blows
havoc on the crops!

Oh . . . (*Moaning.*)

I *cannot* die here.
God is stronger than Fortune—surely!
Help me God!

> *Light suddenly streams from above as the trap door is thrown open and, with the sound of the crowd roaring, the Rope comes dangling down.* FRANÇOIS *stares at it, fascinated, then cries out in panic.*

No! No! ! No! ! !...

GEMINI (*above*): He's at it again! Hey! Wake up, below! You're next on the list, François, old fish! (*As he dangles the rope over him.*) Hook on! Bite! Next on the list!

FRANÇOIS: No! No! No! (*Backing away from the pursuing rope.*) God, I appeal! I have done nothing really wrong! I've lived as this world made me live! If there is a divine justice, I appeal!

GEMINI: Look! Do I have to come down and get you! Hey! Villon! Mouton! Montcorbier!

FRANÇOIS clings to the ground away from the snaking rope.

FRANÇOIS: The world is upside down! It is the devils who are above! Here, below, angels writhe in agony! Save me!— God of the Depths! God below!

As he beats the earth with his fists.

GEMINI: Mad as a coot! Hey, François!

FRANÇOIS: Hear me! I appeal! I appeal! I can't be dragged up to Hell! I'll not come! You can't make me!

GEMINI: Don't you want to go free? Stand up, you fool! And cry " God save the King! "

FRANÇOIS: You can't make——(*Stopping short.*) What?

There is a sound of distant cheering and, faintly approaching, the Music of the King's Progress.

(*In a hushed voice.*) What did you say? The King? Free?

GEMINI: The new King! He's come by Meung. You win. You're free!

FRANÇOIS: Free? (*Hoarse with emotion.*)

The Music grows.

GEMINI: Didn't I say *free*? Hook on! Wrap it round your guts.

FRANÇOIS reaches in a daze for the rope.

FRANÇOIS: I called upon my God! And he heard me. Fortune has been defeated in me. My luck has turned! Pull away!

With one bare foot in the loop he clings to it with all his remaining strength as GEMINI *and those above begin hauling him up.*

Pull away, Gemini! (*Going up.*) Free! Free! Free!—as the wind! I'll go back! I'll go back to the Forbidden City! I'll be François the Fortunate now! God help Catherine! God bless France! God save the King! ! ! . . .

As the CURTAIN *falls the cheering and music swells up and— the scene changes. . . .*

Scene II

Paris—Catherine's room—some weeks later.

Before rise of curtain there is the Sound of the Wind.

On rise of curtain the room looks bare and almost derelict; the shutters hang askew on broken hinges; creepers grow in through the window. A prie-dieu and madonna are noticeable additions to the room.

Catherine sits, sleeping, in a great chair, wrapped up like an invalid and facing away and towards the window.

Marthe comes in from the outside with a basket of bread and an armful of aromatic herbs. As she takes off her cloak the Great Bell of Sorbonne tolls in the distance and Catherine stirs.

Catherine (*without looking round*): I must have slept while you were gone.

Marthe: The physician says sleep is the best thing. I got the sweetherbs. And (*Proudly, as of an achievement.*) I got bread.

Catherine: I dreamed. (*Wearily.*) And as I dreamed I seemed to hear the great bell of Sorbonne.

Marthe: You heard the bell itself. For it is a South-West wind, and a wild one. It is sweeping Paris sweet again.

> Marthe *sprinkling the herbs over the floor and chatting, though she herself looks very worn.*

As I waited in the great queue for bread I watched a cloud of crows in the sky: like a shoal of fish against the stream they all flew westward, yet seemed to stay constantly over Notre Dame. (*Looking out.*)
>
> You can see them still.

Yes—It is wild.

> What is wrong?

Catherine (*as though sensing something from the open window*): There is a strange scent in the air. No, not the rosemary—no—an acrid, yet a sweet, perfume.

MARTHE: Yes—in the garden I made a fire and burned all the clothes you wore during the sickness. But the wind is blowing the smoke from the house.

CATHERINE: Perhaps it has changed?

MARTHE: No. (*At window, looking out.*)
It was the same from dawn, and it is constant now.
Yes, even the signs of these three vacant inns,
which stand over on the far side,
all hang at one angle and do not sway:
The Spotless Leopard, The Lion, and The Lamb.
It is a strangely constant wind, they say.

> *Turning to her.*

Perhaps when its pressures die away
the world shall have Spring.

> *Moving to chair.*

I'll make your chair. Come.

> *As she helps* CATHERINE, *painfully, to rise.*

CATHERINE: Spring—when I shall watch all other things grow; in a house without mirrors. You threw the last away?

MARTHE (*nodding*): Your beautiful hair will grow again.

CATHERINE: God will not award my flesh a new skin.

> *As* CATHERINE *turns we glimpse the fact that she wears some sort of protective mask.*

MARTHE: Thousands died, Madame.

CATHERINE (*moving to window*): That was my hope. Yes, I see your constant crows. I see the doves too. Those that survived. What a flash of silver their wings all make, when turning—when all their feathers take the cold sun. (*Adjusting the mask.*)

MARTHE: If the mask is troublesome to you, need you wear it in my presence, Madame? The physician says constant wearing may—

CATHERINE (*cutting her short*): The physician thinks too constantly of the wrong side of the mask.

> *As* CATHERINE *turns to move from the window we see the Mask fully.* (Its intention may have been medical, but she has made of it something more. It has an almost inhuman beauty.)

If God did not choose to have me die, He must allow me a little vanity—to live upon. Everything else has been taken away. I have my pride. (*Stopping.*) What was that sound?

MARTHE: The wind on the garden door, Madame. It will not lock. The surrounding wood has rotted away.

CATHERINE: Everything is slowly crumbling about me. Except you. (*Touching her.*) Will the priest come again today?

MARTHE: If you wish it, Madame.

CATHERINE: Marthe, I know every inflection of your voice, and what it means—as opposed to what you say. Shall I tell you what you are thinking of me?

MARTHE: If you have already thought it, Madame, do.

> *As* MARTHE *guides her back into her chair, which now faces outwards, from the window.*

CATHERINE: You think that this conversion is not of the heart. You think that Time, and now this Plague, has so ravaged my beauty that I have become pious of necessity. You think that, like a lost woman, I am soliciting religion.

MARTHE: The thoughts are yours. I only think of your peace.

CATHERINE: The priest offers me peace. But I find one great obstacle to this: I cannot confess. I cannot, Marthe, bear to be completely discovered to anybody. For I think that pride is more primitive in me than all the hungers.

MARTHE: It might, Madame, bring ease to confess; but to be forgiven—that is peace.

CATHERINE: By whom?

> *Totally unexpectedly* OLD WILLIAM VILLON *shuffles into the room.*

MARTHE: Oh! (*Standing in front of* CATHERINE *to shield her.*)

WILLIAM: I ask your pardon. But since there was no door—Does Madame de Vausselles live here?

MARTHE: Yes.

WILLIAM: So many have gone in fear, and I was afraid——Are you Madame de Vausselles?

> *He speaks and looks with all the uncertainty of someone whose senses have begun to play tricks with him.*

CATHERINE (*speaking from behind* MARTHE): Why have you come?

WILLIAM (*to* MARTHE): I did not catch what you said, Madame?

CATHERINE: Why have you come here?

WILLIAM: Ah, Madame de Vausselles!

> *As he locates the voice on coming forward.*

I am glad *you* have stayed. I too have not deserted the city. I too have waited patiently behind my red door, while the Plague has swept through our grass-green streets But why have you stayed?

> CATHERINE *does not answer immediately.*

Perhaps for the same reason as myself: just finding it impossible to go, eh? But he has not returned, has he?

CATHERINE: Master William, why have you come?

> *He stares short-sightedly and perplexedly at her face.*

WILLIAM: Oh, Madame, you must not stare at me. I am dressed so because I am on my way out of Paris. Yes—it is the new King who is sending me out of Paris—to Malay-le-Roi. Oh, it is only a small village, but there I shall be King's Magistrate. Yes. And there, you see, I shall have to *enforce the Law*. So, before I go, I should like to know, for certain, that François is dead. Do you know if François is dead?

MARTHE: We don't know, Master William.

> *The old man turns away and in his anxiety paces the floor; talking away:*

WILLIAM: Madame de Vausselles, had it ever occurred to you that François was " irresponsible "? You must not smile at me. For I mean much when I say " irresponsible ". In the last four years I have studied the Law, and not without grave and great pain I have reached this conclusion, Madame, that irresponsibility is a potent sin! And it must be punished. And in Malay-le-Roi I will be Magistrate, and obviously it would be better, simply to know that François was dead. Madame, do you understand me? For as Magistrate surely you must see that I must punish felons and where necessary . . . hang them. Why do you stare at me so? I have assured myself that I would have no qualms if it did come to this . . . this eventuality. Of course, my parish is small. But people always say: " It is a small world ", and thereby imply just such an eventuality. Surely, Madame, (*with growing distress and fervour*) you can see, that once in a position of responsibility— and faced with my own gallows tree—I could not choose, could not refuse that tree its legitimate fruit, could I? *And I will be responsible!* For, Madame, I do assure you that the whole Kingdom seethes with vice and that there now remains only one way—the rack, " the question ", the gallows tree, to drag them up to where they may be destroyed and sent to Purgatory! Why must you stare! I will *not* forgive him now! For there comes a time when to forgive François is to commit every crime which I have given him the liberty to commit!

> *At the top of his voice he suddenly stops, and there is silence, as he realises that her face has the mask of someone with the plague.* WILLIAM, *lost, looks from her to* MARTHE.

I . . . (*confused*) . . . I am sorry . . . (*gently*) . . . I am sorry that you have no news of him. It may always be so un- certain for us. And that, as you know, creates strain. But I have concluded, and I shall go to Malay-le-Roi. (*At the door.*) There I shall enforce the Law . . . *mercilessly.* God have mercy on us. . . .

> *Awkwardly, and shocked, he goes by the stair.*

CATHERINE: Marthe!

As she seems to be going to help the old man down the stairs.

Don't leave me!

MARTHE: I think that his François was the whole of that old man's life. Yet it would be a blessing to be able to tell him now that that life is ended.

CATHERINE: I had thought he had come to tell me so. But it is not ended, Marthe.

MARTHE: We none of us know. (*Going to her.*) And it would be unwise to dwell on this now.

CATHERINE (*bitterly*): I think I must lie down again.

MARTHE: Madame, you're trembling. Come—rest. We must wait for greater warmth to the sun, before we sit at the window again. The fault was mine. I want you well too soon.

CATHERINE: Marthe . . . (*Taking her arm.*) If I were now to die.

MARTHE: Madame . . . (*Stopping.*)

CATHERINE: Oh, I shall not take my own life—painful though it is to me. But, if I were to die, what, Marthe, would you do?

MARTHE: Beyond the weeping, Madame, I do not know. But there are always people who need care. Come in, and you shall play and I shall sing. The lute is in there.

MARTHE *assists* CATHERINE *across the room to the bedroom door.*

CATHERINE: . . . Marthe, (*Turning at door.*) you have risked even this plague to give me a compassion I cannot deserve. I have not dared ask you why, not till now. Why, Marthe?

MARTHE (*quietly*): Why, Madame, to be at peace. I *need* to help.

CATHERINE: Marthe, (*With difficulty.*) . . . never before, at any time, have I said what I am about to say—not to any creature. It has been hard for me. Marthe . . . I love you.

MARTHE: Madame, (*With infinite, gentle, casualness.*) I know.

> MARTHE *leads* CATHERINE *off.*

You will sleep.

> *The door closes behind them.*
>
> *Sound of the wind and the door creaking.*
>
> *Suddenly from the stair entrance* FRANÇOIS *comes in, followed by the* WOLF.
>
> *They stand waiting for possible trouble.* FRANÇOIS *is dressed in the most gallant of clothes which, pathetically in contrast to his haggard self, are as much a " mask " of comedy as* CATHERINE'S *mask is of tragedy.*
>
> WOLF *hiccups.*

WOLF (*solemnly*): I don't like this.

FRANÇOIS: So far, I do. We have achieved our goal with no alarm bells rung. (*Looking around.*)

WOLF (*shaking head*): No, I don't like this.

FRANÇOIS: Wolf, you don't like anything—except strong drink and weak women. (*Tapping flask.*) Sniff around. Sniff around and see that the trap isn't set this time. Sniff around . . . while I improve my anatomy with more spirit.

> *He takes a long pull at the flask.*

Mm. (*Wiping his mouth.*) I'd rather be as sober as a judge on this Judgment Day, but I wouldn't be able to move at all, except for this borrowed buoyancy. Sniff, I said.

WOLF (*sniffing*): I *am* sniffing.

FRANÇOIS: But what, Wolf, do you sniff?

WOLF: Perfume!

FRANÇOIS: Aha! You're on the trail. Where from?

WOLF (*after following the scent by various sniffs to its source*): From *you*!

FRANÇOIS: Saint Sophia scented! So it is. It's from my borrowed plumes—my foster feather. Stop sniffing me, animal.

WOLF: But I like *this*!

FRANÇOIS: Stand away. (*Pushing him off.*) You may go, Wolf. How René would have loved to see me now! Is there no mirror in my lady's chamber now? Eh?

> *Music of the lute is heard within.*

WOLF (*drawing back*): I don't like that.

FRANÇOIS: Wolf, slope away (*Whispered.*)—slope away. Leave the rest to me. Here's your bone. (*Giving* WOLF *his purse.*) I shan't need money any more.

> THE WOLF *goes by the stairs.*

For Pity's sake! (*Whispered.*) Not sweet music now! (*Cried out.*) Stop!

> *The music stops, abruptly.*

FRANÇOIS: No. No sweetness, but that which comes with . . . revenge. (*As he stands back waiting for the door to open.*)

> MARTHE *comes out.*

MARTHE: Oh! . . . (*Catching breath at the apparition of* FRANÇOIS.)

> *Quickly she closes the door behind her.*

> MARTHE *and* FRANÇOIS *confront each other in silence.*

FRANÇOIS (*doffing his plumed bonnet*): I have called to collect the rent . . . for accommodation in my heart, which madame-within has occupied for four years, and for which time I have received no recompense. Woman, don't you know me?

MARTHE: Master François?

FRANÇOIS: The same—but oh, so different! Fortune dotes upon me now. For she has allowed me this—this!—which I am pleased to see as my great moment. Though it may well be my last. (*Coughing.*) Marthe, you have heard people say " I am on my last legs ". Well, my legs this morning passed away; and all above below I'm mortgaged to two bottles of burgundy. I float, Marthe, between Heaven and Hell—and there's a deal of judgment still to do. So! Produce for me La Belle Dame within. (MARTHE *makes no move.*) Are you paralysed?

MARTHE: We thought you were dead.

FRANÇOIS: How convenient for " we ". Tell her I live—precariously (*Coughing.*)

MARTHE (*pityingly*): Oh, Master François!

FRANÇOIS: Marthe, surprisingly lovely though you may seem, it is Mistress Catherine that I want. Bring her in. Tell her her candle of beauty burns here but with a searing flame. Tell her the moth's now a butterfly of unbounded passions. which adversity has dragged beyond dreams. Tell her . . . anything; but bring her out.

CATHERINE (*calling off*): Marthe! (*Through door.*)

  MARTHE *turns decisively and locks the door.*

FRANÇOIS: Marthe!—would you be my latest crime? Give me the key.

CATHERINE (*off*): Marthe, who is it? (*Knocking.*) Who is it?

FRANÇOIS: Madame, it is I—(*Calling.*)—I, Fortune. And I would have you see Fortune face to face. (*To* MARTHE.) The key!

MARTHE: Please, Master François, please go away! Please believe me when I say that this may be disastrous for you.

FRANÇOIS: But I thrive on disaster! I must, Marthe. For nothing else has been offered me for ten years. The key—the key.

MARTHE: I cannot. She is not well.

FRANÇOIS: Neither am I.

MARTHE: But she has been near to dying!

FRANÇOIS: No nearer death than I!

MARTHE: In Paris it has been dreadful.

FRANÇOIS: Marthe—in Hell—it has been terrible! Give me the key!

MARTHE (*in despair*): But she is so sick!

FRANÇOIS: Woman, *I die!*

CATHERINE (*off*): Oh, God.

FRANÇOIS: What did she say?

MARTHE: She called on God.

FRANÇOIS: He's on my side of the door. Let her come out, woman! (*Collapsing in the chair.*) Marthe, (*Laughing piteously.*) I may threaten you with bloody despatch, but really I've not the strength in me to kill off a November fly.

CATHERINE (*off*): Marthe! Open the door!

MARTHE: But, Madame, he is . . .

FRANÇOIS: Open the door!

CATHERINE (*off*): Marthe! Do you hear me?

MARTHE: Very well.

> As FRANÇOIS *stands back, ready,* MARTHE *opens the door. Slowly* CATHERINE *comes out and faces* FRANÇOIS.

FRANÇOIS: No . . . (*Seeing the mask and as though fighting a dream.*) No. . . .

CATHERINE: François . . . (*Desperately keeping composure.*)

FRANÇOIS: What is it? What does it mean? Can you no longer trust your face to belie what lies deeper? Take that damnable mask away. Take it away!

CATHERINE: François, for the love you once bore me—

FRANÇOIS: Love! Ha! It was not love.
After five days torture at Orleans
I threw that illusion away.
For your face burned through and through the pain,
and every time the mist grew
it was simply an indefinable you
acting for life to make me see
that I was you and you were me
and nothing but death could break away
that dependence! To that degree,
Love is not love! It is hatefully
the whole of life, and look at me!—
I am dying of it. Would you mock Death? No!
Take the mask away. Take it off!

> CATHERINE, *half in fear, half in resolution, raises her hand to her face.*

MARTHE: Don't, Madame! Don't!

FRANÇOIS: *Take that mask from your face!*

CATHERINE (*desperately*):
> I have never asked anything of you,
> and what you have given me
> has been a great burden. I ask you now—
> to kill me if you will. But then go—
> go and keep in your memory
> what was the beauty first brought you here.
> Forgive me—and go—on in your own world of dreams
> Only, leave me as I am—as I am, François!

MARTHE: François, go. Go.

FRANÇOIS: Just—go? Now?—
> when for four hunted, animal years
> I've seen that face you'd keep from me
> framed in the mirage of memory
> by candlelight?
>> *As he advances on* CATHERINE *and his appeal becomes more*
>> *and more impassioned.*

MARTHE: Madame, go in.

FRANÇOIS: Wherever, however, I lay down;
> in the night rain beneath a tree,
> in wild hyacinths under the moon,
> in noon-day stupor by a stream—
>> (*Thrusting* MARTHE *aside.*)
> wherever Fortune beat me down;
> wherever I dared kneel to say
> my Ave Marias, Maria, for me,
> was the woman who stands before me now
> and pleads in black hypocrisy
> for sweet forgiveness! No!—

CATHERINE: François—

FRANÇOIS (*reeling on his feet*): Look at me!
> I am this crazed thing because of you!
> For your face has haunted me night and day
> till—(*Gasping for breath.*) Take it off!

MARTHE: Oh, Madame. (*Fearfully as* CATHERINE's *hand goes up.*)

FRANÇOIS: *Take it off*; Take it——(*Stopping aghast.*)

> CATHERINE, *with a great effort of will, has stripped the mask from her face and turned away to face* FRANÇOIS *fully.*
>
> *There is Silence and all we can see is the horror and perplexity on* FRANÇOIS'S *face at what he sees under the mask.*

(*In a hoarse whisper.*) I am an evil thing.

Oh, God, forgive . . .

> *Slowly and in silence* FRANÇOIS *turns and—with all strength gone out of him—he totters towards the door, muttering.*

I am evil. I am evil.

> *He stumbles out of sight down the stairs. Both women stand, unable to make a move.*
>
> *There is the sound of the street door thrown open. The Mask falls from* CATHERINE'S *fingers upon the floor.*
>
> MARTHE, *about to move, hears the Alarm sounded and voices shouting in the street below. She looks to* CATHERINE.

CATHERINE: Yes. Go after him. I need no help now.

> *As* MARTHE *hurries out,* CATHERINE *drops her head into her hands and utterly sobs her heart out.*
>
> *The Scene Curtain falls and the Alarm Bell rings on as the scene changes. . . .*

SCENE III

Outside the Red Door in the Yard of St. Benoit—immediately after.

As the curtain rises FAT MARGOT *and* THE WOLF *come in arm-in-arm. The ever-fearful* WOLF *stops and looks back.*

WOLF: I don't like it. He could . . . Look!

MARGOT: Talk of the devil! François!

> *Both fall back as* FRANÇOIS *comes in and, like a desperate man on a tightrope, walks with his eyes fixed upon it, towards the Red Door.*

WOLF: Don't go near him.

MARGOT: He could have caught it.

WOLF: He could have killed her. I don't like this. Come on.

MARGOT (*as they go*): Poor old François. Did I tell you what he once asked me to do? (*giggling*).

> *As* MARGOT *and* THE WOLF *go,* FRANÇOIS *reaches the door and steadies himself against the door post as* FAT MARGOT's *bawdy laugh teeters into the distance.*

FRANÇOIS: Oh—Old William—all the wonder's gone. The Truth must be old. Take me in.

> *He knocks, weakly, on the knocker.*

Take me in, (*sobbing*) and tell me what to do. I will obey. I *will* obey!

> *He knocks louder.*

Take me in! Put out my wondering eyes! Chain me to The Great Book! I *will* be wise!

> *Beating on the door with his fists.*

I will be!——

> *The door gives way and swings open. Fearfully,* FRANÇOIS *goes in.*

(*Off.*) Uncle William? (*Calling.*) Uncle William?...

> MARTHE *hurries in. She sees the door hanging open and is crossing to it when—*
>
> FRANÇOIS *reappears in the doorway.*

(*Faintly.*) Gone.

> *As he collapses on the steps,* MARTHE *reaches to help him. She carries a bottle of wine.*

No! (*Fending her off.*) Don't touch me! I corrupt. One touch of this corruption in me might stain a whole continent of snow. No—God bless you for your clean linen. Have me buried one world deep—deep. It's all over.

MARTHE: No, François, no. Listen. Your uncle is not dead. He has left Paris—for Malay-le-Roi.

FRANÇOIS: Malay-le—Oh . . . (*With a faint smile*.)

MARTHE: Do you know the place?

FRANÇOIS: Know the place? I once stole a pig in Malay-le-Roi. Stole a pig. Oh . . . what an innocence crime may assume Marthe, when faced with corruption. I corrupt. Let me be.

MARTHE: No, François, (*Trying to rouse him.*) if you don't get out of Paris now it will be too late. They'll torture you. You'll go back to prison.

FRANÇOIS: Oh, not that, no.

MARTHE: They'll close all the gates. You'll be shut in. You must get to old William. He will shelter you. For he does love you.

FRANÇOIS: There's no meaning in the word, Marthe.

MARTHE: Oh, but there is. There is. I know. Take this wine, for strength. You must try. You must try. (*Getting him on his feet.*) Go out by the Porte St. Jacques. Then North. Quickly, before they—Look out!

> MARTHE *bundles* FRANÇOIS *aside and conceals him behind her as a* SERGEANT *and* TWO GUARDS *hurry in, see the open door and continue straight into the house to search it.*

FRANÇOIS (*struggling at last to go*): No—not that again. I'll try, Bless you. There will be a sort of confusion in my mind. Marthe, between the image of the Mother of God and you.

MARTHE (*impatiently anxious*): Go! The other way! Malay-le-Roi!

> *He nods and begins to hobble off painfully.*

Oh, run!

FRANÇOIS: Like the wind?

MARTHE: And may God speed you.

FRANÇOIS: Ah—(*Wearily.*) God will have to go slow.

> FRANÇOIS *goes.*
>
> MARTHE, *exhausted, sways and steadies herself, leaning back against the wall by the door and as the* SERGEANT *and the* TWO GUARDS *come from the house she stumbles into their path, to impede them.*

SERGEANT: Who are you? What are you doing here, eh? (*As she does not answer.*) What's the matter with you?

> 1ST GUARD *seizes her.*

1ST GUARD: You hear!

MARTHE: Don't touch me now.

2ND GUARD (*suddenly fearful*): Don't touch her!

SERGEANT: Why? No—(*Realising and drawing back.*)

MARTHE: Yes—I believe I have taken the Plague.

1ST GUARD: God above! (*Thrusting* MARTHE *from him.*)

> MARTHE *stumbles into the door-way.*

SERGEANT: Inside!

> The SERGEANT *draws a dagger, threatening her, and as* MARTHE *goes into the empty house, the* SERGEANT *slams the door closed and, plunging the dagger into it as a sign, joins the* TWO GUARDS *as they all hurry off.*
> The Bell of Sorbonne peals solemnly as the scene changes. . . .

SCENE IV

Malay-Le-Roy, the Village Green some days later—sunset.

Before rise of curtain a sound of hammering can be heard and someone whistling the tune of " God help both Popes ".

On rise of curtain, a CARPENTER *is discovered at the foot of where a long ladder slopes off and up. He mops his face and begins to gather up tools as he calls to his mate, hammering off.*

1ST CARPENTER: She'll do now! It's just on curfew! Let it be, will you!

> The hammering stops and 2ND CARPENTER comes in, mallet in hand.

2ND CARPENTER: Saints in repose! but it's close, eh? Thunder about? Well—(*Surveying their work, off.*) There she stands!
—as firm a tree as never took root. In Paris, up on

Monfaucon, they swear that the old gibbet *did* take root, *and*—that the mandrakes grew from the same. S'right! And—(*Looking off and up*.) Aye-aye! I see you've fixed the noose up too?

1ST CARPENTER: Anything wrong with that? Used to need a rope on a gibbet in my day. Get your tools.

2ND CARPENTER: Well—we can test it in the morning.

1ST CARPENTER: Test it! What d'ye mean?

2ND CARPENTER (*quoting*): " Must be tested to ascertain that it is entirely capable of taking the maximum strain intended."

BOTH: Guild regulations!

1ST CARPENTER: And I suppose—me being the heavier of us two —that tomorrow morning you expect me to take a hearty breakfast, climb up there, push my neck through the perishing noose, kick the suffering ladder away, and strangle myself for the sake of " Guild Regulations "? I'm hanged if I do!

2ND CARPENTER: That's right. You are. If you do. But you don't.

1ST CARPENTER: Then who does?

2ND CARPENTER: I do.

1ST CARPENTER: What! With that neck?

2ND CARPENTER: No! I just puts the noose round my fundament —like a child in a swing—and jumps from the ladder. It gives the real strain, like when the whole dead-weight of the . . .

1ST CARPENTER (*stopping him*): . . . All right! All right! Stop! Let the ladder be . . .

2ND CARPENTER: But it belongs to . . .

1ST CARPENTER: Nobody will steal it! There'll be a Guard on the green all night and . . . (*Suddenly recollecting*.) Holy Mary! I've just remembered that I am for duty tonight on that old devil's Night Guard! Get your things together.

2ND CARPENTER: But does he make you all do guards?

1ST CARPENTER: Do you know what he brought all the way out of Paris?—a silver trumpet. Just like the ones they blow at the Palace of the Louvre. And he has a trumpeter to blow it for his Curfew.

2ND CARPENTER: Trumpets too! A bit off-centre, eh?

1ST CARPENTER: Between you and me and the old gibbet there, he's been slowly slipping off the hook. Don't cut yourself! But the new King put him there and the new King'll have to shift him. And anyway he's doing what the new King wants: whipping up every perishing vagrant or petty thief and clapping them straight in irons. And from today it will be hangings not floggings. What's this?

> As an almost unrecognisable and battered FRANÇOIS comes in and painfully drags his feet towards them.

2ND CARPENTER: Something for legal disposal, eh? (*Moving off.*) God save you, brother carcass.

FRANÇOIS: Is this Malay-le-Roi?

2ND CARPENTER: What?

FRANÇOIS: Is this Malay-le-Roi?

2ND CARPENTER: All of it, brother.

1ST CARPENTER: Oh, don't encourage him.

FRANÇOIS (*hoarse with exhaustion*): Wait, brother. Do you happen to know where the Seigneur William Villon lives?

1ST CARPENTER: Do we happen to know!

2ND CARPENTER: Yes, uncle. Why?

FRANÇOIS: I want to see him.

1ST CARPENTER: Oh, no you don't. (*Turning away.*)

2ND CARPENTER: What he means to say is that if you knew Old William as he does, you'd not want to see him.

FRANÇOIS: Why?

2ND CARPENTER: Because he's the magistrate here. And he has a nasty way with vagrants.

1ST CARPENTER: So move on or never move again! Come on, or his blessed trumpet will blow before I've had my supper.

FRANÇOIS (*to* 2ND CARPENTER): Is it William Villon of Paris— of St. Benoit?

1ST CARPENTER: Why? (*Becoming suspicious.*) Do you know him then? Eh?

FRANÇOIS (*turning away*): No. I . . .

    He stops short seeing the gibbet for the first time.

2ND CARPENTER: What's the matter, brother?

    As FRANÇOIS *looks like one hypnotised at the gibbet.*

FRANÇOIS: That.

1ST CARPENTER: Never seen a gibbet before?

FRANÇOIS: But it's new.

1ST CARPENTER: Well, even a gibbet's got to begin. Come, (*to* 2ND CARPENTER) if you're coming.

    1ST CARPENTER *goes.*

FRANÇOIS: Wait! (*Detaining* 2ND CARPENTER.) Who had that new gibbet put up?

2ND CARPENTER: The old man, brother cockle.

FRANÇOIS: Old William? (*Looking up at gibbet.*)

2ND CARPENTER: Yes, and they say he's dangerous. And I wouldn't hang around his door. Take this, brother. (*Giving him a coin.*) And go on. There will be a Guard mounting here soon. (*As he sees* FRANÇOIS' *eyes staring up at the noose.*) If you're having any ideas, I'd have you know that rope's not tested yet.

    2ND CARPENTER *goes, whistling* " God help both Popes and Paris too . . ."

    OLD WILLIAM *comes in.* (*He is dressed in his magisterial robes and looks not unlike Moses the Lawgiver. In contrast to François he is the King to the Beggar. They are worlds apart.*) *For a moment* WILLIAM *stares short-sightedly and almost fearfully towards* FRANÇOIS. FRANÇOIS *bows his head and waits. But* WILLIAM *goes straight past him with eyes only for the new gibbet.*

97

WILLIAM: The thing is painless really. It's the mounting the ladder which must be—rung by rung—difficult. (*Seeing* FRANÇOIS.) Is it not terrible too, that such a short drop should take one to the other world—for which we know no location? Eh? (*Turning sternly on* FRANÇOIS.) Answer me! Is it not a sudden change of location—Death? Eh? I can have you whipped for not answering me—and the whole thing be legal! Do you hear me? I'll call the Guard. (*Making to go.*)

FRANÇOIS: Uncle William! It's . . . me.

WILLIAM: What? Speak up! I may not see very well, but God gave the prisoner a tongue. Who are you?

FRANÇOIS: Uncle William, it is . . . me.

WILLIAM: The Tree?—Yesterday they did not all whisper so. They called it the " nevergreen tree " and laughed—and said " It bears forbidden fruit "—God forgive them! They cannot see the shape of . . . the eventuality. (*Looking at* FRANÇOIS.)

FRANÇOIS: It is François.

WILLIAM: Yes. (*Sighing.*) It is François. Yet how did you know? (*Suspiciously.*) Oh, I suppose the whole world guesses by now. It is always so. We think our loves secret. Eh?

> *Distant thunder.*

> As FRANÇOIS *tries to move away from all this which is torture to him,* WILLIAM " *buttonholes* " *him in talk.*

Have you ever thought, my friend, that you were innocent? It's impossible. And so the criminal to a degree must judge the criminal. Confidentially, there is no Law, but Will and the support of the Deity. Do you hear thunder? (*Peremptorily.*) Answer me! (*Suddenly gentle.*) Have you a headache?

FRANÇOIS (*with bowed head*): It is the thunder.

WILLIAM: Yes. (*Turning away.*) The ducks fly high and anxiously. Yesterday it was not like this. There was a wind. Have you noticed how one seems to be relieved of responsibility on a wind-swept morning?

FRANÇOIS: Let the lightning come and single me out. I am Crime. I am Disease, and now I am Insanity.

WILLIAM: What? (*Turning to him, confidentially.*) Do you know —but repeat this to no one—it would be better for everyone's sake if François were dead. For people say "It is a small world" and thereby imply just such an eventuality. I must face it. That is no leafless tree against the sunset. But why must you stare at it? (*With a touch of hysteria.*) Go, it might happen any time now. And I must take a different attitude to you, in preparation. Go. Go! Stop staring at it, or I may repent my leniency. (*Almost shouting.*)

FRANÇOIS (*still looking fascinated at gibbet*): But Master Villon, if François were dead . . .

WILLIAM: . . . There is no "if", unfortunately. Go. The storm is certain.

> *Distant thunder.*

(*Harshly.*) Go, or I'll not answer for what I'll do! It is the awful uncertainty.

FRANÇOIS: Master William, (*Deliberately*). I can give you certainty. (*Turning to him.*) Your François is dead.

WILLIAM (*pause*): The voice has authority—(*Stares at him.*) What did you say?

FRANÇOIS: François is dead. (*Averting his face.*)

WILLIAM: Mm? Yes, there *is* authority. (*Wandering on in a sort of delayed shock.*) But have you noticed how under strain we award every natural sign authority? That curious cloud in grey and red . . . What did you say?

FRANÇOIS: *François is dead.* (*He bows his head away from* WILLIAM's *gaze.*)

WILLIAM (*after a long pause*): Oh! . . . (*With a great sigh of relief.*) Oh, dear! Oh, dear! This should be no shock to me. But one stumbles on the depths of love suddenly. You must not weep. You knew him?

FRANÇOIS: No. I knew everything about him, but him I was in no position to know.

WILLIAM: How did he die?

FRANÇOIS (*looking into red sun at the gibbet*): One red sundown—on a country gibbet—during a storm he . . .
 Thunder close.

WILLIAM: Hanged? Oh, I knew it would be so. But it was his own doing.

FRANÇOIS: Yes. (*Moving to ladder.*) It was his own doing.

WILLIAM: Did he die well?

FRANÇOIS: No. (*Wryly.*)

WILLIAM: No, François would have to be helped to the end—even up that ladder.

FRANÇOIS: He made a fine speech before he went.

WILLIAM: No doubt it was blasphemy. (*Sadly and gently.*)

FRANÇOIS: He spoke of three people.

WILLIAM: Three people?

FRANÇOIS: Yes. One, Catherine, through whom he knew the Passion and the Beauty of Life. One, Marthe, the soul of Compassion, and one—William—whose love in its Constancy was almost godly. Of this William, I heard him say, " He deserved my love which now I feel, but which I cannot show ".
 Suddenly, sharply and clearly the Silver Trumpet for the Guard sounds off.

WILLIAM: Ah . . . (*Catching his breath, then chuckling nervously.*) The trumpet for the Guard. For a moment I thought that Heaven . . . Ah, but praise the Lord! He loved me. God sent you with peace. Here, take my purse. Come to my house after dark. It is the one red door in Malay-le-Roi. But I must mount my guard. Yes . . . but for the last time. And in the morning they can burn down the tree. For it will not now be necessary. (*Moving off.*) He loved me, and it is gone—the dreadful eventuality.
 Thunder in distance and going.
 (*Turning at exit.*) We'll talk of him, eh? But after curfew.

FRANÇOIS: After curfew.

WILLIAM: But I'm afraid you'll have to be gone by morning.

FRANÇOIS: I will.

WILLIAM: But, it doesn't matter, does it? (*Happily.*) Who cares now? Not I!

FRANÇOIS: Nor I.

> OLD WILLIAM *goes, his head high, leaving* FRANÇOIS *at the foot of the ladder.*

God forgive me. (*Looking up at rope.*) Mount, Villon . . . Mount, François. . . .

> *As, with the very last of his strength, he clambers, step by painful step, up the ladder.*

Coming up, René. Keeping it warm? Move over, Casin. Here's no rush, eh? No rush at all.

> *Pausing, exhausted, and looking back down.*

Adieu, the dark earth. Oh, heart—still there? Have a care how you beat up here.

> *Going on up.*

Keep time. Up! (*Up a rung.*) It beats. Up! (*Up a rung.*) It beats. Up! (*Up a rung.*) Up! (*Reaching up.*) It . . . It beats! . .

> *The Trumpet, for curfew, suddenly sounds, loud and clear and—*

> FRANÇOIS, *looking back in startled wonder, loses his grip on the ladder, loses his grip on life, and, slithering back down to earth, lies—dead.*

VILLAGE GUARD (*off*): Cover your fires!

> *One of the* VILLAGE GUARD *comes in, calling and ringing casually and slowly:*

Cover your fires! Cover your fires!

> *Without seeing what lies in the shadow of the gibbet he proceeds, calling and ringing.*

Cover your fires! . . . (*off*) . . . Cover your fires! . . .

as the FINAL CURTAIN falls.

HÉLOÏSE

CHARACTERS

HÉLOÏSE

ABELARD

FULBERT — Uncle and guardian of Héloïse.

THÉO — Friend of both Abelard and Fulbert

HUGO — Servant to Abelard and afterwards to Fulbert

ALBERIC — Rival teacher to Abelard

SUPIRO — A dealer, afterwards a Friar.

ABBESS OF ARGENTEUIL — The old teacher of Héloïse.

A SINGER — A wandering musician.

The action of the play takes place in:—the small hall of Canon Fulbert's house by Notre Dame, Paris ; by a gateway near Notre Dame ; by a gateway at Argenteuil ; by a castle wall in Brittany ; and in the country cell of Abelard at Nogent.

The play is intended to have two intervals, falling after the curtain to Act I and after the curtain to Act II. And the playing time is approximately 2 hours 15 minutes.

Héloïse was first produced at the King's Theatre, Southsea, on 22nd October 1951, and subsequently at the Duke of York's Theatre, London, on 14th November 1951.

It was presented by Michael Powell, by arrangement with Duchess Productions Ltd., with the following cast:

HÉLOÏSE	Siobhán McKenna
ABELARD	Walter Macken
FULBERT	Mervyn Johns
THÉO	David Oxley
HUGO	Esmond Knight
ALBERIC	Nigel Green
SUPIRO	John Byron
ABBESS	Eileen Thorndike
A SINGER	Geoffrey Dunn

The play directed by Michael Powell

Scenery and costumes by Terence Morgan II

Music specially composed by Brian Easdale

ACT I

SCENE I

By a gateway, in the crowded confines of the little island community of Notre Dame de Paris.
A summer morning (about 1115 A.D.).
Before rise of curtain a Song is heard:—

> " ' A woman there will be '—
> so sang the tree;
> ' A woman there may be '—
> so sighed the rose . . ."

On rise of curtain THE SINGER *is seen, kneeling, holding a small lute and a piece of manuscript upon which he concentrates as he sings on:—*

> " ' A woman there must be '—cried the thorn
> —' who comes not to bear but to be born . . ."

SUPIRO, *coming through the gateway, slows down to listen to the song. (He has a richness of garb not at one with the greasiness of its upkeep. He is the medieval racketeer.)*

> " ' not to be known, but be what she knows ' . . ."

HUGO, *passing by, stops to listen too. (He is a heavy, stubborn Breton.)*

> " ' not to ensnare but to set free.
> A woman ' . . ."

SUPIRO *reaches over the shoulder of* THE SINGER, *snatches the piece of manuscript away and stops the song abruptly.*

SINGER: Let that alone or! . . . Oh. (*Changing his tone to one of guarded respect as he sees who it is.*) Monsieur Supiro!

SUPIRO: And how did you come by this song, my thrush?

SINGER: Oh, honestly, Monsieur Supiro.

SUPIRO: Honestly? In Paris, today, the only things come by honestly are perplexity and perspiration.

HUGO: Haw! Haw! (*Heavily.*) Associate me with that remark, Master.

SUPIRO: Disassociate me with that association. (*Turning his back on* HUGO *and concentrating on the manuscript.*)

> *As he is examing the manuscript,* HÉLOÏSE *comes in. She is worrying over a note which she holds in her hands. But she is about to pass on when* SUPIRO *begins reading the words of the song aloud:*

SUPIRO (*reading*):

> " ' A woman there will be '—so sang the tree;
> ' A woman there may be '—so sighed the rose . . ."

> HÉLOÏSE *hesitates and listens as* SUPIRO *continues:*

> " ' A woman there must be! '—cried the thorn;
> ' who comes not to bear but to be born!
> ' not to be known, but be what she knows ' . . ."

> HÉLOÏSE *turns back.*

> " ' not to ensnare, but to set free;
> ' a woman ' . . ." (*Seeing the young woman and stopping short.*) Good morning!

HÉLOÏSE: Oh! (*Confused.*) Good morning, sir.

> *She makes as to go, but hangs back to listen, when* SUPIRO *turns to question* THE SINGER.

SUPIRO (*whispering*): How did you come by this?

SINGER (*whispering*): It was given to me by Master Abelard's servant.

HUGO (*shouting*): That's a lie! (*He starts pummelling* THE SINGER.)

SUPIRO: Woa, turnip! (*Restraining* HUGO.) Woa! Don't thump the fellow. He tells an interesting lie.

SINGER: But it's not a lie, I . . .

HUGO: It is! *I* am Master Abelard's servant, and . . .

SINGER (*shouting*): That obviously is a lie!

> HUGO *is going to thump him again, when* SUPIRO *separates them both.*

SUPIRO: Now. (*Calming them.*) In order of lying . . . (*Turning to* SINGER.) Why did you say that the servant of the greatest thinker of our day gave you such a song?

SINGER: Because he did!

HUGO: But . . . (*About to raise his fist.*)

SUPIRO: Peace, ploughboy! The lesson is in logic. One of you is about to be resolved into a liar—logically. Now . . .

HÉLOÏSE (*coming forward and interrupting*): If I may suggest, sir— may not *both* be lying? For surely Master Abelard does not write such songs? And (*to* HUGO) from your voice you are not a Parisian at all but a Breton and so—

HUGO: —So is Master Abelard and . . . (*Stopping.*) Oho!

> He stands as if some great thought has struck him.

SUPIRO: What's come over you, turnip?

HUGO: A thought has just come into my head.

SUPIRO: Well, for pity's sake, let it out. It can't be happy there.

HUGO: I'm new.

SUPIRO: You? (*Looking him over.*)

HUGO: Yes, and old too. And that's the trouble. I'm an *old* servant of the family just *new* dragged up from Brittany to serve young Master Peter Abelard's needs. Because none of them Paris servants serves. The girl's clever, knowing my voice was from Brittany.

SUPIRO: Oh, she knows the source of more than that. Judgement to you. (*Handing song back to* SINGER.) Costs to you. (*Throwing a coin to* HUGO.)

SINGER: I told you it was Master Abelard's song. (*To* HUGO.) The servant before you sold it to me. The civilised servant.

HUGO: All right! It's my Master's song; and being his rightful property . . . (*He snatches it from* SINGER.) . . . I take it back to him. For it's no proper servant trades his Master's property! So!—

> HUGO *makes his exit, with the song. And as* HÉLOÏSE *is about to drift away* SUPIRO *watches her.*

HÉLOÏSE: But can it be true?

> THE SINGER *tests his lute to see that it has not suffered from the tussle.*

SUPIRO: Can what be true . . . Héloïse?

HÉLOÏSE (*turning in surprise*): How do you know my name, sir?

SUPIRO: Within this little island in the Seine—Our Lady's principality—the names of most people are known to me. I know all the cells in our hive of Notre Dame; and who does, or doesn't, buzz in them. I know your Uncle, Canon Fulbert. And I know your reputation, my dear—for scholarship. And yet—and yet—I am still not convinced that any woman can stay sufficiently at the disposal of Learning to be devoted, in truth, to Truth. She—the woman—will always incline to be devoted to Devotion. Unless, of course, she *does* answer to Abelard's description in this song. But the Lord does not do the world such wrong as to make any woman so divinely right.

HÉLOÏSE: Might it then fall to the Devil? For is not He the more creative in our day?

> THE SINGER, *testing his lute, plucks part of the tune.*

SUPIRO (*looking intently at her*): I see.

HÉLOÏSE: What do you see, monsieur?

SUPIRO: Why all our scholars begin to talk about you, Héloïse, as . . . original. Even our great Abelard—

HÉLOÏSE (*quickly*): —talks about me?

SUPIRO: Yes. (*Studying her.*) What was it you were asking just now—about something being true or not true?

HÉLOÏSE: That song. Could Master Abelard really have written such a song?

SUPIRO: Why not? He does write songs—for recreation.

HÉLOÏSE: Yes—but a love song, sir? The first philosopher of France—the leader of thought in our day—write a love song?

SUPIRO: It would be unwise for a leader of thought *not* to be knowledgeable in that subject. No?

HÉLOÏSE: In Love, monsieur?

SUPIRO: Aye. In Love, my dear. (*Turning to go.*) Though I grant you it is unwise to sing the fact aloud. Especially when, as you say, the Devil is so creative today. God attend you!

HÉLOÏSE (*calling after him*): Monsieur, what is your name?

SUPIRO: Name? Supiro, just Supiro.
> SUPIRO *goes through the gate.* HÉLOÏSE *quickly turns to* THE SINGER.

HÉLOÏSE: The song—can you remember the words? Can you? Please!

SINGER: For a " consideration " I could try.

HÉLOÏSE: Oh, but I have no money. My uncle does not let me— wait! (*As he would move away.*) If you would take... (*Fumbling at her neck.*) . . . this necklace. (*Hesitating.*) I think my mother would not disapprove. They say *she* died singing. And that was a tune which no one has traced to its origin. Here! (*Handing it to him.*)

SINGER: Mm! (*Examining necklace.*) It will do. Now—the words . . .? Let me see!

> He plucks the tune in part—to assist his memory—and then speaks (*not sings*) the words.

> " ' A woman there *will* be '—so sang the tree;
> ' A woman there *may* be '—so sighed the rose;
> ' A woman there must be! '—cried the thorn;
> ' who comes not to bear, but to be born;
> not to be known, but be what she knows;
> not to ensnare, but to set free . . .' " (*Hesitating.*)

HÉLOÏSE: And the conclusion?

SINGER: Conclusion? (*With much surprise.*) It's a *love* song! It just repeats itself.

> " ' A woman there *will, may, must* be! '
> cried the thorn,
> sighed the rose,
> sang . . . the tree."

The Bell of Notre Dame strikes three-quarters of the hour.

(*Rising and pocketing necklace*). Well?—will that be all?

HÉLOÏSE, lost in thought, does not answer. She just looks at the note in her hand.

THE SINGER shrugs, and is about to go when:

HÉLOÏSE, suddenly and deliberately tears up the note and, letting its fragments fall, hurries off.

HUGO almost collides with her as he comes in and comes forward.

HUGO: Hey! (*To* SINGER.) Pst! I've been thinking.

SINGER: What, again? Is that wise?—with the equipment at your disposal?

HUGO thrusts the song at him.

HUGO: Yours!—in perspecuity—for half a crown.

SINGER: Too late, turnip. I've got the words in my head.

HUGO: Oh (*non-plussed*). But there's music notes on it too. Have you got *them* in your head?—straight?—honestly?

SINGER: Well, all right. I'll trade you this necklace for it.

HUGO: Jewellery? Oh, I suppose so.

HUGO takes the necklace but, in his clumsiness, drops it as he passes over the song. In stooping to pick up the necklace he comes upon a torn piece of the note dropped by HÉLOÏSE. He picks it up, then another bit.

Pst! Do you read?

SINGER: Do birds fly?

HUGO: Do I know that name? Is this more of his songs? (*Picking up other fragments.*)

SINGER: No. This is a different tune. (*Reading.*) " Canon Fulbert
would be——". That's the uncle of the girl that was here
now——" would be greatly honoured——"

HUGO: Here's other bits. What does it make?

SINGER: Oh, it's just an invitation from Canon Fulbert to Master
Abelard to come to supper.

HUGO: Supper? When?

SINGER: Tonight, by the looks of it.

HUGO: Tonight! Save us! (*Lumbering off.*)

SINGER (*calling after him*): But the girl tore it up!

HUGO: Well, I put it together again, didn't I?

> HUGO *goes, running.*
>
> THE SINGER *shrugs and goes off, singing the song* . . . " *A
> woman there will be* . . ."
>
> The Song goes into the distance as the scene changes. . . .

SCENE II

*Canon Fulbert's house, near the cathedral, Notre Dame—the small
central hall.*

Evening of the same day.

*As the curtain rises on the scene, the singing of the song can still be heard
in the distance.* CANON FULBERT *is inspecting the room prior to the
arrival of guests.*

*It is an old wooden house and one feature of it is a capacious stone fireplace.
This is canopied and shielded to satisfy the owner's fear of the wooden
house catching fire ; and the authorities' fear of the whole island
joining in.*

As FULBERT *stoops to put on a log, the red glow of the fire adds to the
glow of the candles and lamps in the room and he stands warming
himself at the glow, his shadow throwing out into the room. Round part*

of the room there is a low gallery with a bedroom door leading off and a stair coming down from it on the side opposite the fire.

FULBERT *listens towards the exit to the rear (which leads towards the street door and other downstairs quarters) and calls :*

FULBERT: Héloïse!

> THE SINGER *can be heard singing the song, passing in the street.*

(*Looking out.*) A delicate tune. (*Looking up.*) And a peaceful sky.

> *As the Cathedral Bell tolls the hour he nods his head to the stroke.*

I was only a clerk when they baptized that bell, and raised it up there into Notre Dame . . . to dominate Paris with its tongue. Abelard could only have been a boy. Well, he is up in the clouds now, dominating Paris with his tongue too . . . perhaps the world? Ah, but it's the faith that put the bell so high, and the truth which motivates his tongue, that raises us up! (*Calling.*) Héloïse! But even if she were as brilliant as he, what could she dominate in this age . . . except . . . (*smiling*) . . . me? Héloïse! Where is the child? (*Calling loudly.*) Héloïse!

> *The door on the gallery opens, and* HÉLOÏSE *stands just above him ; dressed for the evening.*

HÉLOÏSE: Here I am, Uncle Fulbert!

FULBERT: Oh. Well. Come down! Our guests will arrive at any moment now. There's no one but myself to answer the door. And I am keeping an eye on the wine. (*Pointing to jugs warming by the fire.*) The woman is preparing the supper and . . . Look at your dress!

> HÉLOÏSE *stops on the stairs.*

Oh! No wonder my hair is turning . . . (*He stops short and stares at her.*) What *have* you done to your beautiful hair? Come down!

HÉLOÏSE: It was getting in my eyes, so I swept it back.

. . . " 'A woman there will be'—
                    so sang the tree;
    'A woman there may be'—
                    so sighed the rose. . . ."

SIOBHAN McKENNA as HÉLOÏSE

WALTER MACKEN AS
ABELARD
AND
NIGEL GREEN AS ALBERIC

ESMOND KNIGHT AS HUGO

FULBERT: But it has *disappeared*! You are like a nun! (*He fusses round her.*) And all the wave has gone!

HÉLOÏSE: Uncle Fulbert! (*Stubbornly.*) The depth of my forehead should matter more than my hair to a philosopher. How old is he?

FULBERT: What? Who? Abelard? Perhaps thirty-five. Why? (*Testily.*) Why ask that now? Does it matter? Eh? And why have you taken your mother's necklace off? Answer me!

> *There is the sound of the Knocker (on the street door).*

What? Oh, the door, child! Answer the door. I'll take the wine from the fire. (*Moving excitedly.*)

HÉLOÏSE: Uncle, (*Not moving.*) how do you know that he will come?

FULBERT: How do I know what?

> *The Knocker is heard again, and louder.*

The door! The door! (*Excitedly.*)

HÉLOÏSE: It's probably only Master Théo. And if the invitation to Abelard happened to go astray. . . .

FULBERT: Well, it didn't. (*Sharply.*) Get along, girl!

HÉLOÏSE (*still not going*): But how do you know it did not go astray?

FULBERT (*exasperated*): How do I know! Because his servant Hugo brought his acceptance. That's how!

HÉLOÏSE: Oh. (*Puzzled.*)

> *The Knocker, again and still louder.*

FULBERT (*losing his temper*): The door!

HÉLOÏSE: Then it *might* be Master Abelard? (*Fearfully.*)

FULBERT: Lord, child, isn't that what I'm telling you. Must I go and let him in myself?

HÉLOÏSE: Oh, no! (*Quickly forestalling him.*) No. I'll go.
> HÉLOÏSE *goes, slowly.*

FULBERT (*watching her go*): What's possessed the child, now?

> FULBERT *is arranging glasses and fussing about the lamp when* HÉLOÏSE *runs back in.*

HÉLOÏSE (*relieved*): It's not Master Abelard at all. But it's Master Alberic of Rheims.

FULBERT: Master Alberic! (*Turning, expecting to find him there.*) How good of . . . (*Finding no one there.*) But where is he?

HÉLOÏSE: Why did you ask *him*? Isn't he an enemy of Abelard?

FULBERT: Hush! A rival—not an enemy. What have you done with him? (*Whispered.*)

HÉLOÏSE: I told him to take off his cloak. He's in the cloak-cupboard.

FULBERT: Told him! But you were to help him, child.

HÉLOÏSE: But I don't like him. Doesn't he support the scheming Bernard of Clairvaux against Abelard? Doesn't he put blind faith before brilliant reason?

> As ALBERIC *appears at the back* FULBERT *sees him, but* HÉLOÏSE *does not, and continues.*

Isn't he one of the blind faithful too?—those wolves in sheep's clothing who fear Abelard, because Abelard is the one teacher in our day who dares use the power of reason to show that God who gave it and not the Church—

FULBERT (*stopping her*): Quiet, child! (*Going towards him.*) Master Alberic!

HÉLOÏSE (*Turning and seeing* ALBERIC): Oh!

> HÉLOÏSE *dashes off upstairs in confusion and slams her door.* ALBERIC *watches her go ; and* FULBERT *watches* ALBERIC *to see how he will take this.*
>
> ALBERIC *has all the marks of an ambitious cleric. He is not quite middle-aged, but as he has courted authority all his life so far, he has become like it—older than he is.*
>
> ALBERIC *laughs and turns to* FULBERT.

ALBERIC: Good evening, Canon Fulbert, sir!

FULBERT: Ah! (*Sighing.*) I never know what she will say next. Please come to the fire and allow me to pour you some wine. (*Doing so.*) I don't know what has got into her today.

ALBERIC: I think perhaps *I* know.

FULBERT: Oh! (*Handing him glass.*) Your good health, Master Alberic.

ALBERIC: Canon Fulbert, you teach your niece yourself, don't you?

FULBERT: I did. She is beginning to teach me. And (*smiling*) not all for my good. For though there are, obviously, things we are too young to know, there are—and much less obviously—things that we are too old to know. She needs a teacher worthy of her intelligence. Now, if you had been teaching in Paris and not in Rheims . . . But we may have struck a solution. Yes. (*Confidentially.*) Abelard may be persuaded to teach her.

ALBERIC: Abelard? And has he shown any readiness to teach her?

FULBERT: Not . . . eh . . . not directly. Oh, perhaps I should confess to you that it has been suggested to him—oh, not by me!—that he might improve his quarters—*and* shorten the journey to the Cloister School—by . . . lodging in my house. Oh, and the rent. I admit—I am not a rich man . . . and he is. (*Stopping.*) You don't approve?

ALBERIC: Lodging here?

FULBERT: Yes, I have a room up there. (*Pointing to stair which leads up from the gallery.*) He is giving it serious consideration. And tonight he may give me his reply—in person.

ALBERIC: Who made the suggestion originally?

FULBERT: Oh, not me—a friend of his . . . (*Seeing what this might mean.*) . . . and a friend of mine, too! He is a former student of Abelard—Master Théo Gola. He is coming tonight, too.

The Knocker sounds again—almost cheekily.

In fact this may be him. (*Relieved to get away from this questioning.*) Or Master Abelard himself, of course. Héloïse! (*Calling.*)

    The Knocker again.

    HÉLOÏSE *comes out from her room on the gallery.*

    (*As she comes down stair.*) The door! Quickly!

HÉLOÏSE: Uncle Fulbert—(*Approaching him.*)—before I . . .

FULBERT: The *door*!

    The Knocker again, in peremptory rhythm.

    What is it? What are you waiting for?

HÉLOÏSE: There was something I ought to tell you before . . .

FULBERT: Oh, I do wish you'd not done your hair that way.

HÉLOÏSE (*angrily*): If every time I try to tell you something serious, you insist on fussing about my hair, I will go to bed and . . .

FULBERT (*cutting her short with surprising violence*): *Go to the door!*

HÉLOÏSE (*meekly*): Yes, Uncle Fulbert.

    HÉLOÏSE *goes.*

FULBERT: I'm sorry. (*To* ALBERIC.)

ALBERIC (*urgently*): Canon Fulbert, before Abelard comes there is something I would like to ask you.

FULBERT (*a little surprised*): Yes?

ALBERIC: In the conflict which is dividing our world—on which side do you stand?

FULBERT: Side? Is there no place for simple charity?

ALBERIC: When the world is cleft in two those in the cleft will be soonest in Hell. (*Dogmatically.*) To put it simply: are you on the side of Reason or on the side of Faith?

FULBERT: Master Alberic, I am too old to take sides over such things.

ALBERIC: I see. Then in trying to get Master Abelard so interested in your niece, what are your *personal* motives?

FULBERT: My personal motives? (*His eyes falling under* ALBERIC's *scrutiny*.) Well ... yes ... I do confess that I am swayed not only for what it must mean to her ... but for the honour it may bring to me.

ALBERIC (*incredulous at his simplicity*): The honour?

FULBERT: Yes ... the honour. Master Alberic, would you advise me against this?

ALBERIC: No, no.

FULBERT: Many people think him almost a saint.

ALBERIC: Yes, I know. That should be disproved. And Canon Fulbert, I believe that in introducing Abelard to your gifted niece, you are performing a service in the cause of Faith, far greater than you can ever assess. Your charity is truly simple.

FULBERT (*uncertainly*): Thank you, Master Alberic! . . . Thank you. . . .

> HÉLOÏSE *ushers in* THÉO.

THÉO (*as he comes in*): . . . And I smell roast duck! Oh! (*Seeing* ALBERIC.) And Fulbert, is someone roasting you?

FULBERT: Théo! Have you met Master Alberic before?

THÉO: No. But Abelard has often told me that Master Alberic is to be ... respected. (*He bows, not too seriously*.)

> THÉO *is a resilient, rather impulsive Irish-Spanish mixture. Physically strong.*

FULBERT: This is Master Théo Gola, of whom I spoke. (*To* ALBERIC.)

ALBERIC: You are a friend of Peter Abelard?

THÉO (*pointedly*): I know of no one who could be his enemy for good reasons.

FULBERT (*afraid of trouble*): Théo is friends with everyone, aren't you, Théo?

THÉO: Sometimes I do fall out with myself. But today he and I are friendly. I had understood, Master Alberic, that you were in Rheims.

ALBERIC: I had occasion to come to Paris and I could not resist meeting a young woman whose reputation has even reached Rheims. (*Looking to* HÉLOÏSE *who has been hanging back, behind* THÉO.)

FULBERT: Of course! Of course! You have not been properly introduced. This is Master Alberic of Rheims, my dear.

HÉLOÏSE: We met at the door.

ALBERIC: We have met before. But on that occasion you did not see me (*As she looks puzzled.*)—at the Cloister School —earlier today.

HÉLOÏSE: Oh! (*Dropping her eyes.*)

ALBERIC: Allow me to congratulate you on your victory.

FULBERT: Victory? (*Worriedly.*) At the Cloister School?

HÉLOÏSE: Uncle Fulbert, I *did* try to tell you. Your invitation to Abelard . . . I took it to the School . . .

FULBERT: Yes, child, I know.

HÉLOÏSE: But I took it right in. Well, you did not tell me I shouldn't. And it was no stupid " victory ". I am afraid I was rather rude. But I was angry. And he should not have said what he said and neither should I and I shall apologise to him—if he apologises to me—if he comes.

FULBERT: If! *If* he comes!

HÉLOÏSE: Well, I have told you that I was upset and . . . and I may not have given him the message . . . yet you say that he will come and . . . (*Almost to tears.*) . . . and I don't know that I want him to.

  HÉLOÏSE *runs upstairs and into her room.*

THÉO (*smiling*): Well, *this* wasn't quite according to plan?

FULBERT: Oh, dear, what can she have said now!

THÉO: Well, shouldn't Master Alberic be able to tell us that; if he was there?

  Both turn to ALBERIC *who is enjoying this.*

ALBERIC: Yes. It happened just after lectures. One of the students asked Abelard a question. It ran something like this: " If

God made Adam perfect—being His supreme creation—
and Woman was made from Adam's rib, might not the
way back to perfection lie in becoming one with a woman
in God, id est, marriage? "

FULBERT: Oh!

THÉO (*with a whistle of surprise*): How did he deal with that?

ALBERIC: He said that marriage was of the earth, perfections of
heaven, and the link with perfections yet to be found in
female form. Héloïse had come in. And unseen by him,
she heard him say—in his rather superior way—" and
women are the bearers of men; that is sufficient subjection
to them—the rest is sheer necessity ".

FULBERT: Oh! (*Shocked.*)

THÉO: Oho! And then?

ALBERIC: The laughter that followed was cut short by her
ringing voice: " Master, are women not also the bearers of
women—because men subject them so? And by whose
' necessity ' are we to see this the lesser creation? " There
was complete silence. " Who spoke? " he asked. " *My*
name is not greatly respected, Master, but what *I* say I
think you will agree is not *irresponsible*! " And she turned
like a hot wind; and swept away, down the cool cloisters.

FULBERT: Oh! (*Horrified.*) Oh, dear!
      Loud Knocking on the street door.
    Oh! (*Starting.*) It is he.
      HÉLOÏSE'S *door flies open and she comes quickly down.* (*She
      has changed her hair style.*)

HÉLOÏSE (*anxiously*): Uncle Fulbert, please may I answer the door
May I?

FULBERT: Good gracious, no! You must be kept out of sight.
I must apologise for you and . . . Master Alberic, I wonder
if you would mind? . . . Héloïse has some work to show
—an illuminated manuscript. It would interest you, don't
you think?

ALBERIC: I would be delighted. . . .
      FULBERT *bustles* ALBERIC *off with* HÉLOÏSE.

THÉO: Shall I go too?

FULBERT: Oh no, no! (*Fearfully.*) Stay and support me, Théo. Have a glass of wine ready. And Théo—Théo, try to be tactful.

THÉO: I'll make the attempt.

> *Loud Knocking again.*

FULBERT: I'll let him in! I'll let him in!

> FULBERT *goes out to door.*

> THÉO *pours wine, and helps himself liberally with an eye to the entrance.*

THÉO (*drinking*): . . . " Women are the bearers of men . . . the rest is sheer necessity. " I hope she doesn't apologise too soon.

FULBERT (*off*): This way, Master Abelard.

> ABELARD *is shown in by* FULBERT, *who fusses round him. He has that combination of physical grace and intellectual brilliance which makes authority natural and pride hard to hide. He is at the height of his popularity.* (*And in that day the philosopher was "the star" and "disputations" had their "world premieres".*)

(*Ingratiatingly.*) It is a great honour you do me, Master Abelard.

ABELARD: Oh, I am afraid I do not so inevitably convey honour, Canon. Théo! (*Seeing him and going to him.*)

THÉO: Master Abelard! Allow me! (*Handing him wine.*) I have been appointed Master of the Cellar!

ABELARD: A not inappropriate appointment, Canon.

> FULBERT *in his relief at the master's good mood, laughs inordinately.*

But it was not Canon Fulbert's wine that I came here to pay homage to. Was it?

FULBERT: Oh. (*Hesitantly.*) You cannot mean my niece, Master Abelard?

ABELARD: I can. I do. Is she not to appear?

FULBERT: Well . . . (*Glancing at* THÉO *for help.*) . . . that is for you . . . Master . . . to say.

ABELARD: Then she cannot appear too quickly.

FULBERT: Do you mean that you would like me to get her now?

ABELARD: If I dare be such an importunate guest, I do. I have only till midnight to set the world aright in that quarter.

FULBERT: Oh! (*Gratefully.*) You are very forgiving, Master Abelard.

ABELARD: Forgiving? (*Suddenly serious.*) Canon Fulbert, one lesson only of me:—I love praise—not flattery.

FULBERT: Oh, Master Abelard, I am your willing pupil too. I'll fetch her right away. She is in her study showing Master Alberic of Rheims a manuscript she has written which he . . .

ABELARD (*suddenly*): Alberic? Here? (*Completely changing his tone.*)

FULBERT: Er . . . yes. I had not the authority to say no. (*Retreating from trouble and hurrying off.*) I'll fetch her! I shan't be long!

       FULBERT *goes.*

ABELARD: Alberic? (*Turning to* THÉO.)

THÉO: Dog-eared Dogma in person—yes.

ABELARD: Why do you suppose he is here?

THÉO: Perhaps to find an answer to the same question about you.

ABELARD: Why I am here?

THÉO: Yes.

ABELARD: You say that, Théo, as if *you* did not know.

THÉO: Well . . . (*Gently.*) . . . do I?

ABELARD: But I told you—(*As he takes in his surroundings.*)—to gain knowledge.

THÉO: I thought *she* was to be the student.

ABELARD: I have much to learn in this context.

THÉO: Evidently—if you were serious in what you said at School on the subject of Woman.

ABELARD: Oh. The remark was for men. She was then, we might say, " out of context ".

THÉO: And now that you have seen her face to face—and the " context " here—do you think that she is going to take your " pursuit of knowledge " philosophically?

ABELARD: Théo, (*Turning to him.*) why have you assisted me to this point?

THÉO: Because, to this point, I have trusted you to know far beyond my ignorant care. At this point I must care. Why *are* you here?

ABELARD (*considering every word*): Théo—
    I believe love of woman may be
    a unique liberator of light.
    Should I shun that light, and run away,
    when my life is dedicated to Light?——
    Not to one lamp lit once a day
    to one faith.
                I intend to see
    if this passion—with all perception kept keen—
    in truth—and, if necessary,
    to the point of personal agony—
    discovers a truth about God in all men,
    which is hitherto hidden from me:
    perhaps from the world.
                That is why
    I have prayed for a such a one. She has come.
    Trust me, Théo.

THÉO: Then you *love* her?

ABELARD: I have seen her spirit rise. What do I really know, but the height of my hopes? In all hopes I pursue knowledge of God in God's creature. Not as you know—for self's sake.

THÉO (*grimly and quietly*): Then, God help you.

ABELARD: I have that hope too.

> *As he can hear the others returning he turns away and speaks out.*

This is an excellent wine, Théo!

ALBERIC (*off*): Beautiful work! A beautiful hand!

FULBERT (*off*): I am so glad you like it! So very glad!

> FULBERT *returns with* ALBERIC *and* HÉLOÏSE.

Oh, Théo, I hope you have cared for Master Abelard.

ABELARD: *He has* cared. (*Looking past at* HÉLOÏSE.)

FULBERT: Master Alberic, you and Master Abelard are old friends

ALBERIC: We have studied together.

ABELARD: Yes. (*Facing him.*) And to a quite remarkable degree we keep coming across each other, don't we?—in the most unexpected places, Canon.

FULBERT: Yes. And this . . . (*Switching from possible trouble.*) . . . this, Master Abelard, is my niece . . . Héloïse.

> *She stands with bowed head before* ABELARD.

(*Testily.*) Well, have you nothing to say to Master Abelard?

HÉLOÏSE (*looking up slowly but defiantly at* ABELARD): I hope I am forgiven, Master, for what I said today.

ABELARD (*gently*): I hope you will forgive me for being so weak as to give you such good cause to attack. I was tired at the time.

HÉLOÏSE: I hope you were *exhausted*, Master . . .

FULBERT: Héloïse!

HÉLOÏSE: . . . or I should be disappointed in the strength of your arguments when you were strong.

THÉO: Well spoken, pupil!

ALBERIC: Could Master Abelard have seen the text you have been illuminating now, he would see from where you draw *your* strength.

FULBERT: Oh, the text on the manuscript! Yes, yes. I mean, no (*On second thoughts.*)—not now.

ABELARD: Why what was the text?

ALBERIC: Anselm of Bec on the Proving of the Christian Creed: " . . . The result of examination by Reason must always be in the affirmative; if in any respect it is negative then the reasoning is by that fact proved false, . . . not the creed ".

THÉO (*impatiently*): We are out of School, Master Alberic!

ABELARD: But not out of the battle—ever. (*Turning to* ALBERIC.) Master Alberic, if the Christian Creed is true, how could attack by Reason—which is the very force of Truth—be other than affirmative?

ALBERIC: If . . . Master Abelard? *If* it is true? Do you doubt it?

ABELARD: By doubting we enquire, and by enquiring we know. I came to hear this young woman dispute—not you. (*Turning to* HÉLOÏSE.) This text you have chosen to illuminate . . .

HÉLOÏSE (*quickly*): Oh, it is not *my* choice. Uncle Fulbert chose it for me. But the illuminated edge with the Greek design, and the bright colours—these were my choice. (*Turning provocatively to* ALBERIC.) For, you see, I think the text *does* need a reasonable amount of " illumination ", don't you?

ABELARD: Young woman . . . why do you study?

HÉLOÏSE: Why, Master Abelard? (*A little afraid of his sudden simplicity.*)

ABELARD: Yes . . . why?

HÉLOÏSE: Why . . . (*simply*). To understand, Master, what I do.

ABELARD: And the doing comes before the understanding, does it?

HÉLOÏSE: We were created, Master, and must discover why *after* the event. For, in all that we do, is not God the prime mover?

ABELARD (*as she drops her eyes under his look*): Canon Fulbert, (*Meaningfully.*) I have five thousand pupils in my new Cloister School, and yet I envy you this one in this old house.

FULBERT: Oh, Master Abelard! Do you? (*Overjoyed.*)

> *A Handbell is rung, off.*

Ah! The supper is ready now! Héloïse. Guide Master Abelard in, through our crazy old house. And mind your Master's head as you go.

> ABELARD *offers her his arm and* HÉLOÏSE *and he go, together.*

Come, Master Alberic.

ALBERIC (*to* FULBERT): They make a fine pair, Canon Fulbert. (*And turning to* THÉO.) Don't you think so, Master THÉO?

THÉO: Like Adam and Eve? (*Flatly.*) No. They *both* reach for the fruit of the Tree of Knowledge; and I know they have good digestions.

FULBERT: Théo! (*At this irreverence.*)

THÉO: And so have I. (*Sniffing.*) And I *love* roast duck!

> THÉO *goes.*

FULBERT: Master Alberic, I am so happy—For I think that he will teach her, don't you?

ALBERIC: Yes—and she him.

> *As* FULBERT *and* ALBERIC *go the Big Bell of Notre Dame chimes the quarter.*
>
> *And—as the love song is again heard—the scene changes. . . .*

SCENE III

The same. Evening, a few weeks later.

Before rise of curtain the tune of Abelard's love song is heard.

On rise of curtain the Cathedral Bell chimes the hour of five.

HÉLOÏSE *is arranging pens, parchment, etc., on the desk which is now a prominent part of the furnishings. She sits humming the tune of the love song, as though by repetition of it she would recall the words.*

FULBERT *comes in and she jumps up guiltily.*

FULBERT: What are you doing, child?

HÉLOÏSE: Preparing his desk; for my lesson.

FULBERT: So early? Surely he isn't back yet. He musn't neglect his students entirely for us—must he?

HÉLOÏSE: No, Uncle Fulbert.

FULBERT: Have you everything he needs? (*Going to desk.*) Pens, parchment, manuscripts. (*Looking.*) What's this?

HÉLOÏSE: Oh, just a flower.

FULBERT: Then take it off his desk. He's not teaching you the natural sciences. Flowers and Philosophy!

HÉLOÏSE: I see no contradiction.

FULBERT: My treasure, you are insolent.

HÉLOÏSE: My uncle, you are ignorant.

FULBERT: Oh! (*About to bridle up, then suddenly, as they both break into a smile.*) Supposing I admit my ignorance, mistress. Instruct me. Instruct me as he instructs you. I sometimes feel out of it now. (*Smiling.*) You be Abelard. Instruct!

They are, at this point, both like children playing a game.

HÉLOÏSE (" *playing Abelard* "): It is true, pupil, that I like flowers on my desk. It is also true that they distract the eye from the written word; but, in doing so, they remind me that learning is only a part of Nature and Nature only a part of the Universe and the Universe . . . part of . . . (*Hesitating and lapsing into her own seriousness*).

FULBERT: Go on! Go on! The Universe a part of what?

HÉLOÏSE: Of Man.

FULBERT: The Universe? A part of Man?

HÉLOÏSE: So a part of " nothing tangible, but simply a quality of man, the custodian of reality ". (*Now quoting her teacher.*)

FULBERT: The Universe a quality of Man? Does he say this? (*She nods.*) And do you understand this? (*She shakes her head.*)

HÉLOÏSE: No (*smiling*).

FULBERT: Then you should. You just haven't taken it in. You're lazy and he's too indulgent to you. (*Half seriously.*) I will authorise him to beat you when necessary. (*Picking up a handbell on the desk.*) And this?

HÉLOÏSE (*quickly*): Don't ring it!

FULBERT: Why?

HÉLOÏSE: It bring his servant running.

FULBERT: Oh, I'd be surprised if anything brought *him* running. He's something we didn't bargain for. He almost offsets the rent of the room. Have you everything else required, Mistress Philosophy?

HÉLOÏSE: Yes—except my Master. Unless, of course, he has come in quietly and gone up to the room.

FULBERT: Come in quietly? Impossible. Do you know that I myself had to go out on the door-step last week to disperse the students who followed him home. They are quite jealous of you. All the youth of Paris loves and follows him.

HÉLOÏSE: And his teachings will spread all over the world.

FULBERT: Yes, (*Looking up out of window.*) but from Paris. From here. (*Looking around room in pride.*) From here. (*Indicating desk.*)

HÉLOÏSE: He will be the greatest teacher since Aristotle.

FULBERT: You think so? Perhaps even greater? For Abelard will be within the Church and have its height on which to transcend the old heights.

HÉLOÏSE: Within the Church? (*Troubled.*)

FULBERT: The very highest positions are open to him.

HÉLOÏSE: Then he would be a priest. Uncle, (*Hesitantly.*) priests must now be bound by the new rule of celibacy, musn't they?

FULBERT: Of course. Oh, my dear, (*Smiling tolerantly.*) this man was always all spirit, all mind, have no fear—the transcendental is under our roof and we shall rise with it.

HÉLOÏSE: The key. The key in the street door, Uncle.

FULBERT: Then it must be him. I heard no students. Did you?

HÉLOÏSE: No . . . at least . . . (*Lying.*) . . . a little cheering only.

FULBERT: Cheering? Really?

HÉLOÏSE: Well, you are getting a little deaf, you know.

FULBERT: Am I? And of course he is early. It wouldn't do for his students to feel neglected. Hugo! (*Calling at door.*) I'll tell his servant to see to his supper and go to bed early. So I'm getting deaf? Well, keep note of all he says. It may affect the world; and you have good ears. Hugo!

    FULBERT *goes.*

    ABELARD *comes in. He is deep in thought and as he walks about the room it might be that he has not seen* HÉLOÏSE *sitting attentively on a stool by the desk.*

ABELARD: I have been thinking, as I walked—of what might bind this broken world into one belief—bind those who long for Truth, but will not try beyond blind longing, and those who cry " We will not tolerate the lie in blind Faith ". (*Stopping.*) I was wondering what concept can contain all conflict so that the conflict may be not to the death but eventually to the new life of Man; what can bind us yet leave us so dangerously free that we are reason-

MERVYN JOHNS AS FULBERT, WITH HÉLOÏSE

HÉLOÏSE The Nun

DAVID OXLEY AS TH
WITH HÉLOÏSE

Photographs of Héloïse by Fred Daniels

able to the same degree that we are divine. That is the crux and . . . Good evening, pupil. (*He sits and stares at her.*)

HÉLOÏSE: Good evening, Master. And, in thinking, have you reached a conclusion?

ABELARD: Yes, I have. (*Still looking at her.*)

HÉLOÏSE: You know of a concept which might contain all conflict for humanity's sake?

ABELARD: Yes, I do. (*Still looking at her.*)

HÉLOÏSE: And are you able to formulate this concept, Master?

ABELARD: Yes, I am.

HÉLOÏSE: What is it, Master?

ABELARD: Love; in all forms.

> *As she turns her head away he produces the necklace, which* HÉLOÏSE *had given to the* SINGER.

In tracing the history of this necklace, it had occurred to me that this concept—at least set to music—must be of interest to you. (*He smiles.*)

HÉLOÏSE (*turning to see necklace*): Oh. (*Confused.*) But you were thinking, were you not, of Christian Love, Master?

ABELARD: Christian Love? And what, pupil, is *Christian* Love?

HÉLOÏSE: Well . . . (*Sitting watching him.*) Is the supreme example of Christian Love not God's sacrifice of His Son?

ABELARD: That God, by the sacrifice of His Son, made payment for the World's Sin? Payment? To whom? To whom could God make payment?

HÉLOÏSE: To whom?—(*Reflectively.*)—could God make payment, Master?

ABELARD: Yes, whom could He deal with on equal terms? Who . . . but the Devil? A sordid bargain that the Father should buy Satan off with His innocent Son to save his worldly possessions—men.

HÉLOÏSE (*shocked*): But I do not see it in that way.

ABELARD: Good. Nor do I. For it was not that God so loved the world but that the Man—Christ, containing God, commanded Man's love to a greater degree than any man has done till now. It's the loving. It's love, in all its forms, which is irresistible. Nothing will be defeated which is Love.

HÉLOÏSE (*disturbed*): Have you taught your students these things, Master?

ABELARD: I teach my students what I know. Then, coming home, I teach you, by the process of getting to know things which were beyond me. Perhaps you teach me. (*Coming close to her.*) For look at you. You have sat there and said scarcely anything. But from your being there has arisen, for me . . .

HÉLOÏSE (*interrupting*): The subject for tonight was Philosophy, Master.

ABELARD: And it is. (*Changing tone and standing over her, the necklace dangling on his fingers.*) Have you a pen sharpened— pupil?

HÉLOÏSE: Yes, Master.

ABELARD: And parchment?

HÉLOÏSE: Yes.

ABELARD: And ink?

> *She nods.*

Then write me down an answer to this question:—What other forms of Love do you know besides Christian Love, that is, besides Sacred Love?

HÉLOÏSE (*hesitating*): Is this within the subject, Master?

ABELARD (*looking straight at her*): It is, I believe, at the heart of it.

> *She writes.*

(*Repeating slowly like teacher at examination, while playing with necklace.*) What other forms of Love than Sacred Love? (*Looking over her shoulder at what she writes.*) " Profane . . ." Stop! Stop! That's enough! "*Profane* Love!"

HÉLOÏSE: Is that what you wanted, Master?

ABELARD: No. It is what I expected. (*Taking up parchment.*) Now answer me this: What in the simplest terms does this "profane" mean? In putting this word before the word "Love" what sort of love do we really imply?

HÉLOÏSE: I suppose, Master, worldly Love.

ABELARD: And what is the most potent form of worldly Love?

HÉLOÏSE (*after a moment of hesitation*): The love—I suppose—between women and men.

ABELARD: And do you see such love as profane—in the most obvious sense? Well, do you?

HÉLOÏSE: Master, my answer to that question can only be a matter of opinion.

ABELARD: Then opine, pupil. Opine. I repeat the question. Do you see such love as inevitably profane?

HÉLOÏSE: Yes, Master.

ABELARD: Oh.

HÉLOÏSE (*and, as he seems surprised*): For is the profane not an inevitable part of all women and all men? And does not the word profane derive from "pro fanus"—meaning "*before* the *temple*"? *In* the temple—that is, within the church—a man and woman must become less than man or woman, and then the love must be for a third person— the Deity. But otherwise it would be false not to be profane; being worldly beings and . . . Why are you staring at me so?

ABELARD: Nothing! Nothing. (*Continues looking at her.*)

    In embarrassment she turns her head away. He leans forward and puts the necklace around her neck.

HÉLOÏSE (*turning and raising her eyes to his, a little desperately*): Shall we continue studying?

ABELARD (*still looking intently at her*): Studying? I am. I am.

HÉLOÏSE (*rising*): Master, I must refuse to be the subject of study.
    HÉLOÏSE *turns and runs upstairs.*

ABELARD (*calling after her as she mounts the stairs*): Even, my pupil, in the pursuit of Truth?

> *Going into her room she slams the door. One may even hear her weep.*

> ABELARD *stares at the door for a time then, looks down at the parchment, moves the handbell and sitting, begins to write.*

> HUGO *comes in.*

HUGO: Supper's ready master. Supper master . . . (*seeing* ABELARD *so absorbed in his work he checks himself*).

> HUGO *shrugs and withdraws.*

> *Scene Curtain as the music of the second love song plays (" Said the rose to the virgin ").*

SCENE IV

The same. Later the same night.

On the rise of the curtain the Bell of Notre Dame is striking eleven.

The hall is quite dark, except for the small lamp on the desk where ABELARD *still bowed over his manuscripts, works on.*

But he has noticed the bell, and on the last few strokes he raises and nods his head, counting silently.

The bell completes its strokes.

ABELARD: Eleven! (*He stretches himself and rises.*) The lamp. I must not forget the lamp tonight. Oh!

> *In reaching for the lamp he knocks over the Handbell, which falls to the floor loudly.*

Oh! (*As in recovering the bell he lets it ring again.*)

> HÉLOÏSE *appears at her door, with a light in her hand. She is in her night-clothes with her hair about her shoulders.*

HÉLOÏSE: Who's there? Oh!

ABELARD: Heloïse! (*Struck by her appearance.*)

HÉLOÏSE (*reprovingly*): Master Abelard, the house is sleeping. Or it was, till you rang.

ABELARD: I knocked over the bell on my desk.

HÉLOÏSE: It is late to be working, Master.

ABELARD: I had forgotten to keep count of time. (*Unable to keep his eyes off her.*)

HÉLOÏSE: Is it possible that you may forget to go to bed, Master?

ABELARD: What? (*Moving to stairs.*) No. I am going up now. (*He goes up the stairs.*) And God grace you for . . . light.

(*In weariness, he stumbles on a step.*)

HÉLOÏSE: You work so late so often. And even you cannot do without sleep, Master.

ABELARD: Now that you have taught me so much, you must not call me " Master ", my dearest.

HÉLOÏSE (*a little in anger*): Then you must not call me " my dearest ", must you?

He looks at her without answering.

(*Annoyed.*) And you have come up and left your lamp burning again.

ABELARD (*lightly*): The moral in this might surely be that I should not be separated from my source of light. (*Then again seriously.*) Héloïse, cannot we be . . . equals?

HÉLOÏSE: In our respect of each other I hope that we are. Goodnight, *Master*. (*She goes in.*)

ABELARD, *turning to go up the steps to the upper rooms, recollects the lamp. He is about to come back down when* HUGO *shuffles in below.*

ABELARD: Who's that?

HUGO (*sleepily*): Hugo! Marster! You rang the bell. (*Muttering.*) Where in Christendom is he now? Mas—! (*About to shout.*)

ABELARD: Sh! Up here. Put out the lamp on my desk and get to bed. There's a good fellow.

HUGO: Here's a good dog. And was that all that you rang for, Marster? (*Annoyed.*)

ABELARD: I did *not* ring for you. And speak quietly.

HUGO (*loudly*): But I heard the bell, Maa-rster!

ABELARD: Will you be quiet! I knocked it over. And did you take the Seneca back to Master Théo's lodgings?

HUGO: The red-bound vellums? No. She has them. The young mistress has them in her room beside you there.

ABELARD: Oh.

HUGO: Was that what you rang for Marster?

ABELARD: No! In the morning I shall want my " Civitate Dei " —which I believe is . . . Oh yes. Yes.

HUGO (*nods*): . . . " Cheevy Day "? She has him too.

ABELARD (*impatiently*): I know! I know!

HUGO: She has him but you rings for me. Do I have to go in and get it for you, Maa-rster?

ABELARD: No!

HUGO (*taking the lamp and muttering*): Someone ought to tell him what he wants.

ABELARD: What did you say?

HUGO: I said, she seems to have everything you want, doesn't she? But she'll give it you when she goes to bed—if you only ask.

ABELARD (*losing his temper and shouting*): Get to bed you animal! Get to bed! Do you hear me!

HUGO: Should think the whole of Paris hears you—(*Going.*)— ringing bells and shouting and calling people names, as if this was an island of dogs. . . .

> HUGO *goes, taking the lamp.*
>
> *And as* ABELARD *turns in darkness to mount the stairs* HÉLOÏSE, *again disturbed by the noise, comes to her door, holding the light.*

HÉLOÏSE: What is it now, Master Abelard?

ABELARD: It was Hugo. He thought I rang the bell, and then he said something which angered me. I am sorry that I should so raise my voice. Forgive me.

HÉLOÏSE: Why—what did he say?

ABELARD: Something foolish. You have learned enough for one day. You need sleep too.

HÉLOÏSE: Wait, Master! (*As he is turning away.*) What Hugo said . . . was it about me?

ABELARD: No, not only you. In the morning . . .

HÉLOÏSE (*persisting*): . . . But if it was not only about me, was it, Master, about . . . *us?*

ABELARD: Us? (*He hesitates.*)

HÉLOÏSE: Surely, Master Abelard, you do know that your neglected students talk idly of . . . us? That that is why they no longer follow you home—in pursuit of Truth.

ABELARD: Indeed. And what sort of thing do they say?

HÉLOÏSE: What, Master, did Hugo say?

    ABELARD *slowly turns to face her fully.*

ABELARD: Must the last lesson begin so soon?

HÉLOÏSE (*after a pause*): What did Hugo say?

ABELARD (*sighing*): Very well. (*Then, speaking as Master to pupil.*) Has Hugo a delicate mind?

HÉLOÏSE: No.

ABELARD: Does Hugo talk delicately or crudely?

HÉLOÏSE: Crudely.

ABELARD: Why?

HÉLOÏSE: He can do no better. He has a crude mind and a coarse tongue.

ABELARD: So that if Hugo were faced with something fine to say—with even the most delicate thing on earth—that delicate thing would still become crude on Hugo's lips. Is that not so?

HÉLOÏSE: Reason leads us to conclude so, Master.

ABELARD: But Hugo, with all his crudity, leads us beyond reason. Shall we proceed?

> *She pauses—the light trembling in her hand.*

HÉLOÏSE: What did Hugo say?

ABELARD (*slowly*): That it was not really my books I wanted— but you; not Knowledge—but knowledge of Héloïse.

> *The sound of someone singing or playing the first song (" A woman there will be . . .") comes from the street.*

HÉLOÏSE (*with trembling lips*): But that is not true?

ABELARD: There is a song they sing in the streets today, *and* at night; for the subject never sleeps. And *I* wrote the song, and the cause was *you*.

HÉLOÏSE: Me? Then I was The Woman? (*Turning to go in.*)

ABELARD: You *are* this woman. (*Stopping her.*) We must face the truth of this.

HÉLOÏSE: You taught me that Reason was necessary in the pursuit of Truth. Was your teaching false?

> *The song persists in the distance.*

ABELARD: No. (*Holding her with his eyes.*)
But teaching you is not teaching at all;
It is having a light pour in on my soul,
like sun on a resurrected tomb;
and everything must be considered again
in this new light. For out of my brain
the bats fly up from darknesses I
had not admitted, and as they fly
they strike the new light, suffer and cry
out, " Withered dogma! " then fall; then die;
And the temple crumbles with the tomb.
And it may not ever be redesigned.
till you are not only the light of my mind,
but of my . . . body. Do you understand?

> *The song fades away along the street.*

HÉLOÏSE: No. (*Fearfully.*) Might it be more true to be more crude—like Hugo, Master? For this must be true. And what is the truth of this?

ABELARD: Oh, Héloïse, millions of men
> have strained all sense to sound the sweet bell
> which tells this truth. How dare I
> hope to make that great bell toll?
> Yet . . . (*With intensity of thought and emotion.*)
> think of what *you* feel . . . when I say . . . " soul ".
> Think of what *I* feel, saying so.
> These two self-aspiring sensations now
> somehow merge into the one; invent a sky
> of indescribably delicate blue
> in which two unbelievable clouds combine,
> to merge into one momentous delicacy—
> the gentlest cloud phenomenon of all time.
> *That* is the height, and the tenderness, of this;
> and the purity.
> > Or is it better to say,
> " I love you "—and leave the imagining to you,
> in hopes that our imaginations too
> coincide?

> *Gently he takes the light from her hand.*

> I have taught you to reason. I cannot teach you now
> to throw reason away. But, Oh, my love,
> we may *outreach* it.

> *She passionately embraces him.*

> The light.

> *He puts out the light, and, as the Curtain falls, he takes her
> into his arms.*

> *And once again* THE SINGER *comes slowly to pass the dark
> house and we hear the second love song:*

> " Said the rose to the virgin,
> > ' Praise not me;
> Praise not the beauty I unfold;
> Praise me not for purity.
> I unfold for unfolding—not for thee.
> Praise the process,
> > and the bee ' . . ."

SCENE V

The same. Some days later—early morning.

On rise of curtain the hall is empty, but the Lamp is still burning on Abelard's desk.

FULBERT *comes in and sees the lamp still burning.*

FULBERT: Hugo! Hugo! (*Querulously.*) Hugo! Hugo!

HUGO (*off*): Hugo! Hugo!

> HUGO *comes in.*

Oh, it's you!

FULBERT: Hugo, why is this lamp still burning here in the morning?

HUGO: Because it wasn't put out last night. I can't keep up with him. (*Moving to it.*) This is the third time this week that I've had to put it out in the morning.

FULBERT: You should have seen to it before you went to bed. It is your duty to look after your Master.

HUGO (*turning*): Yes. And whose duty is it to look after your niece?

FULBERT: I will not have you talk to me like this!

HUGO: You will not have anyone else do it. But I'm not afraid of you. Why does he forget everything—including the money owed me? Why does he leave his lamp burning all night? And why (*Pointing to* HÉLOÏSE'S *door.*) is her door always bolted now and his never? Eh? That'll be another song for market. (*Reaching for manuscript.*)

FULBERT: Don't touch his lamp or his papers with your filthy hands. (*Raising his arm.*) You! . . .

HUGO: Nah! I warn you not to raise your hand to me, Canon. (*Moving off.*) Not till you come to a conclusion why your niece's door is bolted now *on the inside*. Now I'll go to my Morning Mass with a better conscience than anyone else in this canonical coop of a house.

HUGO *goes*.

FULBERT: God forgive him! But he is just an animal—and sees us so.

> FULBERT *moves to the desk and before putting out the lamp, he takes a look round to see that no one is there, then looks through some of the manuscripts.*

What a strangely irresolute hand for such a mind. Why, I write better! What's this? (*Reading.*)

> " Said the rose to the virgin,
> praise not me;
> praise not the beauty I unfold;
> praise me not for purity;
> I unfold for unfolding—not for thee.
> Praise the process, and the bee."

A song? An obscure song—a strange song . . . " praise me not for purity . . ."?

> *He puts out the lamp, and puts down the manuscript.*

(*Turning it over in his mind.*) " I unfold for unfolding—not for thee . . ."

> *He looks up at* HÉLOÏSE'S *door.*

" Praise the process . . . and the bee. . . ."

> FULBERT *hesitantly mounts the stairs and goes towards the door of* HÉLOÏSE'S *room.*

(*Calling, gently.*) Héloïse!

> *He tries the door and finds it bolted. He is surprised. He knocks.*

Héloïse! Héloïse! (*Then he panics and turns.*) Master Abelard!

> *He runs up the stairs and disappears towards* ABELARD'S *room.*

The door of her room opens and HÉLOÏSE *comes out, and as she does she speaks to someone in the room.*

No. *You* must not.

Drawing the door closed behind her back, she stands waiting in a sort of defiance as FULBERT *comes back down the stairs, in appalled silence.*

HÉLOÏSE: Uncle. (*Shaking her head and searching for the words.*) You are wrong. The world is wrong.

FULBERT: No. (*Broken.*) It is true. Everything they said is true. And you have deceived me. I opened the door of this house to a great and good man . . . a saint, they said. . . . But these were wrong . . . a pinnacle of height and purity . . . and he . . . he is Satan in my house!

HÉLOÏSE (*deathly tense*): If my Master is Satan, then is Heaven Hell; and all I ever want to be is deeply satanic.

FULBERT: Christ!!

FULBERT *strikes her.*

She does not flinch. And as she stands firm he goes completely to pieces.

Oh . . . (*Stumbling down the stairs.*) . . . Héloïse . . . (*Weeping.*) Oh, Héloïse!

As he stumbles out of the house.

Héloïse!!

For a moment she stands there, then—

HÉLOÏSE: Oh God! (*Like a whisper.*)

HÉLOÏSE *turns and goes blindly into the room as—*
The Act Curtain falls. . . .

ACT II

SCENE I

Over a year later—Brittany—the village of Le Palais—an orchard against the castle wall. Summer.

HÉLOÏSE *discovered, with a rose in her hand.*

Music of the second love song (" Said the rose to the virgin ").

As HÉLOÏSE *puts the rose in her hair,* THE SINGER *crosses the stage singing.* HÉLOÏSE *looks thoughtfully at the scene.*

THÉO, *travel-stained, enters from the opposite direction. With a few quick steps he comes up behind her and puts his hands over her eyes.*

HÉLOÏSE: Oh no? (*Not moving; not daring to think it might be* ABELARD.) No. (*Feeling his hands.*) No. (THÉO *lets his hands fall and she swings round.*) Théo! Oh, how lovely to see anybody from Paris.

THÉO: Just anybody?

HÉLOÏSE: But what brings you to Brittany? What brought you, Théo?

THÉO: A horse.

HÉLOÏSE (*laughing*): Yes, I know. But why? Why did you come?

THÉO: Because you are here.

HÉLOÏSE: Because I am here? (*Uncertainly, then playfully.*) Am I to believe, Master Gola, that I have attracted you all the way from Paris to Brittany?—a five-days' journey?

THÉO: Ah, believe it or not. Truth's indifferent. But I can see no good reason, can you, to limit your powers of attraction to a Sabbath day's journey?

143

HÉLOÏSE: Not even after these months?

THÉO: Not after all the years that you have yet to live.

HÉLOÏSE: To my shame, Théo, I think that I could live quite a time on flattery.

THÉO: To my greater glory I think that I could live till I die giving it you. But I am squire to my knight.

HÉLOÏSE: Peter?

THÉO: And carry his message.

HÉLOÏSE: A message. Oh well, a message is something.

THÉO: Yes, this one is.

HÉLOÏSE: Well, may I have it? (*Eagerly.*) You haven't lost it, have you?

THÉO: No, no. I have it here. It has never been elsewhere. (*Tapping his forehead.*) Now how did it go . . . (*Tantalisingly.*) It was something about waiting till . . . (*Muttering to himself*) . . . waiting till . . .

HÉLOÏSE: Théo Gola . . . I would have you know that I have a son who can be as tantalising as you—but I spank him for it.

THÉO: Yes, mother, I know.

HÉLOÏSE: Then am I to be allowed to have my message from Paris?

THÉO: From Paris? Did I say from Paris?

HÉLOÏSE: Don't Théo. (*Declaring the game at an end.*) His words are my food. And I am starved.

THÉO: You will not go hungry.

HÉLOÏSE: Why, what did he say?

THÉO: That you were to wait here—

HÉLOÏSE: Wait here? You mean in Brittany?

THÉO (*smiling*): I mean here—in this orchard—by this very wall. Here, where as a boy he would look out over his father's fields. You are to wait—just as long as it takes him to kiss his sister's cheek, caress his son's head and cross the orchard.

HÉLOÏSE: No! (*With relief and joy as* THÉO *nods.*) He's here?

THÉO: Yes. I must see to the horses.

HÉLOÏSE: Wait, Théo. (*Restraining him as he turns to go.*) Do you know why he has come back so soon? Is there trouble in Paris?

THÉO: There will always be trouble in Paris—I hope.

HÉLOÏSE: No, but . . . (*Not to be put off.*) . . . Has he told you why he has come back?

THÉO: The great battle has begun—in Paris. Bernard, Alberic, all the foe. This is for the mind of Man. And in that final battle I believe that he wants you by him.

HÉLOÏSE: That is my wish too—but under what conditions could I possibly return to Paris? Fulbert would seize me. He is still my guardian—legally.

THÉO (*deliberately*): Think of one condition; and, when you do, think of what you once said to me:—" The sacred things of life must all, in our day, be renewed by a sort of profanity ". Here he is.

> ABELARD *comes in, looking more like the knight he was by birth than the philosopher he was by vocation. He almost takes her off her feet into his arms.*

ABELARD: Ah, Loïsa! Loïsa! Here is Heaven!

HÉLOÏSE: Does it follow, Master, that Paris was Hell?

ABELARD: Hell? (*Looking at* THÉO.) Has Théo said anything?

THÉO: No, no. (*Quickly.*) Though I could say that the few days on horseback in between were sheer Purgatory. The dust I swallowed!—His. Which way to the stables?

ABELARD: They'll announce themselves (*Laughing.*) They lie up-wind! (THÉO *goes.*) Théo is so happy to see you. And in the family here there seems nothing but joy about the child. And Oh how they love you.

HÉLOÏSE: And how they adore you. Did you waken my master?

ABELARD: The little Master? Of course. By this means. (*Kissing her forehead.*) Let's sit in the sun. For two weeks I need do nothing more than adore you according to the mood, the time of day, the weather, and the way you do your hair. Sit here. (*Sitting by the wall.*) Come. Sit by me, silent one. I didn't really awaken my rival in love. Sit. (*Patting ground by him.*) I let him sleep. I let him dream on. For I hadn't the courage to challenge him for your attention.

> *As* HÉLOÏSE *subsides beside him and intently looks at his face.*

Yes, but not all that amount of attention.

HÉLOÏSE: Why have you left the field of battle?

> *As he turns her head gently away from looking at him, and lays it on his shoulder, without answering her.*

ABELARD: There's a scent of roses round your hair. Ah, the source! (*Consciously trying to break her serious silence.*) The rose itself. Why? Aren't you happy that I have come back?

HÉLOÏSE: Beyond words. This is a moment in my dreams.

ABELARD: For two whole weeks it will be Heaven.

HÉLOÏSE: Heaven, is no fortnight affair, Master.

ABELARD: Would a lifetime serve better, Mistress?

HÉLOÏSE: No. No better than a moment. In eternity only the quality counts for time.

ABELARD: Yet the heavenly moment, like a drop in a pool, starts earthy consequences. I have seen the ripples spread and the reeds in the mud begin to tremble.

HÉLOÏSE: Fulbert? (*As he nods in silent assent.*) We are bound to stir the unseen reed on the unsought shore. Don't covet responsibility where the withered reeds tremble.

ABELARD: He is all but insane. Yes. And this we have done. It is as if, in him, our dream had turned to nightmare.

HÉLOÏSE: It had to be.

ABELARD: But must we claim no responsibility for the creatures created by our dream?

HÉLOÏSE: In the place where dreams occur, the dreamer is the
  stranger. He may not authorise his dream.

ABELARD: Yet he must be true to himself—and to the final
  Authority—and His Charity.

HÉLOÏSE: Which is love—not pity.

ABELARD: But mercy.
  Héloïse—when I was a little boy,
  this castle was a magic castle to me.
  And from a room high up in this very wall
  my father's voice, instructing me,
  would merge with bird-songs in that tree:
  the voice of a soldier who was a saint.

HÉLOÏSE (*dreamily relaxing into his arms*):
  Your sister has told me how fine he was.

ABELARD: The finest man I will ever know.

  (*Peering out over the country.*)

  With his consent I would sit alone in that room—
  the old shields shining, and the boar's head on the wall—
  looking from my legendary cell
  across the historic country.
                              In the trees,
  beyond that ribbon river, I would see
  a dress in the sun, or cloaked figures in the rain,
  move between village and village and—moodily—
  I'd brood on my Princess.

HÉLOÏSE: Your Princess? (*Almost teasingly.*)

ABELARD: Yes.
  For castles were not made—
  not at that age—which were not meant to be
  sanctuaries for damsels in distress.
  But this grave brooding prince was not content
  with princesses. His Princess would be a saint.
  Oh, (*As she turns to see his face.*)
  there was the sadness in it, even then,
  that saints must suffer; but in *his* suffering
  he had to redeem her.

Oh, there was the improbability too—
in saintliness—that any Princess could be
found to fill the nature of his dream.
But, (*Looking into her troubled face.*)
now that she has come, would it not seem
natural that she should be his Queen,
and a marriage . . .

HÉLOÏSE: No! (*Interrupting.*) No, Peter. (*She rises.*)

ABELARD: But why not marriage? Is it no honour to you to be acknowledged as my wife?

HÉLOÏSE: We think of honour differently. No honour could add to the glory for me of having been your mistress. You must be free to rise. Not bound to me.

ABELARD: Would you rob Fulbert of reason?—and me of respect.

HÉLOÏSE: Respect? Would you rob me of honour, in robbing the church and the world of you?

ABELARD: But this marriage would be secret.

HÉLOÏSE: Secret? Oh, Peter—you are a child.

ABELARD: But to this Fulbert has agreed, and on oath to keep the secret.

HÉLOÏSE: Fulbert has agreed? (*Incredulously.*) But—no. (*Afraid.*) This is nightmare already. Peter, how could such a secret be kept? No. Don't let this happen.

ABELARD: It is too late. I had not thought you were unready to be my wife. My oath is already given.

HÉLOÏSE (*fiercely*): You had no right to commit me to this!

ABELARD: But you do not understand . . .

HÉLOÏSE: . . . I do! I do. This was my sphere of wisdom—not yours. And have you not at all times taught me that only Love can both bind and set us free? Was Love not to be our one tie? Christ in His Mercy!—what have you done?

ABELARD: Héloïse, listen to me. (*Gently forcing her to face him.*) I am not afraid to be tied to you by all possible bonds. Are you?

HÉLOÏSE (*after a long pause*): Yes. This is one which would drag us both down to God knows what depths. You were to be a priest, the high priest of Truth. And through me you were to gain nothing but truth. And now care will weigh you down and I shall be that care. If you can think of Fulbert, think of me—and that honour.

He looks at her as though torn with doubt.

ABELARD (*turning*): Stay here with the child. I shall return to Paris, I shall break my oath: and risk the outcome.

HÉLOÏSE: The outcome? (*Fearfully.*) Oh, what possessed you to commit us to this? If you break oath with him now, he may do something dreadful. I know. I know the dark passions which sweep through that man. Don't go back to Paris. Don't ever go back to Paris again. There is all of Christendom open to you!

ABELARD: But the battle is joined. And at the centre of the world. To desert Paris now would mean utter defeat to all those who trust me—even to you. All the scheming spiders would come, and crawl through Paris and gradually the brain of the mind of the world would become enmeshed in their web. No, my sword is in the sun. And I had seen you stand by my side. I need you there. With Fulbert at peace, you can join me. I need you.

HÉLOÏSE (*resignedly*): If this is your way to live for your world and to love me, then I will come to Paris and I will be married in secret. While I am near my uncle I can be your protection against his treachery. For over him I do have power. And Oh, I need that you need me.

ABELARD (*taking her in his arms*): Trust the goodness in this, to lead us away from possible nightmare.

HÉLOÏSE: God is more than good. It is He, if He chooses, will punish us.

ABELARD: But surely you do not see our love as a sin?

HÉLOÏSE: Not our love. To be married in shame; that is our sin. Thank God that your sister loves the child. For he dare not be seen in Paris. He must stay. Peter, let us start tomorrow.

ABELARD: Tomorrow? (*Amazed.*)

HÉLOÏSE: Or tonight—while I am still strong—or weak. It is to be secret? Then—I think I shall be married in black at midnight. I hear him crying. He will be hungry. (*As* ABELARD *hesitates.*) Come.

> HÉLOÏSE *goes.* ABELARD *follows slowly after her, as the scene changes. . . .*

SCENE II

Paris—some weeks later—a gateway—the East entrance to the Cloister School.

Before rise of curtain the Bells of Paris grow in clamour, then as the Great Bell alone begins to strike a resounding six, the curtain rises.

On rise of curtain, SUPIRO *stands by the gate and* FULBERT *comes in, happily and as if chattering to himself, though one cannot be sure for the noise of the deafening bell.*

SUPIRO (*calling after him*): Good afternoon, Canon Fulbert!

> FULBERT *looks at him—but, the words being drowned by the bell, and possibly anything in content, he keeps going.*

(*Louder.*) Good afternoon!! Canon!!

> FULBERT *stops, suspiciously.*

FULBERT: What did you say?

SUPIRO: I . . . (*Shouting.*) . . . said . . . (*Then as the bell completely drowns him he indicates the competition and gives up.*)

> FULBERT *turns to go. But as he does so, the bell stops. Cautiously he turns back.*

FULBERT: Monsieur. . . . (*Almost whispered.*) . . . what did you say?

SUPIRO: I said, " Good afternoon ".

FULBERT: Ha! (*With relieved laughter.*) Why? (*Suddenly suspicious again.*) Should I know you?

SUPIRO: Supiro is the name. I had the honour—through your servant, Hugo—to recommend the Spanish doctor to you.

FULBERT: Honour. Who? O, Hugo! He is only mine by adoption. It is my way to acquire life, it seems, eh. The Spanish doctor? He tells a strange story, the Spanish doctor. But she is back again, and there is no necessity. He is just a man. You understand, I do not know you. What was it you said. Oh, yes——Good afternoon!

> FULBERT *moves off.*

SUPIRO (*to self*): I don't believe he heard a word I said.

FULBERT: Oh, yes I did. (*Returning.*) Monsieur Supiro, I apologise for seeming rude. You must take no offence, but occasionally something comes between me and my hearing. It is a thing which is peculiar to me, she says. Yes—(*Reflectively.*)—a sort of bell. Even as they read the marriage vows I heard a bell . . . (*Stopping, confused.*) The bell is often the real bell. The Great Bell. (*Looking up, to Notre Dame.*) My niece is at home and waiting for me, so . . . Good afternoon. (*Moving off.*)

SUPIRO: Any time I can be of service, Canon!

> FULBERT *hurries off, almost running away from him.*

(*To self, and satisfied.*) "Even as they read the marriage vows . . ." It adds up. It adds up. And the total will be absolute certainty. Oh.

> *As* ALBERIC *comes out through the gateway.*

Here comes The Absolute—uncertainly.

> *As* ALBERIC *uncertainly approaches him.*

ALBERIC: Monsieur—

SUPIRO (*indicating gateway and building beyond*): Archdeacon—have you been to school to our teacher?

ALBERIC: I have been to sample his teachings. Monsieur, we need no introduction, nor do I need to tell you how the Church is offended, our youth misled and the mind of generations under taint today from teachings that are the fruit of a tree whose roots you may well know are serpentine.

SUPIRO: Oh, I have some knowledge of the knowledge of such a tree.

ALBERIC: And I am empowered by Holy Church when I ask you why Canon Fulbert visited you at the height of summer and what on that occasion he said; and what words he had with you just now.

SUPIRO: Oh, just now we had words—two, " Good " " afternoon ". Oh, I shan't run away. What he said to me in the summer well—very little really in addition to what I already knew about certain parties to a certain contract.

ALBERIC: Why, what do you know?

SUPIRO: I come by knowledge, Archdeacon Alberic, at a certain spiritual expense to me. I part with it at a profit, if it profits the man who would relieve me of a certain strain in holding it here. (*Tapping his brow.*) But I know the church—that's a certainty.

ALBERIC: Do you mean that you know our institution, the Church —or a particular building.

SUPIRO: Oh, both, both. And I could be more particular still about a certain Church ceremony: a secret ceremony. But I am very particular and I am sure it is distasteful to us both seeking certainty in the street. You will find on this piece of parchment a time and a place to pursue our acquaintance. Yet I must warn you that it may be expensive. But you should know the profit and loss of damnation, surely.

> ALBERIC, *after a moment's hesitation, takes the piece of parchment and goes off, as a bell sounds within the gateway.*

Oh, (*Sighing.*) how I wish my clients would show a little more resistance. Yet, that one at least lets his conscience know that he knows where it is. He's not afraid. And the worst sin in the world may yet be the taking up of an appeasing policy to your own conscience. Aha! Here comes the new star—falling.

As ABELARD, *deep in thought comes through the gate, moving quickly.*

I must make sure that it doesn't fall on me. Master Abelard!

ABELARD: Well, sir . . . (*Stopping.*) What is it? Who are you?

SUPIRO: You have not yet the misfortune to know me, but I have the misfortune to know Hugo, your servant.

ABELARD: He is no longer, thank heaven, a servant of mine. He serves Canon Fulbert. What of him?

SUPIRO: He drinks strong wine, Master, and—

ABELARD: And so do I. (*Impatiently.*) And I detest gossip. Good day!

SUPIRO: But in drinking he talks . . .

ABELARD *hesitates and turns back.*

And, as in drinking you say he shares with you, so in talking he obviously shares with the Canon something he shouldn't share with others—should he? But he does.

ABELARD *looks him in the eye and* SUPIRO *is not at all put out.*

ABELARD: I think I understand you, Monsieur. Is money your object. Because——

SUPIRO: No, no—not immediately. My object is to serve—for what I am. And I am on the side of Reason and can wait a reasonable time. I am like a bridegroom, sure of his bride, Master. I can wait. Good afternoon—Master.

SUPIRO *goes.*

As ABELARD *stands, irresolute, the sound of his scholars coming from the school is heard. He moves off, taking refuge from this approaching sound as—*
The Scene Curtain falls. . . .

SCENE III

Fulbert's Hall.   Soon after—the same day.

HUGO *sits, helping himself to wine.*

FULBERT (*off*): Hugo! Hugo! (*Calling.*) Hugo! Hugo!

HUGO (*mimicking him*): Hugo! Hugo! The old miser.

FULBERT (*approaching*): Hugo! Hugo!

HUGO (*mimicking*): Hugo! Hugo!

> FULBERT *comes in and looks puzzled.*

FULBERT (*disturbed*): Hugo, who was calling your name?

HUGO: My name, Canon Fulbert? (*Innocently.*) You was.

FULBERT: Yes, I know, but . . . It must be my hearing. I imagine
things. Hugo, where is she?

HUGO: Out. (*And as* FULBERT *seems not to hear.*) Out! !

> He shouts at the deaf old man and it is obvious that HUGO
> feels he " rules the roost ".)

FULBERT (*querulously*): But I told you not to let her go out alone.

HUGO: Am I serving for her watch-dog too?—And on the same
pittance, eh? Eh?

FULBERT: Go and find her, Hugo, please. Go and—

HUGO: Sick-nurse to you, nursemaid to her, and porter to him!

> (*Turning to go.*)

FULBERT: Him! Was he here?

HUGO: My late master—the husband? How should I know?
Aren't his comings and goings secret, eh?

FULBERT: Yes, no one must know—and they don't know, do
they, Hugo? If they did, he might even have to go,
mightn't he?—out of Paris—out of Christendom, perhaps.

HUGO: Woa, turnip! He might say I did that too. So, when you're outside and you feel the pain in your head for godsake you stop talking.

FULBERT: Surely I'm capable of controlling my tongue ... I ... (*Worried.*) Have I said anything strange ... now? Have I?

HUGO: No.

HÉLOÏSE *comes in.*

FULBERT: Am I likely to have said anything strange outside? Anything forbidden?

HÉLOÏSE: Uncle Fulbert!

HUGO: She's come herself. (*Going.*) And watch that clapper, Canon Bell. (*Pointing to his own tongue.*) Sometimes you don't hear it wag now.

HUGO *goes*, with wine glasses.

HÉLOÏSE: Uncle Fulbert ... (*Standing in the doorway.*)

FULBERT: ... Come here, my love. What a beautiful woman my girl has become. I like your hair that way. What? What is wrong with me? (*As she looks intently at him.*)

HÉLOÏSE: How is it that people know about my marriage?

FULBERT: Sh! (*Looking round.*) Do you mean that they have guessed already?

HÉLOÏSE: I mean that they have been told.

FULBERT: Oh. I swear that I did not break my oath. I kept my tongue ... I ... (*Suddenly changing.*) Yet ... if it *is* known, why should we deny it? Eh?

HÉLOÏSE: I wonder if you know what you do?

FULBERT: But why deny it? You did not want this marriage. Did you? Did you? And why should we care what happens to him? You have been good—oh, so good! You have done all you can. And now he will be driven away and it will all be as it was before and you will always stay with me. No. I took oath and I held my tongue. But if it *is* known I will not deny it! I will not lie!

HÉLOÏSE: You must be mad!

FULBERT: You keep on saying that! Why? Do you want me to be? Sometimes I think my madness is you—and that you want to drive me mad. Stop looking at me so or . . .

> *Cries of pain off (from* HUGO).

Oh! (*Troubled.*) What was it? Did you hear something?
ABELARD *comes in.*

ABELARD: Yes, Canon Fulbert. It is a weakness in me to have usurped the wrath of God. May He forgive me but— (*Advancing.*)

HÉLOÏSE: Peter! What have you done?

ABELARD: Thrashed a servant for breaking an oath. (*Advancing on the frightened* FULBERT.) Should I stop at Hugo? He says not.

FULBERT: Oh! (*Cowering fearfully.*) Yes, strike me! Strike me down! That is all that is needed now. Strike!

ABELARD: If this is your doing you *will* be struck down—but not by me. You are in God's hands now. I have exercised what mercy I could. (*Turning to* HÉLOÏSE.) Héloïse . . .

FULBERT: Oh! (*Holding his head.*) I tried not to hate you. I . . . Oh, Hugo! (*Calling.*) The pain! It is the bell—the bell is beating again! (*Going.*) Hugo! Hugo!

> FULBERT *goes.*

HÉLOÏSE: Oh, Peter, why did you ever choose this way?

ABELARD: God knows—I hoped. (*Then hurriedly.*) I have come to tell you to prepare to go. Come to my lodgings as soon as it is dark. It is now dangerous to stay. The light is beginning to go now. Come soon.

HÉLOÏSE: I was already prepared. (*Sadly.*) But I dare not remain at your rooms. Where shall I go from there?

ABELARD: Argenteuil—it may have to be early in the morning and Théo will . . .

HÉLOÏSE: . . . Argenteuil?—The village?

ABELARD: The convent—I had arranged with the Abbess—your old teacher.

HÉLOÏSE: . . . You had arranged?

ABELARD: Yes. Oh, there is not time to explain now. It will be safe. Because she will let you wear the vestments of a nun —less the veil, of course—and that will gradually kill the report which Fulbert has spread about our marriage. We can then . . .

HÉLOÏSE: . . . Gradually? Shall I be there long?

> ABELARD *looks at her.*

How long?

ABELARD: I shall come to see you frequently and we shall walk together in the country.

HÉLOÏSE: In the winter, too?

ABELARD: Oh, my love, it shall be as short as necessity demands. Go upstairs now and get ready.

HÉLOÏSE: It would be better if we went separately. I can slip away. Go now!

ABELARD: But if you do not reach my lodgings within the hour, I shall come back for you.

> *They embrace and* ABELARD *goes.*
>
> HÉLOÏSE *runs upstairs into her room.*
>
> HUGO *comes in cautiously.*

HUGO: It's all right, Canon. I think he's gone, and she's nipped up into her room. Canon! (*Calling off.*)

> FULBERT *comes in and stands, trying to speak.*

FULBERT: She . . . she . . . she . . . she said . . .

HUGO: What's the matter with you? I told you not to get excited. (*Shouting at him.*) Fulbert! Do you hear me!

FULBERT: I heard a bell, Hugo.

HUGO: What the . . .!

FULBERT (*with unnatural calm*): Under the stairs in the deep cupboard, Hugo, we have twelve tall glasses and three bell-shaped decanters? Eh? Am I right?

Hugo (*looking at him*): You're a strange creature, Canon.

Fulbert (*calmly*): I have a clever memory, that is all. There, (*Pointing.*) under the stairs. Come, you will see that I am right. I said, come! (*With sudden authority.*)

Hugo: All right! All right! (*Rather sobered by the evident madness.*)
  Fulbert *leads* Hugo *to, and opens, the cupboard under the stairs.*

Fulbert: In these things I am never wrong. Now, look in. (*Smugly.*)

  As Hugo, *afraid to refuse, does so,* Héloïse *comes from her room, does not see them, and moves to the stairs to come down.*

Was I not right?

  Stepping back he sees Héloïse *who is dressed to go out and has a valise in her hand.*

Oh!

  There is a silence as he looks at her.

Héloïse (*fearfully*): Uncle, I . . . I am going out for a little.

Fulbert (*gently*): Hugo, go away. (*Fiercely.*) Go away!
  The Bell strikes the half hour.
  Hugo *goes, looking back at them both standing motionless.*

Fulbert (*with frightening calm and gentleness*): So, you are going? Come down. Great hurt creates great calm. Come down. (*Gently.*)

Héloïse (*not moving*): It was never my intention to hurt you, but now that you are so . . .

Fulbert (*quickly*): . . . so strange? Eh? *You* have always been strange. But I had believed it genius, but instruct me in the brilliance of this deceit—this insistence on my insanity? Eh? Come down.

Héloïse: But I have not said that you were insane.

Fulbert: But you said that my mind would strike me down. Come down!

HÉLOÏSE: I did not say so. And I hate to go on hurting you. I *must* go now—out of your world.

FULBERT: Is there another world for you not Hell? (*Fiercely.*) Come down!

> HÉLOÏSE *comes fearfully down and stops.*

Now, (*Gently as to a child.*) Héloïse, my little one, have I not often been good to you?

HÉLOÏSE: Yes, but . . .

FULBERT: . . . and educated you well?

HÉLOÏSE: Yes.

FULBERT: Given you comfort and good food? (*Step-by-step losing his calm.*)

HÉLOÏSE: Yes.

FULBERT: And liberty, *and* affection?

HÉLOÏSE: Yes, yes.

FULBERT: Then what have I done wrong? (*Crying out.*) Why have I deserved such anguish?

HÉLOÏSE: I do not believe that suffering comes to us by our deserving.

FULBERT (*excitedly*): Do you mean that if it had been in your power you would have spared me this? Answer me. Please!

HÉLOÏSE: I do. (*Moving down past him.*)

FULBERT: Then Héloïse, my darling one, (*Moving after her.*) spare me now. Don't go away! I *need* you. I need you more than anyone else in the whole world needs you now!

HÉLOÏSE (*frightened*): Let me pass!

FULBERT (*blocking her way*): He dare not keep you now. And why should we obey him?

HÉLOÏSE: Have you not made him my husband?

FULBERT: But the whole world does not know he is your husband Would you go out into the world and seem to be his mistress—his harlot?

HÉLOÏSE: For his sake—would to God that I were.

FULBERT: Oh! (*Appalled.*) Then you are possessed of the Devil! And I have wasted my life upon you. For I have set my course by how you would go. And now that you are going to Hell must I follow you too, fiend! ! !

> *He strikes her, so that she stumbles and in doing so drops the key of* ABELARD's *rooms.*

HÉLOÏSE: Ah! ! ! ! (*In pain.*)

FULBERT (*piteously*): I did not mean to strike you. Oh, rise. Rise! (*He goes to her but she thrusts him away. He picks up the key.*) Where does this key fit? Where would you go? Héloïse! I must know where you will be. Stop! (*He struggles with her.*) Where will you be, my love? Where will you be?

HÉLOÏSE: Argenteuil!—the convent—(*weeping*)—as I did, as a girl—to learn.

> *As he is taken by surprise and shock at this he relaxes his grip.* HÉLOÏSE *slips away through the doorway.*

FULBERT: Ar-gent-euil! ! (*Stunned.*) Héloïse! Come back! Héloïse!

> FULBERT *runs out, to the door.*

(*Off.*) Héloïse! ! ! Héloïse!

> HUGO *enters.*

HUGO: For godsake, Canon, don't bellow so with the door open.

FULBERT (*off*): Come back!

> HUGO *hauls* FULBERT *back in.*

HUGO: The whole of Paris will hear you, with the door open.

> HUGO *puts him in a seat and runs to shut the door.* FULBERT *sits staring ahead of him.*

FULBERT: So she's gone. Argenteuil! He has made her a nun. He is burying her in the black veil. (*In his strange calm again.*) But this widower Satan shall never again have anyone, anyone.

> *Bell of Notre Dame strikes three-quarters. He looks up and out.*

If the bell lost its tongue. It would have to come down—
come down. St. Augustine touched the bell . . . " and so
never living never dead, but ever dying. This is the worst
thing that can happen to a man " . . .

HUGO (*uneasily*): What are you talking about now?

FULBERT: When Satan was lodger in my house he paid me as
highly as his plunder was deep. I set it aside for—for
learning.   The Spanish doctor says it is costly, so—
Hugo—Supiro—get me Monsieur Supiro.

HUGO: Supiro? Why?

FULBERT (*shouting*): Do as you are commanded! !

> *As* HUGO *faces him and the Scene Curtain falls one may hear
> the Nuns' voices chanting—*

> Lacerata
>   Jacent membra
> Parvulorum
>   Et tam lacte
> Quam cruore
>   Rigant humum . . . (*fading*.)

SCENE IV

Fulbert's Hall.   The next evening.

*On rise of curtain, it is dark but for a glow from the lamp by the desk
and the red light from the fire.*

SUPIRO *is there, taking stock of everything in the room, especially the
desk where* ABELARD *used to work; this* FULBERT *has kept un-
changed. The handbell is still there.* SUPIRO *lifts it and tinkles it
gently.*

HUGO (*off, calling*): Canon! He's here! Supiro! He's here!
> SUPIRO *quickly puts down the bell, darts back to the fire and
> his wine.*

HUGO *comes into the dark room.*

He's on his way up. He's down in the cellar at his money box again. Oh, and he says he doesn't want the lamp lit. So you'll just have to make do—like I do. (*Drinking also.*)

HUGO *has been making rather free with* FULBERT'S *wine.*

SUPIRO: You don't seem happy, Hugo. And in a comfortable place like this? With such amenities. (*Indicating wine.*)

HUGO (*thickly*): I never wanted to come to this place—never wanted to come to Paris at all. Happy? Huh! My Master beats me for what this one did, and neither of them pays me what they both owe. I'm sick of slavery, I am. Sick of it!

SUPIRO: There's only one answer to that sickness, Hugo. Be your own Master—like me. It pays. I only do what I am implored to do by a world which evolves its fate in a way who am I to criticise? Eh? But oh! . . . the dirty work Humanity requires of me. The disgust I feel at what I have to do! I pay dearly, in disgust—so I make people pay—in cash.

HUGO: I'd like to make him pay for beating me; then run away to Brittany. What did you say? Drink up! (*Sighing.*) Brittany.

SUPIRO (*expanding*): If I take the risk for the wicked world of eternal damnation then surely I am entitled to *compensations*, Hugo? And I have them. Money?—stacks of it! Women?—corollary to stacks of the same! Food?— mn-ah! . . . Heavenly! I can't afford to live badly. For in the end, as soon as breath leaves my blissful bones, the Avenger will pounce like a plummet and I shall be rent in Hell. And I'll deserve it. Oh, it needs courage, Hugo. But the rewards are sure. Are you sure of Heaven? Are you sure of Hell? Honestly? Not honestly!

HUGO: No, not honestly . . .

SUPIRO: Look at our Abelard. Is *he* sure? Honestly. I tell you, Hugo, there's no proof! And even if there were, who wants to suffer in hopes of Heaven when he can get

heavenly pleasures here . . . without hope. Eh? Hugo?
In a month you could be like me—gem-studded!
(*Flourishing rings, etc.*)

HUGO (*looking unsteadily at him*): But everybody hates you.

SUPIRO: Three women adore me! Oh, men may hate me, but
life is a complete scheme here below and I am no small
part of that scheme. Condemn me and you condemn it
all! But share my risks and you share my power.

HUGO (*sulkily*): Don't want power. Only want money enough
to live.

SUPIRO: Then, begin to live now. (*Producing coins.*) Hold hypo-
thetical damnation at bay with a little pile of gold. There!
(*Putting money in* HUGO's *hand.*)

HUGO (*fascinated by what's in his hand*): Gold! (*Slowly.*) What do
I do for this?

SUPIRO: Do? Just watch me, learn and then . . . do. Oh, there's
technique in doing, Hugo. Sh! Canon Fulbert!

> As FULBERT *shuffles in holding something heavy under his
> gown,* SUPIRO *sits, and waits for the old man to begin.*

FULBERT (*with quiet intensity*): Monsieur, I come before you with
a special mission to perform—having recourse to your
reputation for doing what might be done. (*Sighing.*) It
is dreadfully simple, monsieur, and very specific; only,
I cannot make it seem so. For I must perforce be circum ·
spect and vague. And—

SUPIRO: Naturally, Canon. Won't you sit?

> FULBERT *is staring into the dark where* HUGO *sits at*
> ABELARD's *desk.*

FULBERT: There is someone behind you, monsieur. Oh, it is
only Hugo. Poor Hugo! Light the lamp, Hugo. (*He
sits.*) How can I explain? I do not find this easy, monsieur.

SUPIRO: You have my sympathy.

FULBERT: Now isn't that strange? Do you know, I have everyone's sympathy. But it will not do. Nothing short of
surgery will do. One must be clinical . . . " If the eye

M   163

offend ". . . . (*Leaning forward.*) You know a surgeon. I should like . . . Oh, " like " is not the word. I need to speak to you alone. Hugo, go away!

SUPIRO: Yes, Hugo, go away.

HUGO (*thickly*): I'll go away, I'll go away—(*Going.*)—to Brittany if you'll show me the way.

> HUGO *goes unsteadily.* FULBERT *sits and* SUPIRO *draws his chair close up so that he may be heard more easily.*

FULBERT (*to self*): There was a child too. She was a child. That must not go on.

SUPIRO: Now, Canon, speak your mind.

FULBERT: My mind? Oh, yes—my mind. I am aware that I am accounted mad. Oh, yes, I am! In fact it is highly probable. I have suffered so . . . but this rings like reason, does it not, to you?

SUPIRO (*uneasily*): Of course, Canon.

FULBERT: And being " out of one's mind " one might logically say, what a golden opportunity for being objective? But one can only be reasonable. And this is reasonable. I am the servant of Reason. Do you understand?

SUPIRO (*beginning to realise his madness*): I begin to, Canon. Yes—I understand.

FULBERT: Then. (*Quickly opening his gown and taking casket out.*) I have money here. Here! (*Proffering it.*)

SUPIRO: But I have done nothing yet.

FULBERT: You have understood. And in understanding you may have to cry out for great compensation.

SUPIRO: Compensation? Canon Fulbert (*Standing up.*)—you did me an honour to call me here. But I never take money or instructions from a sick man.

FULBERT: Sick! (*Rising.*) Monsieur Supiro, I am not sick—unless being so terribly wronged destroys tissue. Look! In this casket is *all* my wordly wealth.

> He holds it for SUPIRO to see.

SUPIRO (*impressed*): It is a great deal. I had no idea you held so much.

> *For a moment* SUPIRO *hesitates, then sits.*
> What would you require me to do?

FULBERT: Do? I have heard that you have the services of a surgeon, who can relieve a man of the sinister power of reproducing his form in the flesh. And so in this occasion here if . . . I find this difficult to say, monsieur, without crude reference not applicable to the dreadful delicacy of the task, such as . . . gelding . . . of animals. Oh, this is not revenge! (*His voice rising excitably.*) Is that clear? It is a duty I would gladly forswear. But it falls to me. And I hope that Rome is too robust today to accept saints gelded. For his ruin, which is inevitable now, must not be the Church's ruin. No. For I love my Church just as much as I hate this man! And I love her. (*Confidentially.*) Can it be done?

SUPIRO: May I ask the name of the patient?

FULBERT: That I consider unnecessary, don't you? It is the surgeon's business. I shall supply the opportunity *and* the patient. I only purchase skill, monsieur. You are not, you understand, ethically involved. I hope you will feel no responsibility; but I know of no other so qualified as you to achieve the thing. Frankly, Monsieur Supiro, I implore you.

SUPIRO (*with resignation*): What the world demands so desperately, that I always do, Canon. And *where*, will this take place?

FULBERT (*evasively*): Ah. I appreciate your anxiety, but . . .

SUPIRO: Well, then, *when* shall it take place?

FULBERT (*sharply*): Tonight!

SUPIRO (*daunted*): Oh. Must it be so soon?

FULBERT: Oh, please! (*Looking round fearfully.*) This strain must not carry into another day. And I have assured myself where he will be tonight. But tomorrow . . . (*Fervently.*) No! I insist that it be tonight.

SUPIRO: These things take time to arrange. However, (*Rising.*) I suppose you can give me a rendezvous?—for the Spanish doctor?

FULBERT (*quickly*): Not in this house!

SUPIRO: No. Shall we say the East entrance to the Cloister School?

FULBERT (*suspiciously*): And why should it not be the other end of the town?

SUPIRO: Why not?

FULBERT: Oh, I concede. I concede. In the courtyard there is a small gateway with a carving of the Trinity over the lintel. I shall be there at the last quarter of ten, and let the thing be done as the bell strikes eleven, so that no one may hear if . . . I shall pay you now. (*He hesitates.*) Take the whole box. To count the cost might seem to presume a scale of consequence. Do you complain? (*To* SUPIRO *who is taken aback.*)

SUPIRO: I never complain. But such generosity, Canon, eases my burden.

FULBERT: Have you a burden too?

SUPIRO: What the world requires me to do is burdensome.

FULBERT: Perhaps we could arrange to meet afterwards . . . no. (*Turning to go.*) At eleven. As the bell strikes. I shall come from the cathedral.

SUPIRO: As near eleven as may be. There is little time. Could I borrow your servant to run with a message now, Canon?

FULBERT: Hugo? Yes. (*Calling.*) Hugo! (*Moving off.*) God forgive me—and you too. I shall be credited with courage and all I know is a desperate necessity. I must prepare my mind—my mind.

> FULBERT *goes as* SUPIRO *goes to* ABELARD'S *desk, puts the casket on the desk, takes a piece of parchment and pen, and writes quickly.*
> HUGO *comes in.*

SUPIRO: Hugo!

> HUGO *starts, seeing him sitting at* ABELARD'S *desk, and goes to him.*

Tell the doctor to come to my house straight away—that the case is a very critical one—but not a matter of life and death. Show him this sign by my signature.

HUGO (*peering at it by the lamp*): What is it?

SUPIRO: I said show it to the doctor. And look, Hugo, (*Opening casket.*) we're rich! And the old man's gone—out of the house; and out of his mind too.

HUGO (*whistling*): But if he's gone out and given you the money already, you don't have to do it.

SUPIRO: Hugo, (*Firmly.*) what the world demands so desperately, that I *do* do.

HUGO: Are you cracked too?

SUPIRO: No. (*Fingering the gold.*) My bell has a golden note. (*Handing him the note.*) Take it. And quickly! We have till eleven to . . . do. Go!

HUGO: It's something to do with my Marster.

SUPIRO: Master? You have none . . . if you do as I say.

HUGO: But what will happen to him?—my Master, I mean.

SUPIRO: You have no master. A peculiar pride precedes a most peculiar fall. But who are we to interfere? For what has been is all of the Lord's creation. And when God asked Adam, " Why did you eat of the Tree? " He said, " It was the Woman Thou gavest me ". And when God asked Eve, " Why did you do it? " She said to Him, " It was the Serpent told me to ". But did God have the courage to ask the Serpent why? And if He did, did the Serpent say . . . " Lord, who made me so? "

> *Bell of Notre Dame striking ten.*

HUGO: I want to know what will—

SUPIRO: Sh. Listen! . . . Three, Four, Five, Six, Seven, Eight, Nine, Ten . . . (*Pause.*) Ten! We have a lot to do before it strikes another hour. Run Hugo. Run, I say! But *I* do not beat you.

> HUGO *goes in great doubt with the message.*

> SUPIRO *gathers up the casket, blows out the lamp and as he goes he knocks the bell from* ABELARD's *desk. Letting it lie* SUPIRO *goes.*

> *The Scene Curtain falls slowly and rises slowly.*

Time Passes

> *There is silence, but for a voice muttering a prayer "Agnus Dei ". The red light of the fire suddenly glows up, then slowly and steadily it dims and* FULBERT's *voice can be heard clearly intoning the prayer repetitively.*

> " Agnus Dei, qui tollis pecata mundi—
>   Agnus Dei, qui tollis pecata mundi—
>
>   (*Tailing off.*)

> *The darkness is complete, and as the Act Curtain begins to fall the Great Bell of Notre Dame tolls eleven peals each louder than the preceeding.*

ACT CURTAIN

ACT III

Scene I

Fulbert's House—the hall. Some weeks later.

Before rise of curtain the Great Bell of Notre Dame strikes three-quarters of an hour.

On rise of curtain the house is seen to be derelict and the hall empty. The daylight is shuttered out.

The handbell still stands on Abelard's desk.

All is silent.

Slowly, into the hall below comes HUGO. *He moves painfully, and fearfully and looks like a mud-stained and hunted animal. He moves to cross but Abelard's desk abruptly stops him. By the way in which his hands grope about the desk to find out what it is, it becomes obvious that* HUGO *is blind. His groping hands strike against the handbell and it clatters to the floor.*

HUGO *panics and runs against the gallery wall, then, stumbling back into the open, he stands crouching, waiting.*

THÉO *appears on the gallery, coming from the stairs to the upper rooms.*

THÉO (*in grim amazement*): Hugo!

> THÉO *comes quickly down the stairs while* HUGO *faces to where the voice had come from.*

(*Picking up the bell and advancing on him.*) Hugo! You . . . swine! . . . (*Almost as if he'd fell him with the bell*).

HUGO (*turning and falling on his knees and putting up his arms to shield his head*): No! Master Théo! No!

THÉO: Get out of here or God help you! For what you did there's no fit punishment. Get up! Stand up, you animal! Stand up!

HUGO *stands and fearfully faces him.*

(*Appalled.*) God in Heaven! What have they done to you?

HUGO: It was the students. But it's all right, Master Théo. It's healed up now. It took time. I had to lie up (*Nearly weeping.*) in a sewer for . . . six weeks it must be. But now it's healed.

THÉO: But what in God's name made you come *here*?

From a room above a regular to and fro of footsteps is heard.

HUGO: I still had the key. I had to get off the streets. I'm just trying to get back—back to Brittany. I tried that night. But his students had closed all the bridges so that they could track us down like rats in a ship. They did worse than this to Supiro. Don't send me out into the street. Let me stay till it's dark.

THÉO: No, God help you! You'll have to get out of here.

HUGO (*resisting as* THÉO *tries to guide him to the passage-way*): But I thought no one else would want to be here. I thought the house was standing empty. He hasn't escaped his punishment has he? He's not here?

THÉO: Fulbert? No. (*Guiding him across the hall.*)

HUGO: And is he dead?

THÉO: He's mad beyond human punishment. Come.

THÉO *puts the bell on the table by the dead fire and uses both hands to lead* HUGO.

HUGO: Master Théo, let me stay, please. (*Whining.*) They think the house is shut up. They won't look here. (*Struggling to stay.*) Don't put me in the street!

THÉO: For godsake, be quiet! (*Fiercely.*) Damn you, you've got to go!

HUGO (*struggling in panic*): But why? Why?

THÉO: Because your Master is here.

HUGO: My Master? Master? Oh! . . . (*Fearfully.*) Oh dear.

THÉO: He's up above.

The footsteps cease their pacing.

HUGO: Guide me to the door, Master Théo. Put me in the street. Tell him what they did to me. I didn't know what they would do to him. I didn't know. (*As he is being led to the exit he " freezes ".*) Sh!

THÉO: What is it?

HUGO: The key in the street door. It's somebody coming in from the street. Hide me! Hide me!

THÉO: Quickly! Get in there. But who could it be? Get in! And keep quiet or God help you!

> THÉO *hides* HUGO *within the great empty fireplace while he himself steps aside and waits, watching the entrance.*
>
> A NUN *comes in, and stands, listening.*
>
> *In the silence, one can again hear the restless footsteps of* ABELARD, *pacing up above. She looks puzzled.*

(*Coming forward.*) Sister of Benedict!

HÉLOÏSE: Oh! (*Catching her breath.*) Théo!

THÉO: Héloïse! (*Amazed.*) But . . . but the veil . . .!

HÉLOÏSE (*taking it off*): God forgive me! It was only a disguise to shield me coming through the streets. I could not bear that the crowds might recognise me . . . and laugh at me . . . Yes . . . (*Bitterly.*) laugh, Théo. When I saw the crowds of scholars still crowding his door I could not go on. So I came here. (*As he looks at her.*) But why are *you* here?

THÉO: So you don't know?

HÉLOÏSE: Know what? (*Afraid.*) I only know what everyone knows; for he has sent no word to Argenteuil. (*Agitatedly.*) But, Théo, why are you here? Is he left all alone? What is it? Is he—

THÉO: No, no. He's alive. Héloïse, listen. Listen. (*Indicating the sound above.*)

The sound of the footsteps.

HÉLOÏSE: Yes, I heard. I wondered . . . Théo! (*Suddenly.*) It's not him?—not Peter?

The footsteps stop.

THÉO: Yes. It was his suggestion to come to the deserted house. No one would think of looking for him here . . . and he is as afraid of the crowds as you.

HÉLOÏSE: Yet, how strange, Théo—to choose to come here.

THÉO: No—not for him . . . (*Stopping himself.*) Héloïse, you should not have come. You should have stayed at Argenteuil. You must go back there and wait.

HÉLOÏSE: Wait?

As she moves restlessly about the room, nervously fingering the veil, THÉO *stands with his back to the fireplace.*

I cannot just wait.

The footsteps are heard again.

For how do I know that he too may not just wait? And both of us stand away on either side of this calamity, fearful to move for the other's sake—and no move ever be made? No. I must see him. Oh . . . (*Referring to the footsteps which throughout this persist above.*) Does he never rest! He must tell me what to do.

THÉO: Héloïse. (*He leads her to where she may sit.*) Will you sit here and listen to me? Please! You look so tired.

The footsteps cease.

HÉLOÏSE: Would to God that I were exhausted. No. I cannot sit still. Does he sleep? Does he eat? Oh, I can bear the complexities, but I am tortured night and day with the simplest things. What is it you are trying to say?

THÉO (*with difficulty*): Héloïse, the person pacing up in that room is forever out of reach of our hearts.

HÉLOÏSE: What do you mean? Théo! . . . he's not mad! Not mad!

THÉO: God curse my clumsy tongue—no! But he is almost another person.

HÉLOÏSE: Why do you say this? (*Fiercely.*) Why?

THÉO: Because going up that stair might be for you a sort of descent into Hell. You musn't try to see him. Oh, he does not look differently and he talks in the same moving way with the same voice; but what moves him to talk and what he will say are quite different. It appals me.

HÉLOÏSE (*completely perplexed*): But for all that has happened to him, Théo, it must still be our Peter. His person, his spirit could not change!

THÉO (*wearily*): I had thought so.

HÉLOÏSE: And . . . (*Fearfully.*) . . . do you think differently now?

THÉO: Oh, I'm no thinker, Héloïse, but I must conclude from what I see that the spirit of a person must surely be—and this, this frightens me—the spirit must depend on the body so, that this flesh, in God's esteem, must be precious beyond everything. And I have squandered the gift in every way. But yours—your sweet body—guard it! Oh, (*As she recoils from this intensity.*) not from me—and guard it in what way, I do not know, but here, beyond any doubt, I know that it is in danger of real death.

HÉLOÏSE: Théo. (*In hushed voice.*) What are you trying to tell me?

THÉO (*turning away*): Not simply, with nothing to fill your need in the whole world now, that I love you too.

The footsteps are heard again.

(*Turning to face her.*) And that beyond that awkward confession I . . . am aimless and useless. *And* what I detest saying and yet must say, is that he talks of this calamity as having . . . *saved* him.

HÉLOÏSE: Saved him? But from what?

THÉO: From what else, but from you—your love; from what he now declares to have been . . . blind lust.

The footsteps stop.

HÉLOÏSE (*almost inaudibly*): No. (*Appalled.*) Oh, no. He must not deny truth. No.

ABELARD'S *voice breaks the silence from above.*

ABELARD: Théo! (*Calling.*) What was it? Théo! Come up! Come up, will you!

THÉO: I'll have to go up. (*Quietly.*) Shall I tell him you are here? Shall I?

HÉLOÏSE (*after a long pause*): No. See first what he wants. I . . . I will sit here. I *am* tired.

> THÉO *goes off upstairs while* HÉLOÏSE *waits and sits staring ahead of her, her fingers playing convulsively with the veil.*
> In this silence HUGO, *thinking no one there, slowly gropes his way out from within the fireplace and blindly fumbles his way towards the entrance.*
> HÉLOÏSE—*as if this were all part of the nightmare—watches him go unmoving. As he passes the table his groping hands knock over the bell again. It rolls on the floor.*
> HÉLOÏSE *drops her head into her hands.*
> HUGO *blunders out in panic.*
> THÉO *coming down the stairs realises what has happened, recovers the bell and goes towards her. He carries a folded sheet of manuscript in his hand.*

THÉO (*softly*): Héloïse. (*She raises her head.*) I told him. I told him you were here. And . . . and he immediately gave me this manuscript—to give to you.

HÉLOÏSE: Manuscript?

THÉO: I do not myself know what it is, but he says that he had already written it and was awaiting the courage to send it to you. He says that you are beyond his instruction now, but that this, as you will see, contains his wish.

HÉLOÏSE: His wish. (*As she just stares at it in his outstretched hand.*) My hands . . . are cold, Théo. Break the seal for me. (*He does so.*) No! Do not read it. (*Almost as if she were paralysed.*) Hold it where I can see.

> THÉO *holds it before her. She reads.*

Ah! . . . (*Gasping as if struck on the breast.*)

> Convulsively she seizes it out of his hands and crushes it to her breast.

THÉO: Héloïse! What does it say?

HÉLOÏSE: It is my instruction to remain at Argenteuil—(*She gets up.*)—and to take the veil, finally.

THÉO: No! But he said that he dared not instruct you.

HÉLOÏSE: This is his wish, and he must know that to me it is his command.

THÉO (*desperately*): But this is not your vocation and never could be. It would be utter hypocrisy on your part!

HÉLOÏSE: Théo, I think that life calls for much greater constancy than to be true to oneself. For (*Looking at the stairs.*) if I were only *so* true, I would mount these stairs, and with my nails I'd try to tear from his tortured breast the naked truth . . . and find nothing . . . and kill my love. And it still must live. It still must grow. There will be a way, God knows!—there *must* be!

THÉO (*bitterly*): But it's not right!

HÉLOÏSE (*in exhaustion*): No, nor just, nor even good; but it has become a necessity.

THÉO: Oh, what can I say?

HÉLOÏSE: Nothing, Théo dear. (*Handling the veil.*) But let me not be so hypocritical as to say that it suits me—this veil. (*Sadly.*) I was proud of my mouth. Théo . . . Kiss me! Yes.

THÉO: Oh, Héloïse! (*Taking her into his arms and kissing her head anywhere but on the mouth, and breaking away weeping.*)

HÉLOÏSE: I wish they were *my* eyes that were not dry; but, as I cannot, you must cry for me. God works in strange unities. But this arid desolation now will not last a life-time. And when his tears fall they will water more withered earth than mine. (*Turning at the exit.*) If you visit Argenteuil, ask for me. It will be lonely for me to be among women only. Goodbye, Théo, and God bless you.

She covers her face with the veil and goes.

Théo: Christ forgive him!

> Abelard *appears in the gallery.*

Abelard: Théo. (*His voice is hoarse with strain.*)

Théo (*turning on him*): Yes, you—Master Abelard! (*Shouting.*) Christ forgive you!

Abelard (*tensely*): Then she has chosen to go?

Théo: You gave her no choice.

Abelard: I know. (*Under great strain.*) I know. Nor could she have wished it. Could she, Théo?

Théo (*turning away*): No walls, no rules, no nunnery will hold her spirit. You shall see. For those who will not be humbled today the Church will cast out! You have not put her away. (*Bitterly.*) You have not achieved safety . . . Master!

> Abelard, *taking this bitter attack without evidence of feeling comes slowly down the stairs and proceeds towards the doorway.*

Peter . . . where are you going?

Abelard: Through the streets; to the Abbot of St. Denys; to arrange my taking of the vows.

Théo: You cannot bury yourself. As you go through the streets they will recognise you, and your students will shout your name. They will clamour for you to stay and teach them. And you will know you must. For, ruthless in you stands Truth above persons—above love. When they kneel in your way—what then, Peter?

Abelard: I shall go on.

> Abelard *goes.*

Théo: Yes. For a time. For a time.

A Voice (*off in the street*): Master Abelard!

> *Sound of several voices calling:* " *Abelard*; *It's Abelard*; *Master Abelard*; "

Théo: Fools! Can't they leave him alone! Can't they give him some peace!

> Théo *hurries out after* Abelard *and the shouting grows as the Scene Curtain falls. . . .*

SCENE II

By a gate of the convent of Argenteuil—about ten years later—Spring.

Before the rise of the curtain THE SINGER, *passing, sings one verse of
    Abelard's version of the hymn:—*

CHANT: Est in Rama
                     Vox audite
                     Rachel flentis
                     Super natos
                     Interfectos
                     Eiulantis.

THE SINGER *goes.*

Sound of women's voices chanting takes up the hymn.

On rise of curtain ALBERIC *paces to and fro, thoughtfully.*

The chant concludes:

                     Lacerata
                     Iacent membra
                     Parvulorum
                     Et tam lacte
                     Quam cruore
                     Rigant humum.

       THE ABBESS *comes out through the gateway.*

ALBERIC: Where is she?

ABBESS (*gently*): Archdeacon, I find that I cannot persuade her to
    come.

ALBERIC: Abbess, it should not be necessary to *persuade*, when
    you hold the authority to *order* her to come.

ABBESS: That, Archdeacon Alberic, I do not choose to do. Unless
    you are persuaded to order me.

ALBERIC: I see. So ten years of your rule have not taught her to
    bow to this house's authority.

ABBESS: When one has suffered much one must see that suffering has a sort of authority. I respect it. And I respect the reasons she gives for the further pain this interview must bring. I also respect, that on your part, the pain may still be necessary.

ALBERIC (*with dry humour—as between old hands at the diplomatic game*): One cannot, Abbess, accuse you of lack of *respect*. And what are the reasons she gives for the harm I'd do her?

ABBESS: Well . . . (*Choosing her words wisely.*) Your past conflicts with him who is, in the sight of God, her husband still. And your part in Abbot Bernard's policy of refuting the doctrines of . . . her husband. And your initiation of the trial for heresy of her husband. And with these follows her fear that this questioning may be but another step in a campaign whose final aim she chooses to see as the driving of . . . her husband from Christendom. This allegiance to a husband is something I find difficult *not* to respect.

ALBERIC (*firmly*): And do you find it difficult to see that her first allegiance must always be to her Faith and her God?

ABBESS: No. (*Gently.*)

ALBERIC: Then send her out to me.

ABBESS (*cautiously*): And you order me to do so?

ALBERIC: I do. And with the authority of Abbot Bernard, and your own Bishop.

ABBESS: I see. Then I will convey the order, Archdeacon.

> THE ABBESS *goes off by the gate.*

> *As* ALBERIC *paces, a crippled and disfigured* FRIAR *comes in.*

FRIAR: Sir, can you direct me to the Abbess.

ALBERIC: Through the gate. (*Lost in his own thoughts.*) Her office is just inside. (*Staring at him.*) What is your business here?

FRIAR: Hers, sir. (*Hobbling past him.*) And his who sent me.

ALBERIC (*looking more carefully at him*): Brother! (*Calling after him.*) What is your name?

FRIAR: Just Brother, brother. (*Going on towards the gate.*)

ALBERIC (*troubled*): Is your name not . . . Supiro.

FRIAR: Name. (*Turning at gate.*) I lost my name with my memory
And until my real name comes to me, I'll not use any.
But it will come. They call me Brother Adam—but that's
a generality. I should be a particular person and I am.
I am. (*Going.*) I must speak to the Abbess.

> THE FRIAR *goes in through the gate with difficulty.*

> *As* ALBERIC *looks after the* FRIAR, HÉLOÏSE *comes out and
> stands waiting. Her head-veil is drawn over her face and she
> avoids Alberic's eyes.*

ALBERIC: Prioress, I learn from your Abbess and others that
you—while you have been here at Argenteuil—have
performed great services and good works; and that you
have been greatly loved.

HÉLOÏSE (*in subdued voice*): I have done little to deserve that love.

ALBERIC: But I think you have. However, duty drives me now
to ask you a difficult question.

HÉLOÏSE (*quietly*): I am used to difficult questions. (*As* ALBERIC
hesitates.) Well?

ALBERIC: Héloïse, my sister, why is there still no visible sign
that you have fully repented of all the sin into which Peter
Abelard once led you?

HÉLOÏSE (*restraining herself from anger*): All that was sin I have
repented.

ALBERIC: Then why do your sisters and the Abbess know that
you still treat as sacred what happened to you? (*Trying to
goad her to retort.*) That even when you were first hid in
this place, and wearing all but the veil you wear now, even
that!—when borne by his hellish lust you desecrated this
place . . . even that! you refuse to see as of the Devil! Is
that not so?

HÉLOÏSE (*quietly*): This was not of the Devil—nor of God; but
of both in conflict. The conflict goes on—and in the end

of this conflict there may be a glory which you cannot see
—and which I know I dare not deny.

ALBERIC (*shaking his head*): How can you expect to retain your
authority over your sisters?

HÉLOÏSE: My authority is their love for me—which I did not
expect.

ALBERIC (*quickly*): And in loving you they emulate you and in
doing so they are led astray! For they cannot see that
the beliefs you hold are those of a monk they will one day
see branded as arch-heretic!

HÉLOÏSE (*tenssly*): But not by me. And my sisters find no heresy
in me.

ALBERIC: Then I do! (*Throwing aside all restraint.*) Was the
Tractate on the Trinity, written by Peter Abelard, not
ordered, *with all copies extant*, to be destroyed by fire?
And was that order not confirmed by the Pope? And do
you deny that even now, under the vestments which you
wear, and warmed by your guilty heart, there lies a copy
of that book?

    HÉLOÏSE *clutches her breast.*

Do you deny it?

HÉLOÏSE (*quietly but defiantly*): No.

ALBERIC (*shouting at her*): Why must you defy your Church so?

HÉLOÏSE: I do not! (*She throws back her veil.*) I defy *you*! (*Suddenly
attacking fiercely.*) For why were you unable to support the
charges which you brought against this book? Why had
you to resort to a trivial charge to have the book burned
at all? Why? Because it is dangerous to you! Dangerous
to all who now try to suppress the new truth! The truth
which grew by letting the light of Reason show the
darkness in Dogma.

ALBERIC: Truth! This book maintains that there is not One
God, but Three! Is this Truth? That Father Son and Holy
Ghost are separate in their Trinity!

HÉLOÏSE: Separate, but held in the human mind as One Concept
—One thing! One Deity!

ALBERIC (*furiously*): In man's mind! Is Man then the container
of God? Does God have to wait upon Man to have his
Being?

HÉLOÏSE (*passionately*): Was God not made Man in Christ, so that
we might contain him? And where then shall we worship
God? In the inhuman Heavens from which He came, or
where He is now?—broken and crying out to be remade
within Humanity in the Cause of Love! (*Trembling.*) Yes,
I love my Earthly Master! I love him! Not more than
God in Heaven, for what I love is God in Man with all
my passion! And so shall I do, till my human morsel of
divinity finds its peace; or until I die, in this withering
agony of its denial!

ALBERIC (*appalled—and quietly*): Woman, from what can this
damnable blasphemy spring? Not from the instruction
of the Holy Word, but from the instruction of your
husband who in his instruction drives not only you but
thousands of Christians into Hell!

HÉLOÏSE (*slowly with trembling voice*): I have received no instruct-
tion from him for . . . ten years.

ALBERIC: Prioress, how can this be true?

HÉLOÏSE (*swallowing her emotion*): I cannot blame you for doubting
that. (*Turning to avoid showing her emotion.*) God be with you
(*Making to go.*)

ALBERIC: Prioress! (*Halting her.*) It had been decided that if you
could not find your way to deny what you have so asserted
now . . . you would have to leave Argenteuil.

HÉLOÏSE (*turning*): Leave? (*Shocked.*) If I go my sisters will desert
this place to follow me.

ALBERIC: This convent has always been the property of the
Abbot of Saint Denys. He will be glad to find it empty.
And I shall be glad to be relieved of the necessity of
evicting you.

HÉLOÏSE: But where could we go?

ALBERIC: We do not know. You have chosen your way. The pity is I cannot say "God go with you". And yet He may.

> ALBERIC *goes.*
>
> *As* HÉLOÏSE *stands, desolately alone* THE ABBESS *comes in and holds out a message to her.*

ABBESS: I cannot any longer keep them away. And now this crippled Friar has brought some new instruction for you.

HÉLOÏSE: Instruction?

> *As the Nuns off take up the hymn again* HÉLOÏSE *opens the message then turns towards* THE ABBESS.

Mother (*intently, radiantly*). He has sent for me.

> *They both go off through the gate as the hymn concludes and the Scene changes. . . .*

SCENE III

The country near Nogent-sur-Seine—" The Paraclete" (which is a primitive collection of cells forming a sort of hermitage, built by Abelard and his followers)—Abelard's cell in " The Paraclete".

Some weeks later.

Before rise of curtain THE SINGER *can be heard singing and playing the first love song:—" A Woman there will be . . ." The cell has one door, and one square, open window, where the sun shines. It is Spring.*

THÉO, *in monk's garb and bearded, is repairing a fishing rod.*

He takes a flagon of wine and has a hasty and guilty gulp before he hears THE SINGER *outside singing. He listens, puzzled, and as the song stops he goes, flagon in hand, to peep out of the window.*

As he makes to peep out, THE SINGER *peeps in.*

THÉO: Oh.
SINGER: Oh. } (*Then recovering from his surprise* The SINGER *says.*)

They told me this place was deserted.

THÉO It was. (*Looking at him suspiciously.*) It isn't.

SINGER: Why, who's in it now?

THÉO: Me.

SINGER: Whose was it before, brother?

THÉO: Abelard's, brother.

SINGER: Oh. That's strange. I was thinking of him as I came along singing. (*Looking longingly at the flagon.*) There's warmth in the sun. Is it far to the river?

THÉO (*pointing*): There!

SINGER: Is it drinkable?

THÉO: Yes. (*Pointedly.*)

SINGER: Someone went round and into that other cell just now. Who is it?

THÉO: Here; (*Suddenly.*) Take it and stop your pipe with it for godsake! Let your ears sing! There's nobody here, not even me. Now go on! Move on!

> SINGER *takes the flagon and goes while* THÉO *again busies himself with the rod.*

> *Without knowing it he is whistling the tune of first song, "A woman there will be . . ."*

> ABELARD *comes in while* THÉO's *back is turned and stops, listening.*

ABELARD (*clenching his hands*): Théo!

> *He shows signs of the ten years of adversity. He is gaunt, bearded and obviously broken in health. But he has if anything more dignity.*

THÉO (*guiltily*): Yes, Abbot?

ABELARD: What possessed you to whistle that tune now?

THÉO: What tune? Oh! A wandering singer passed just now singing the tune and somehow I . . . Oh, dear God above! (*Realising what tune it is.*) Your song. Oh, Peter, I'm sorry. Lord, how the years erase the meaning from the surface of things.

ABELARD: Time does not erase—it covers up. See (*Leading him to window.*) now, even the rock carving of the Trinity is almost covered over with moss.

THÉO: Yes. (*Looking out.*) Do you remember when we built this place—when right down to the river it was all scrub, and we had to cut our way through and . . . (*Stopping.*)

ABELARD: What is it, Théo? Is someone coming?

THÉO: It was the singer going to the river. He has met with a party of nuns at the ford . . . probably crossing the fields to St. Ayoul. (*Turning.*) I must admit I'm glad to be back in our Paraclete. And with the summer before us. But will dear Bernard and Alberic and all these smooth-handed weavers of webs leave us alone?

ABELARD: Théo, I have not been honest with you. I came back here only to arrange that this place—which as you know is so dear to me—will not be left derelict when I go.

THÉO: Go? Go where? (*Grimly.*) Where are we being driven to now?

ABELARD: I shall not ask you to accompany me this time. I shall be going alone.

THÉO: Alone! Not even me? Peter, where are you going to?

ABELARD: Spain.

THÉO: Spain! (*Incredulous.*)

ABELARD: At first. But my destination is further East.

THÉO: Further East! But surely if you go further East it will take you right out of Christendom?

ABELARD: Yes, Théo. (*Counting the keys.*)

THÉO: But . . . (*Slowly.*) . . . you'll come back?

ABELARD: No. (*And as* THÉO *takes this in with difficulty.*) I have tried to teach Truth to Christians, Théo. You know the results. Outside Christendom I may yet find an innocence which might be better ground for the seed I must sow. For out of the thorn the rose must grow, all over again.

THÉO (*turning to the window again*): But, Peter, why were we cleaning up the place if you are going? Is someone else coming here to take your place?

ABELARD: Yes. The Prioress of Argenteuil and some of her nuns.

THÉO The Prioress of . . . (*Amazed and delighted.*) Héloïse!

ABELARD: Yes. I have hopes that she will take my place. I had written to her some weeks ago. Yesterday she reached Nogent. (*Crossing to look guardedly from the window.*) These will be her nuns, and she . . . the tall one . . . moving round now . . . into the sun.

THÉO: Oh, Peter. (*Excited as a boy.*)

ABELARD (*drawing back*): They are coming now.

THÉO And does . . . does the Prioress of Argenteuil know what you mean to do? Go East.

ABELARD: No. (*Quickly.*) And it would be quite useless to try to get her to alter my mind, for I am afraid that she does not know it now. Fetch the Prioress here, to be instructed in the ways of this place.

THÉO (*happily*): I'll send her. You won't want me here.

ABELARD: You will come with her! There are rules of this house concerning women, and these rules shall be strictly observed in this.

THÉO (*meekly*): Yes . . . Abbot. I'll fetch her.

> THÉO *goes out but as soon as he gets out he loses all restraint and can be heard calling:* "Héloïse!" (*Going.*) "Héloïse! Héloïse!"
>
> THE SINGER *can be heard in the distance singing,* "*A woman there will be . . .*"
>
> ABELARD, *whose agitation is obvious, goes painfully to his knees in prayer.*
>
> *Slowly* HÉLOÏSE *comes in.* ABELARD *rises. She stands facing him. Her head-veil is back from her face. Above her face-veil her eyes search his for some sign of what is expected. She gets none. The singing of* THE SINGER *dies away.*

HÉLOÏSE (*almost in a whisper*): Brother Théo sent me in.

ABELARD: I see. You had my letter in good time?

HÉLOÏSE: Yes. (*Tonelessly.*)

ABELARD: The instructions and conditions embodied in it were clear? (*He speaks hurriedly and tensely.*)

HÉLOÏSE: Yes.

ABELARD: It was advisable to be brief here at the expense of being tedious in the letter. (*Hurrying on.*)

HÉLOÏSE: I see.

ABELARD: You are prepared to take over immediately?

HÉLOÏSE: Yes.

ABELARD: How many are you?

HÉLOÏSE: Myself and eleven.

ABELARD: Yourself and eleven. (*Dropping his eyes and moving to avoid her scrutiny.*) There remains no need for me to do more than to extend to you and your sisterhood my poor blessing. I shall now show you round the property and welcome your sisters before I go. This cell . . .

HÉLOÏSE: . . . Go? (*Interrupting him.*) Do you go back to St. Gildas immediately . . . Abbot?

ABELARD: I have left the monastery of St. Gildas. Poison was put in my chalice.

HÉLOÏSE: Oh!

ABELARD: This cell was my own and I hope . . .

HÉLOÏSE: . . . Abbot! May I ask where you will go?

ABELARD: I am afraid that that is rather hard to say. It will be your duty—if you see it so—to care for this place. I am afraid it is rather primitive. But with your reputation for works I am sure that you will improve upon mine. And may I say that, with others, I am proud of you and what you have done for the Glory of God. (*Quietly.*) I was not wrong.

HÉLOÏSE: No . . . (*Simply.*) With others, you were deceived. (*He turns.*) For although I have won some praise from men I deserve none from God. For what I have done—which seemed as for Him—was inevitably done for you, for whom my love must always be more real.

ABELARD (*avoiding her eyes*): Thereby you offend both God and me. (*Trying to escape.*) I will now show . . .

HÉLOÏSE: No! (*Stopping him.*) Why . . . after ten silent years, have you sent for me?

ABELARD (*still avoiding her eyes*): The plan to evict you from Argenteuil was reported to me. I had this shelter to offer. I hope it will do—(*Tensely.*)—for I have no more that I can offer you.

HÉLOÏSE: Oh. (*All her hopes crumbling.*) And when you go, will you return to visit us soon? (*Putting her hopes again in the future.*)

ABELARD: I am afraid that I cannot.

HÉLOÏSE (*passionately*): Then I must know where you are going!

ABELARD: I am going out of your world.

HÉLOÏSE: Peter!

ABELARD (*quickly*): By your world, Prioress, I mean Christendom —and not this life. I am going to the East. I shall not return.

HÉLOÏSE: Oh no! I cannot allow you to do this!

ABELARD (*raising his head*): Your care exceeds your authority.

HÉLOÏSE: I do not think so! (*Passionately.*) I have the *highest* authority to care!

ABELARD (*defiantly*): If that authority is suffering then I . . .

HÉLOÏSE: . . . No! ! *It is still Love.*

> ABELARD *turns away and his hand goes to his head as he leans wearily against the window's edge.*

ABELARD (*hoarsely*): Prioress, I am tired—more than tired. I am utterly weary of this world, and, physically, I am not well. My motive in asking you to come here was Christian charity. It was not without pain that I had to suppress and discipline inferior motives in me.

HÉLOÏSE: Inferior! (*Appalled.*) It was not, Abbot, without pain that I have had to suffer ten years alone, waiting for word.

ABELARD: It was not for you to say if my words could ever have expressed the utter impossibility of my position.

HÉLOÏSE: It was perhaps for neither of us to judge.

ABELARD (*turning to her*): No.

HÉLOÏSE: And you had seemed to make judgements. (*Bitterly.*) You had seemed to convey that our love was a crime, and Fulbert's crime an act of God designed to bring us back to Grace! (*All her pent-up emotion rising as she proceeds.*) But if cruelly now you are going away, I would not be misunderstood. I took this veil not for God, but for a sacred something which God had given to the quality of our living when in love. I have not spent these ten years in prayer . . . I have not made a success of a vocation foreign to me, for the world's good or for mine—but for you!—your protection and your grace! For atonement not for what we'd done—which to me can never be sin—but for *you*! —atonement for *your* suffering! And now you . . .!

ABELARD: For God's sake! (*Crying out pitifully.*) Stop!

HÉLOÏSE: Oh! (*Suddenly showing her exhaustion too.*) What have I done to you to deserve this desertion?

ABELARD (*with trembling voice*): What you have done for me, no other creature could. For it is by you that I have reached God.

HÉLOÏSE (*wearily*): My heart was not a ladder; my body not a stair; nor was God out of reach before.

ABELARD: Bitterness is too common to both of us. And (*In both impatience and weariness.*) what I'd do in leaving Christendom is not desertion. I have no longer the strength both to teach and to fight.

HÉLOÏSE: I can give you strength. God knows, God gave me more energy than this narrow existence employs. Stay and let me make for you some peace in this place—this Paraclete. Do we not deserve that peace?

ABELARD: They would make a scourge of even such peace.

HÉLOÏSE: And need we—under scrutiny of God—care what men and women say?

ABELARD (*despairingly*): You do not know the powers of the world. You do not know what they have done to me; imprisonments, public ridicule, stoning, false trial, attempts on my life, poison, mutilation, and now . . . out of this ordeal what do I bring but burned books, confused trust and a saga for the sensationalists? What have I brought to stay in the world?

HÉLOÏSE (*slowly*): This truth in many forms; that without the freedom to doubt and to think and to be at one with his spirit, Man is committed to darkness. Peter, if you run away, you do the will of a world which now demands its darkness deeply. I have seen the twisted face of their triumph. Stay. And fight on—with me.

ABELARD: The Church in whose kingdom I must fight will not give me freedom to fight at all. It is closing in—the whole web of authority! (*Feverishly*.) Their powers grow. Soon there will be no way through to the Truth, and the Great Spider Superior will seize my beating brain within his slow, cruel, placating claws and I shall bow down and I shall deny the little light I now see to make the darkness so dark that it swallows me. No! For this will not be martyrdom, but mutilation—and mutilation this time, not of my body but of my brain—of my reason!—my reason!—which in all my sins has been devoted to the pure truth! I cannot give that up! God cannot require that that should be so! And that . . . (*Trembling*.) is why I am running away. Oh Christ! I am so tired!

> ABELARD *breaks down and, clenching his hands, bows his head in tears.*
>
> HÉLOÏSE *goes forward, instinctively, to take him into her arms, then, realising the bitterness this would mean to him, she holds herself away.*

HÉLOÏSE (*gently*): Abbot, this dreaded darkness will come, upon the whole face of the whole earth. But the truth you teach is the love I know, and the love *will* survive, and take that truth through the days of darkness. This, in love, I know. Dare you deny this love now? Dare you go?

ABELARD: Would you seek my death?

HÉLOÏSE: Master, must we never die? Live—in me.
        ABELARD *slowly raises his head.*

ABELARD: Woman, (*Looking in her eyes.*) what is your authority?

HÉLOÏSE (*with difficulty*): Master, in what does authority lie?

ABELARD (*hoarsely*): The Love of God.

HÉLOÏSE: Master, in what does authority live?

ABELARD: Truth in all forms.

HÉLOÏSE: So have I authority as I love my God in you, and find Truth in the forms of that love.

> *And unable to control her emotion further* HÉLOÏSE *turns and falls on her knees in an attitude of prayer.*

ABELARD (*looking down at her and with great compassion using her name*): Héloïse—If this is your love then it is mine, and His, and we are one, in One—come what may.

> ABELARD *kneels by* HÉLOÏSE.

> *Finding him there, she raises her head and her face towards the heavens.*

HÉLOÏSE: Then, let the darkness come on.

THE CURTAIN SLOWLY FALLS.

ADELAISE

CHARACTERS

ADELAISE	of Louvain, second queen of Henry I of England.
HENRY	The First, of England.
STUFF	his Fool.
ALBINI	his Cupbearer.
ROGER	Bishop of Salisbury and Chancellor to the King.
MAUD-MATILDA	Daughter of Henry by his first wife.
AGATHA	Former nurse and teacher to Adelaise.
PETRONILLA	Personal maid to Adelaise.
UNIVERSAL	} Two monks.
PARTICULO	
A SHIPMASTER	of Bosham.
THE YOUNG HORNER	to the King.

The action of the play takes place in and around Arundel Castle, Sussex: the Solar—or King's private apartment; the shore by the mouth of the river Arun; Pyneham Wood.

The play is intended to have two intervals, falling after the curtain to Act II and after the curtain to Act III. And the playing time is approximately 2 hours 10 minutes.

Adelaise was first produced on 24th September 1953 at The Studio Theatre, Ashburton, S. Devon; in a try-out production with the author working throughout to produce the final script. It was presented by The Buckfast Players with the following cast:

ADELAISE	Jean McLeman
HENRY	Lewis Gedge
STUFF	Geoffrey Matthews
ALBINI	Donald Moffat
ROGER	Peter Clapham
MAUD-MATILDA	Paddy Bendell
AGATHA	Maud Hays
PETRONILLA	Moyra Babington
UNIVERSAL	A. E. Sproston
PARTICULO	Frederick Bolton
A SHIPMASTER	Michael Armstrong
THE YOUNG HORNER	Gerald Armstrong

The play directed by Moyra Babington

Costumes by Eric Gibbins and Elizabeth de Heveningham

Settings and lighting and special effects by Arnold Parker

Music specially composed by Brian Easdale

ACT I

SCENE I

By the sea at the mouth of the river Arun, Sussex—Autumn of 1120—
around sunset—sea mist.

*Before rise of curtain there is the sound of a horn, blowing steady blasts
at regular intervals.*

*On rise of curtain the horn continues, and the blast is heard in the back-
ground at irregular intervals throughout the scene.*

Two MONKS *come in. One is a large man, one is a small man.* UNI-
VERSAL *is the larger.* PARTICULO *stops to listen; as the other looks
out through the mist towards the sea and mounts a stump to see better.*

PARTICULO (*diffidently*): What is that sound, Brother Universal?

UNIVERSAL (*expansively*): A hunting horn, Brother Particulo.

PARTICULO: Yes, but whose horn, Brother Universal?

UNIVERSAL: The King's horn, Brother Particulo.

PARTICULO: Oh, the King! I see.

The Horn sounds off.

No, I don't.

For why should it be blowing down here
by the sea?
Has his stag leapt into the river's mouth
and gone swimming towards Normandy?

UNIVERSAL (*making every point doubly clear, as to a dullard*):

It is not blown for the hunt at all.
Up in the castle—up in Arundel—
the King, it seems, thought that he saw
the Great White Ship. You know,
the ship with his son, which was following him;
following him home from Normandy.

But when they had all galloped down here
the mist met their steaming horses. And now
they are on foot, on the shingle, looking out to sea.
Does that lift the mist, Particulo?

Horn off.

PARTICULO: Yes ... but why the horn?

UNIVERSAL: Well, to be still more Particulo,
the King sent his horner to the river's mouth;
and where it churns channel mud out to sea
he keeps blowing.

PARTICULO: Oh, I see. Why?

UNIVERSAL: Both you—and the reason—are beyond me.
But, if his beloved son *is* becalmed out there,
might he not by the judgement of his princely ear
guide the White Ship in here?—
despite all mist? But with the sun almost down
and no moon to come . . . Oho!
                    (Seeing something off.)
Here comes hot air.

PARTICULO: What? Where?

            STUFF *calling off.*

STUFF (*off*):   Ho, cassocks! Ho, beads!

PARTICULO (*turning away*): I wish the King had left that Fool over
the sea.

STUFF *comes in while Particulo's back is turned. (He wears a coat
of small bells which makes a sort of mail.)*

He's a pagan. But so are they all today
on this island. Oh!

As STUFF *thrusts under his nose what would be his cockscomb
but in his case is the fool's sceptre, with a small silver fish on
the end.*

STUFF: Where is my King—thing?

UNIVERSAL: On the shingle—jingle.
What's the state of the realm?

STUFF: The state of the King—
which is peace here and now, and better to come.
For, with the royal life's-work done,
he's contracted to pure pleasure upon
a piece of pure peace: young Adelaise of Louvain.

UNIVERSAL: Contracted to marriage again?—The King?

STUFF: He says of her hair that it is " seaweed brown ".
And if that's not old man's folly issuing in
a new age of peace—I'm fish-food.
Eh, fish-face? (*To* PARTICULO.)

PARTICULO: Yes. I mean no. But the King—
he has no need of heirs. He has his son—
out there in the mist—

The Horn still blowing in distance.

—and his daughter too:
Maud-Matilda—in Germany.

STUFF: No need of heirs—no.
But what of graces, Particulo?
A sceptre needs sway. Ah! (*Looking off.*)
It's the King.
It *is* my sceptre!—sepulchral with mist.
Disperse fog!
He abhors holy perplexity.
Disperse!

Bundling them off.

UNIVERSAL: But who is this with him, Stuff?

STUFF: Young Albini—young William Albini.
Above the high-tide mark with you!
Exeat!—my high and my low—
my Universal and Particulo!

He sees UNIVERSAL *and* PARTICULO *off and turns to issue in
the* KING *and* ALBINI.

Aha!—out of the mist walked Majesty!
Out of the red orb of the sun,
orbicular, came the golden one!

197

KING: What's this, Bells? Who is so orbicular?

STUFF: You, my orb. Too many lampreys.

ALBINI: Not one! Not one.
That fish is forbidden fruit now.

STUFF: Oh? . . .
Is the new butler here so forbidding?

KING: No, Nature. Pure poison now. Yes.
I must eat no lamprey. But you—
if you'd eat less anything you'd jingle more
and I'd not have lost you in the mist.
Where have you been?

STUFF: With the salacious Bishop of Salisbury
and your Young William's little French bride.

KING: Why, where are they now?

STUFF: Sitting by the quay drenched in wet sun;
the lady longing and longing for the ship to
     come—
for reasons not unnatural to a bride—
and the Bishop looking at her and longing as one
who remembers his youth, but may very soon
forget his age. I'd move them on.

KING: Then go to them " Archbishop Stuff ",
and tell Bishop Roger that both he
and my dear son's little bride are to go
riding back to the castle now.
The sun allows us barely an hour.
But Albini and I shall wait for the ship,
and all gallop back. Don't eat my supper!

STUFF: And don't forget your horn,
or the rising tide may reduce him to
a salt sea gurgle! Adieu!

STUFF goes.

ALBINI: It does all of England good to know
that you return so happy.

198

KING: I have such good cause.
How happy your father would have been, eh?
—peace on both sides of the sea.
But the fruits of the father must pass to the son.
Thank God I have such a gifted one;
and as beloved of the people as by me.

ALBINI: And how much that love is. (*Watching out to sea.*)

KING: Much?—Aye.
All causes for joy—except one;
and that's contracted for.

ALBINI: The new Queen?
As new cup-bearer may I say how delighted I am.

KING: I chose for delight. Have you seen her?

ALBINI: No. (*Peering out to sea.*) It was only a whiter wreath
of mist.

KING: I meant had you seen my Adelaise?

ALBINI: Never, no. (*Still looking out to sea.*)

KING: You must choose a wife soon, Young William
Albini.
And when you do, how will you choose?
I knew your father's answer, and there are you
—proof to your mother's quality.
But for what qualities will you choose? Eh?
Let's play a game, while we wait.

                              (*Sitting on the stump.*)

ALBINI: A game?

KING: Yes. Suppose, William, that within
that nearest scallop of wet shore
your ideal woman were to rise up now—
coming calmly from the calm sea—
how would she come?—what qualities?
—what graces and shapes—what total form?

ALBINI: Form? . . . (*Laughing.*) Do I then presume, sir,
that as she comes straight from her sea-bed
she comes without wardrobe?

KING: Without one terrestrial stitch.
New clothing all lies ready for her
above the high-tide mark there.
that's English hospitality.
I'll keep my eyes open for the ship.
You conjure your Venus out of the sea,
till that red sun goes or the White Ship comes.
Well—I am waiting.

ALBINI: I see . . . (*Laughingly taking up the game.*) . . .
I see . . . at the seventh slow wave from the shore,
the crown of her head break surface—there.
                                        (*Pointing.*)

KING: Mm. . . . and what's the colour of her hair?

ALBINI: From the sleek crown we see it spread
in slow waves into the green sea,
and its colour is . . .

KING: Red?

ALBINI: No . . .

KING: Black?

ALBINI: No. Brown . . .
seaweed brown.

KING (*turning suspiciously*): Seaweed brown? Mm. . . . Proceed.

ALBINI (*now enjoying the game*):
     As she rises slowly from the calm sea
the long, loose tresses uncoil and sway,
and from its slow suspension where
there was local movement to each hair
the sun-varnished tresses now rise and cling
closely to her oval head.
Her brow appears. It is pale and fair—
like walrus ivory. Her eyebrows . . .

KING: Ah, there! . . .

ALBINI: Is it the ship?

KING: What? No. It's her eyebrows.
There you will be wrong.

ALBINI: Wrong? How?

KING: There's nothing so gives a woman away
as the shape of her eyebrows—
if they're hers—It's true!
It is the most revealing thing.
next to her laugh. Oh! . . . (*Rising.*)

ALBINI: What have you seen?

KING: Out there in the mist—
I thought that I saw . . . Come. Come this way.
Don't stop. Keep your Venus coming from the sea.
But come this way. The eyebrows—well? . . .

            As the KING *goes.*

ALBINI (*following*):
     Neither arched—nor the inverse—let us say
mobile, with a mobility
based on straightness . . .

As ALBINI *goes off,* PARTICULO, *curious, edges in. And from the opposite direction, a* SHIPMASTER *comes in, breathlessly. He starts at hearing the horn, and then again at seeing* PARTICULO. *He taps* PARTICULO *on the back.*

PARTICULO: Oh! (*Starting.*) Are you looking for the King, because . . .

SHIPMASTER: God's Grace!—no, not the King.
Is he here?

PARTICULO: There. Just along the shore . . .
What is it?

SHIPMASTER: Stand still! (*Holding* PARTICULO *as a shield.*) Keep between me and the King. Ah, he's gone into the mist.

PARTICULO: Who are you? And what do you want?

SHIPMASTER: Just a shipmaster from Bosham creek.
But I've got to find the King's Chancellor—
the Bishop Roger of Salisbury.

PARTICULO: But he's just gone!
—with the young Prince William's French bride—
riding up towards the castle.

SHIPMASTER: Then it must have been them I passed in the mist.
(*Turning back.*)

PARTICULO: But here comes the King again and I think . . .
(*turning*) . . . Shipmaster! Where is he?

As the SHIPMASTER *hurries off into the mist, with* PARTICULO *on his heels.*

(*Off.*) Shipmaster! Shipmaster! . . .

The KING *and* ALBINI *come back in, obviously relishing their " game ".*

KING: Yes . . . the shape of her breasts? What of that, eh?
Wait! Did you hear someone call?

ALBINI: No.

KING: Her breasts, I said.

ALBINI: I said high . . .

KING: High?

ALBINI: Oh, not in themselves, whose eminences are
the tenderest of tender twin tumuli,
pale hunter's moon colour. But as I say
in positioning they are high.

KING: Yes. That is true too . . . (*Lost in his own thoughts.*)
And the high-breasted woman worries me.
It leaves such a vulnerable territory
between the hills and the sea;
such slopes of compassion and pity . . . eh? . . .
not meant for children. But neither is she.

ALBINI: What she is meant for you must leave to me.

KING: What? . . .

ALBINI: She is *my* Venus. I conjured her up out of
your sea.

KING: Ha! This game's gone far enough.
Come. The sun's sinking into the mist,
and the White Ship can't make land now
before morning.

ALBINI: I hope, sir, that in no way
my Venus disappoints you.

KING (*dryly*):　　　　　　　　I hope not.
　　　　　For you have conjured up out of that sea
　　　　　the figure of my Adelaise—to a fingernail.
　　　　　And you knew it, young devil! Call the horner.

ALBINI:　　　No, no. Really! For I swear
　　　　　I have never set eyes upon her.

KING (*meeting his eyes*):
　　　　　There is one thing unlike your father in you—
　　　　　you swear very easily. Call in the horn.

ALBINI:　　　But I think you do not believe . . .

KING (*shortly*): . . . I believe you meant no offence.
　　　　　Meet me by the horses. I'll wait for you,
　　　　　and I'll race you to the castle;
　　　　　and I shall win!

ALBINI:　　　　　　　　　　　But, my liege . . .

KING (*angrily*): Call in the horn!

　　　THE KING *goes and* ALBINI *turns and goes to call in* THE HORNER.
　　　Horn sounding over scene-change and ceasing abruptly for . . .

SCENE II

*Shortly after—the Solar, or King's room in Arundel Castle (which is a
raised room apart from the Great Hall. Here the King sleeps and
has his privacy.)*

By a glowing open fire and in the dark ROGER, *Bishop of Salisbury, paces,
waiting.*

The door curtains part and unceremoniously STUFF *comes in.*

STUFF:　　　Where's that elusive shipmaster? Ah! . . .
　　　　　　　　　　　　　　(*Approaching him.*)
　　　　　Bishop Roger! Well, Deputy Sceptre!
　　　　　Well, Conscience of the King,
　　　　　what's on the conscience?

ROGER (*avoiding talk*): When the King comes in, call me.

STUFF: Why, where will you be?

ROGER: With his son's bride.

STUFF: In the bridal room?
Has young William made you his deputy too?

                ROGER *goes out abruptly.*

What's damaged his disposition towards bawdry?

                Distant Horn.

Ah. Well, I hope the Bishop doesn't hear the horn.
I hope the King goes straight to the bridal room,
and finds that ecclesiastical whale
floundering in secular French. Oho!
There goes the bailey gate.   (*Listening.*)
Motte tower gate already too?
The King of the English is in a royal hurry!
Guard-room outer gate—inner—Phew!
Has the King wings? Now he's through
the Great Hall—on the stairs now—
Well, I'll be . . . !

     THE KING *bursts in gasping and laughing.*

                    . . . blown, is the word.

KING: I win! I win!

STUFF: Win what? What's the prize?

KING: Ha! (*Getting his breath back.*)
With almost twenty years given away,
and no better mount, I beat him!—

STUFF: Beat who?

KING: Albini—young William Albini. Oh heart!—
stop galloping now. The ship didn't come.
Any news? Where is everyone? Where's my cup?
Where's my supper? Where's my daughter-in-law?
Where's the Bishop?

STUFF: Retired to the bridal room,

KING: What! With the bride? (*Laughing*.) Oh my heart—
    As ROGER *comes back in.*
    —the race is over—stop galloping.
                Ah, there you are!

ROGER: My gracious King . . . (*solemnly*.)

KING: . . . Good gracious, the clerical air! . . .
    How have you left our little princess?—
    How you found her, I hope.

ROGER: She is . . . not well.

KING: What, sick already? Then you escape blame.
    And young William is his father's son. Eh, Stuff?
    What's come over our Bishop? Why so glum?

STUFF: I think, my sceptre and orb,
    that we see standing there,
    not far from the foot of the bridal stair,
    an unpreferred bishop. She prefers your son.

ROGER: Fool!!

    ROGER *strikes* STUFF *and fells him.*

KING (*astounded*): Salisbury! Roger!
    No man—not even my deputy—
    strikes at my Fool without wounding me.
    God's death! Look at the poor fool's face.
    Get up boy! Get up, Stuff!

STUFF: And that is not the first time
    that he has raised his hand to me.

ROGER: I . . . I'm deeply sorry. God forgive me,
    but I had no intention of hurting the Fool.

KING: Then in God's Name what's come over you!
    What's come over England, if the King's Fool
    cannot make sport of the King's counsellors? Eh?
    What made you do it?

        ROGER *does not answer*

                (*Uneasily*.) What is it?
    Oh there's news of the ship? Mm? Yes, coming up
    my dogs worried a stranger hurrying down.

> . . . a seaman . . .
> I saw that fellow at . . . Barfleur! . . .
> He sailed on my ship or . . . God's death! . . .
> (*Quietly, in awe.*)
> Tell me. For I think I know.

ROGER: In such things God does not deem that we
should be long deceived. The White Ship . . .
is . . . lost . . . is down.

KING: Down? . . . (*Stunned.*) . . . But . . . young William? . . .

ROGER: Our cherished hope, and your beloved son . . .
drowned.

THE KING *tries to speak, clutches at his heart and crumples to the*
floor.

STUFF (*running to him*):
Oh, my poor sceptre! Oh, my poor crown!

ROGER: He has struck his head on the floor. Raise him.

STUFF: Is he dead? Has it killed him?

ROGER: Run below to the Hall. Find the physician.

STUFF: Don't let him be dead!

STUFF *goes.*

ROGER (*supporting the* KING):
Oh, dear heart, what a cruel blow.
Our one vital link is struck away
from all our vast diplomacy.
Our planned peace is all adrift now.

KING: Roger . . . (*Slowly recovering.*)
Roger . . . Oh, Salisbury . . .
It was the sea. It was the sea.
We did not reckon with the sea. (*Raising his head.*)
Where have you put him? Where is he?

ROGER: Where? Why . . .

KING: Aye, in Heaven, I know.
But his dear body. Take me to him. Why,
where is he?

ROGER: Why, my liege, in the depths of the sea.

KING: Oh . . . (*Slowly he rises—shocked, stunned.*) Oh . . .
               my young William.
               Then he conjured up out of the sea
               the wrong figure.

ROGER (*troubled*): What figure? Who?

KING: And she's not to come now. Our anchor's gone.
               She's not to come, Roger.

ROGER: Not to come, no . . .

KING: Aye, Adelaise—she's not to come.

ROGER (*gently, as to an invalid*):   No.

KING (*turning on him savagely*):
               Would you have me feed the voracious sea
               with other sons! She's not to come!

ROGER: No, no, not to come.

   As the KING *turns to go by the door* ALBINI *comes in breathlessly.*

ALBINI: I had to turn back,
               Your horn got torn from the horner's saddle and . . .

                    Seeing the KING's *face.*

KING: Oh, young William Alb . . . (*Stopping.*) . . . No . . .
               Change your name. For God's sake change your
               Christian name! Oh William!

   The KING *goes out, weeping, and* ROGER, *with the confused*
   ALBINI, *goes after him in concern for what he may do.*

ACT II

The King's Solar—Arundel—some months later.
The bed has a moveable screen round it now.
It is late afternoon and a log fire burns in the hearth. Laughter is heard off.
PETRONILLA *runs in lightly and is pursued by* STUFF.

STUFF: Petronilla!—(*Seizing her.*)
my little imported lily of Louvain!

PETRONILLA: I am not lily, nor of Louvain.
At first I am from Germany.
I am transported.

STUFF: Ah . . . so am I!
(*Looking into her eyes.*)
But . . . wo . . . bist . . .
mistress the Queen?

PETRONILLA: My mistress . . . the Queen? (*Puzzled.*)
Oh! My mistress the Queen! Adelaise!
Oh, I shall never become accustom.

STUFF: Never mind. You may yet become a habit.

PETRONILLA: Habit? Habit?
I have not understood you at the last.

STUFF: You have not understood me from the first.
But where is . . . Adelaise?

PETRONILLA: " My mistress the Queen "? Oh . . .
She is walking around the woods of winter.

STUFF: That's a long walk. Sit by me.
As they sit in the window.
Look, I see the Queen and Albini coming in below.

208

       Petronilla, help me, before she comes,
       to understand " Your mistress, the Queen ".

PETRONILLA: Oh, in that is little understanding.
              She is just a girl, Master Stuff.

STUFF: And on your transported tongue what might that
              mean?
              For instance, are you " just a girl "?

              As she laughs wickedly.

              At least that's clear. But wait!
              Wait a moment. You don't mean
              that you are married, my lily?

PETRONILLA: Married? How is . . .?

STUFF: Have no husband? Husband? No?

PETRONILLA: Husband? Hus-ba . . . Oh!

              She slaps his face.

STUFF: Now what might that mean?

              Nursing face.

PETRONILLA (*indignantly*): I would be sitting so making fun,
              If I had a husband?

STUFF: Mmmmm! . . .
              It means conventional fidelity.
              Ah, the cultural chasm between.
              But come closer. We'll try.

PETRONILLA (*suddenly drawing away*): Oh . . .
              You have not a husband? No?

STUFF: Not even a mother. Keep your seat.
              But " Your mistress, the Queen "—
              did she come to England by choice?

PETRONILLA: We come by sea.

STUFF: Inevitably. But why did she come?

PETRONILLA: Why? Why, to be Queen!
              Her father would always be saying she,
              my daughter, must live as to grow as a Queen.
              For has she not the blood of Charlemagne

to course in her nerves? Some day
she is coming to be a Queen!
And here it comes.

STUFF: Yes, but here it comes.
Does she realise why, so suddenly,
she is summoned to England?
                    PETRONILLA *titters*.
Well, that's relatively clear too.
And she is content?—happy?—
simply to provide us with a prince?

PETRONILLA: Oh, she finds England not home. But poof!
She is Queen!

                Rising to arrange room.

STUFF: Well—poof!—that would seem
to be the idée fixe. And you——

                Following her.

Are happy with England?—and the English men?

PETRONILLA: Are you Englishman?

STUFF: No. No . . .
I'm undenominational islander.
A bit of the bocage . . . a bit of the bush.
Your true Englishman is a sort of tree—
immoveable, adaptable; but only to
the seasons, the weathers, the winds from the sea.
Yet, if he *is* moved, " Look out below! "
For he comes up, root, earth and all,
not reckoning the consequence of the fall.
No, not even if he should be
cut up ever so frightfully
to feed the fast devouring flame
of the last lost cause!
For he's true Lord of Battles, and doomed to die
cut into neat pieces and stacked so high
as heaven needs fuel up near the sky
for God's many mansions! *But* make no mistake!
He's not wood all the way through.

His head it is true may be out of view
in the intimate clouds of this island's sky;
and all that foreigners like you may find
to indicate the position of his mind,
is a wreath of laurel, or ivy or holly,
the sound of strange birds in the air;
and that old enigmatic stare,
which is hyperborean. Still! . . .
He's all there—somewhere—some day—
when the world needs must have mad gallantry
and inspired idiots!
And you don't understand a word I say?
Do you, little Petronilla?

PETRONILLA: Yes—
I don't.

STUFF: Ah . . . (*Taking her in his arms.*)
Would that without understanding at all
we might come to the true business of knowing.
For you and I might together aspire
to the Great Non-Sense.

PETRONILLA: Oh, I hear a door coming!

STUFF (*quickly*): Then kiss me before it comes.

PETRONILLA: What? No . . . Ah . . .

As he kisses her.

Another door!

STUFF: Another kiss.

PETRONILLA: Encore une door!

STUFF: Encore une kiss.

PETRONILLA: Nochmal ein door!

STUFF: Nochmal ein . . . Mmm . . .

Kissing her fully.

PETRONILLA: Mmmmm! . . . Master Stuff!

STUFF: Ah, don't draw too much conclusion from this.
That sort of lip-to-lip kiss—

at all hours of the night and the day—
is an English custom.

PETRONILLA: It becomes a " habit " with me.
No?

STUFF: Yes. (*Detaching himself*.)
But here comes " Your mistress, the Queen ".

As they both fall back from the door ADELAISE *comes in.*

She is dressed for out of doors and is followed by AGATHA *and*
ALBINI.

STUFF (*with a flourish*):
Welcome to the critical compartment of this hive
of stone—the King's Solar!

As ADELAISE *proceeds towards the fire.*

ADELAISE (*smiling*):   Ah, there is warmth in here.

STUFF: Potentially there's more than warmth.
Petronilla and I have been adding fuel to your fire.

ADELAISE: It would seem Petronilla should have come
walking in my woods with me. No?

STUFF: Oh, but she has covered some ground.
While Albini, there, was introducing you
to some of England's noblest scenery,
I was introducing Petronilla, here,
to some of England's oldest customs.

ALBINI: I should not myself have left
the selection of old English customs to you,
Stuff, my jester.

STUFF: Nor I, the selection of wood-walks to you,
Albini, my hunter.

ALBINI: My sovereign lady, I leave you now
to the care of your sweet ladies from over the sea.

ADELAISE (*she speaks as one new to the language*): My lord,
you have made this countryside live for me,
in all these strange new names which hitherto
have been mere words taught to me,
by Agatha.

ALBINI: My majesty . . . (*With a bow.*)
you have brought new life and light into
my oldest of loves, England—its earth.
I shall tell the King in council below
that you are come in.

               ALBINI *goes.*

ADELAISE (*thoughtfully*): Agatha . . .

AGATHA (*shortly*): Master Stuff, you may go.

STUFF: I may. I may. (*Not going.*)

ADELAISE: Agatha . . . (*As* AGATHA *is about to dis-
lodge* STUFF.)

AGATHA: Yes, my lamb?

ADELAISE: Agatha, my copybook Queen,
teach me one more English lesson.

AGATHA: Now? But you must change your dress.
You are to sup with the King in the Great Hall.

ADELAISE: Then one question only: Did he not say,
" *My* majesty "?

AGATHA: Lord Albini? He did, didn't he?

ADELAISE: And should he not, as all others, have said,
" *Your* majesty "?

AGATHA: If he intended to be
" as all others " he should, shouldn't he?

ADELAISE: It might have been a " slip of the tongue "?

PETRONILLA: His tongue did not seem slipping to me.

AGATHA: Idiot! Hold your own tongue! It slips too easily.

ADELAISE: But, in the manners and customs of this country,
what might it mean?

STUFF: My Queen . . . (*Coming forward.*)
as an expert in manners and customs . . .

AGATHA: No!
Not in manners, Master Stuff! Go.
You have no right to be here.

STUFF: I've royal right to be foolish anywhere.
                I thought I was being so, but now
                you've made me self-conscious and being so
                I feel the folly and folly should be
                above feeling, don't you feel? I go.
                But my bow is only to Majesty.

ADELAISE: Raise your head, Stuff. No, don't go.
                I would ask you what the Lord Albini means
                in saying to me, " My Majesty ".

STUFF: But it is so simple. He means what he says,
                you . . . are . . . his . . . Majesty.
                For, whatever the apologetic world may say,
                either side of sheer simplicity,
                we all in private or public do bow
                to some sort of majesty—some sort of crown.
                No, my Majesty, do not frown.
                We all must aspire.
                Yet few there are in search of that higher,
                that semper-in-excelsis thing,
                who find in the flesh that which would bring
                majesty to circulate
                within their own orbit. He means to say—
                as I do now—" My Majesty ".
                But there's a difference. For you see,
                he hopes to mean it, but I know—
                beyond all hope of hopes—that I do.

         For a moment their eyes are held.

ADELAISE: What were you before you were a Fool?

STUFF: Oh, I was more foolish still.
                I was a novice.

ADELAISE: In a monastery?

STUFF: In all things.

ADELAISE: But in what order?

STUFF: Oh,
                in the order I have said:
                firstly the Church and then the World.

For in the majestic concept I'd die to defend
the Church is a better start than an end.
But I'll live—and with you.

ADELAISE: Why do you choose to say this to me?

STUFF: Inspiration has little choice;
and I, being a fool, have none at all.
Yet there's much in mere motive.
                     You have a way
of veiling your eyes. So had she
who kept her part of a pact to die,
and stayed on in her nunnery.
But I talk personal history, and I
am no person—not even the Fool.
I am Stuff, the Folly. Adieu!
Notice the difference between a porter and me—
the doors I open I always pass through.
And I leave yours ajar—my Majesty.
           STUFF *slips out.*

AGATHA: Fool!

ADELAISE: A strange sort of Fool, Agatha.

AGATHA: An English Fool—and believe me, that *is* folly!

PETRONILLA: What does a Fool do?

AGATHA: That *you* should ask that!
Sit by the fire, my royal lamb.
I'll fetch the green slippers the King gave you,
in London—the ones with the fishtail toes.

As AGATHA *goes for slippers and* ADELAISE *prepares to change
dress.*

PETRONILLA: Walked you far, my mistress the Queen?
                            (*Helping her change.*)

ADELAISE: As far as a wood called Pyneham.
It covers the opposite hill.

PETRONILLA: Not crossing the great river in the vale?

ADELAISE: Over the river there is what he called a " causeway"
Agatha was so afraid of the waters rushing through,
that he had to carry her across.

PETRONILLA: Carry? What!—all of Agatha!
No wonder he is called Gwylliam of the Strong
Hand.

AGATHA: Idiot! (*Coming back with clothing and slippers.*)
Thank heaven I am in no way so " light " as you.
Fetch the blue bliaut from the chest.
And the green girdle. *And* . . .
Light the lights from the fire.

ADELAISE: I love these log fires. Unbind my hair.
The King calls my hair " seaweed brown ".
I shall love England—the country—Agatha.

AGATHA: And the King of England?

ADELAISE (*turning the question away*): He loves England too.

PETRONILLA: Is this the dress?

AGATHA: Yes.

ADELAISE: Agatha,
move the screen around the fire,
and, within its warmth, I shall change.

The screen is moved by both women.

PETRONILLA: Take care that you do not catch fire.

As her simple but fine garments are passed over to her, ADELAISE's
head and shoulders are seen.

AGATHA: So you love England—its earth—my dove?

ADELAISE: Yes. Oh, Petronilla, the quality of the air!

(*Speaking out over screen.*)

The first winter winds had stripped away
all their Autumn's yellow greenery.
And, in the thorn bushes which lie
on the river meadows between Pyneham and here,
those branches at the hearts of bushes show
the brightest coatings of moss-green;
while outside on the leafless branches there grow
the dark red clusters of the fruit—
like to miniature apples.

216

                              The English say,
          " When fruit is fair and branch be old,
          then Winter will be long and cold."
          Pass the green girdle. Put a light there.

AGATHA: And the King of the English? Was it his wish
          that the young Albini should walk with you?

ADELAISE: The King of England expresses no wish.
          He sighs, smiles and, sometimes, points the way.

As ADELAISE *comes out from behind the screen to have her mantle finally adjusted.*

          Now bind up my hair. (*As she sits.*)
          From the high pines of Pyneham we could see
          this grey tower standing among its trees.
          And all around us the winter breeze
          brushed a sea-sound from the boughs;
          while at our feet from a quarry nearby
          the wind flushed up and threw at the sky
          two great grey doves. They swung away
          and clapped across the valley to where
          schools of . . . rooks? . . .

AGATHA: Rooks. (*Nodding assent.*)

ADELAISE: . . . so busily.
          in black congregations were purposing
          some massive bird-treason.
                              Agatha . . .
          it is no treason to you that I
          should keep my King's confidence.

AGATHA: No, no. You are the Queen. Rise.
          But all is not right with him, is it?

ADELAISE (*turning away*):
          What did you do when we climbed to the wood?

AGATHA: Adelaise, my virgin queen, look at me.
          (*Making her face her.*)
          You are not forgetting a most important thing—
          why you came to England?

ADELAISE: I cannot. (*Quietly.*) But the King . . .
Petronilla, put this oak log on the fire.
It will burn till long after supper.
They call the oak the " royal oak "—
don't they, Agatha? It burns well.

PETRONILLA: Oof! This log is too heavy for me.
I am not Gwylliam of the Strong Arm.
Help me, Agatha.

                         As she does.

ADELAISE: Agatha,
this confidence you may both know:
that the King at Westminster said to me
that our " wedding night " might not be
until we reached Arundel.

PETRONILLA (*jubilantly*):   And here it is!

AGATHA: Quiet, girl! Remember your position in life.
Attend your mistress, the Queen of England.
Attend her to the Great Hall, and to her King.
I shall with my own hands prepare the bed.
And God grant you the mercy of fruitfulness.

AGATHA *does obeisance to the* QUEEN. *And as Music can be
heard from below,* ADELAISE *goes out, with* PETRONILLA *in train.*
AGATHA *takes the screen from the fire and moves towards the bed.*

*Music goes on through the Scene Curtain and into the music of the
next scene.*

SCENE II

The Solar—later, the same night.
Before rise of curtain Music of DAVID THE HARPER'S *song is heard.*
The only light is from the great log fire.

The Song

DAVID (*off*):   Rock me gently where I lie
                    and sightless see the Summer sky
                    clouded with fish.

                    Rock me gently where I lie
                    and hear the silent seabirds cry
                    my drowning wish.

On rise of curtain ADELAISE, *in night attire, comes from the bed and listens to the song:*

(*off*):   Rock me gently where I lie
                    and sense the witch-waves sweep the sky,
                    stealing my light.

                    Rock me gently where the moon
                    with her molten silver spoon
                    is stirring my night.

ADELAISE (*calling, softly*):
                    Agatha! Agatha!

As she returns to the seat by the fire the song begins again:

(*off*):   Rock me gently where the sun,
                    like some gold robe whose dyes have run
                    drifts overhead.

                    Rock me gently where I lie.
                    Rock me to sleep; I cannot die,
                    in limbo laid.

AGATHA *comes in, sleepily.*

AGATHA: Where are you? (*Whispering.*) Why are you still
                    by the fire?

ADELAISE: There is no need to whisper. The King is not here.
            No. He has not come up from the Great Hall.

AGATHA: Not come up! But isn't it very late?
            What's that?

She listens to the music of the song going on in the background.

ADELAISE: It is a tune that David the Minstrel plays.

AGATHA: A dreadfully sad sort of tune
            to play on a wedding night, my love.

ADELAISE: It is a tune that David made for the King
            after the young prince was drowned.
                                        Agatha,
            go out and look down into the Great Hall,
            and tell me what you see. I dare not go,
            for fear he should see me. Please. Please go.

AGATHA: Of course, my love. But why doesn't he come?
            What's wrong with the man?

ADELAISE: Look and see. Look down.

AGATHA: Yes, my lamb. Keep warm. Keep warm.
            Don't stir from the fire.

As AGATHA *goes the song can be heard again:*

DAVID (*off*):   Rock me gently where I lie
                 and sightless see the Summer sky
                 clouded with fish.

                 Rock me gently where I lie
                 and hear the silent seabirds cry
                 my drowning wish . . .

AGATHA *comes back in and the song goes on.*

ADELAISE: Well?

AGATHA: I do not understand this.
            Only the minstrel awake in the Great Hall;
            and all the sleepers along the wall
            huddled under the guttering lights.

ADELAISE: But the King?

AGATHA: The King—yes—
The King of England not asleep, not awake,
sitting alone at the far east end
and staring into the smoulder and smoke,
rocking gently to the tune.
Oh, what stands between you up here
waiting by this blazing fire,
and him in the desolate Hall down there
staring into a dying one?
My white one, tell Agatha.

ADELAISE: I don't know.
But that tune—that tune which rocks him now,
like an empty cradle rocked to and fro
in an empty ship. Can it be so?
Should I not return across the sea—
before it is too late?

The song and the music stop.

AGATHA: Now I don't understand you.
Has this wooded island bewitched you?

ADELAISE: It has stopped.

AGATHA (*listening*): The dogs are roused below.

ADELAISE: Then he's coming up. Go now.
Go before he reaches the gallery.

AGATHA: Goodnight, my sweet one. And God guard you.
I shall not sleep. I shall not sleep.

She goes.

ADELAISE *sits by the fire, apprehensive.*

After a time the KING *comes in. He carries a sword.*

ADELAISE: Oh . . . (*Catching her breath.*)

KING: You wonder why I bring a sword to bed?
No, don't rise, girl.

ADELAISE: I . . . must wonder, sir.

KING: The sword is not for you, nor for me.
The sword's for the unseen enemy.

A king has many.
> *Laying it down by fire.*

But why do you sit by the fire still?

ADELAISE: Why . . . for warmth, sir.

KING: Warmth? Aye.
This body's warmth is a miracle we
don't rightly assess until we see
death chill it.   (*Wearily, sitting by her.*)

ADELAISE: I understand.

KING: Yes. You may. There lies a danger.
May I hold your hand?

ADELAISE (*confused by this simplicity*): My hand?

KING: Aye, your hand. (*Gently.*) Give me your hand.
Ah . . . Mary above! What a comforting thing
is a hand to a hand. (*Staring into fire.*)
Adelaise, I am informed—
and the information's confirmed by my soul—
that I should love you.

ADELAISE: Should, my liege?

KING: Aye . . .
For now, and with soul's confirmation too,
something must always stand between me
and the great risk of loving. Aye.
some say it is a quite different thing—
love of child, love of woman. It's not true.
All love is of one quality;
whatever the sort or the degree,
all's dangerous. One may lose all in all.
So, let us sit and watch this fire;
let's both be brought to one animal warmth
as humble beginning to less, or to more,
than loving. Let's worship simple warmth, eh?
For, Oh! the unobvious end can be
so easily, so wrongly achieved.
                          (*In increasing agitation.*)
And yet from the worst occasion of the dear deed
may spring—from the uncontrollable seed—

the one—the adored one!—the blessed child!
And even then—even then—the miracle be
swept away—cast into the awful sea—
swallowed up by the monstrous Majesty
of . . . Ah, God! . . . (*Breaking down.*)
my son! my boy! my boy! . . .

ADELAISE: Oh, don't . . . don't . . .

KING: Stay out of this, girl. It would drown you too.
No, don't talk to me. Talk of anything.
Talk of the fire. Talk of the fire.

ADELAISE: The fire?

Like a child asked to write an essay.

The fire gives warmth . . .

KING: Aye. (*Bitterly.*)

ADELAISE: But more than warmth . . . (*Desperately.*)
For, in this fire—in this fire I see—
in the centre of this fire—a glowing cave,
which is gnawed by the flame from the solid oak.

*The whole scene now narrows down to the two figures in the glow
of the fire. And slowly* HENRY'S *attention turns to her and to the
fire.*

And across this red cave lies a young, green log.
It's form of fire is orange tongues.
These lick around its little girth,
while from each end there issues forth
hissing sap, and from this
steam mixes with smoke.
Right at the back is a great log of oak,
whose girth, now halfway burned through,
makes a charred arch across the red cave.
And soon this charred arch must break in two,
and each heavy half-log roll away
into the ashen territory
which surrounds the fire.
There lies a grey desert where now and again
little explosions occur and throw
puffs of fine ash up into the air;

        and then little wood-coals glow and grow
        cold and . . . Oh, my liege, I can see no more.
        Why should you weep?

KING: Your hand—the warmth made human again—
        the image raised of another night.

ADELAISE: I see. (*Withdrawing her hand.*)

KING (*quickly*):

        No, no. You cannot see.
        This other night—it had nothing to do
        with woman's love. (*Rising and pacing.*)
                      His mother and I,
        in separate worlds, were asleep in this room.
        For fashion's sake, not compassion, she
        must feed the child herself. And so he lay
        in some low rocker by that fire.
        A bird's night-cry awoke the child,
        and wild with lost sleep she cursed his cry,
        So I climbed from the bed and, savagely,
        in rage at her anger, groped where he lay—
        took him up, felt his cry
        die into shuddering sobs and then sighs
        as I walked till an equal weariness
        solaced me and sealed his wet eyes.
        And in the silence of that night, holding him
           thus,
        I knew what sovereign triumph it is
        to cause defeat to a child's distress
        and force it into sleep. Success
        has nowhere any greater reward
        than when the torpid eyes stay closed,
        the breathing's deep, and the small form goes
        finally limp. Then one knows
        the sweet, the utter value of trust.
                    (*Going to her.*)
        Never once again—so Time's arranged—
        did I hold his sleeping form thus.
        Never once.
             Why do you draw away?

ADELAISE: It has been a sort of agony,
            when in your sleep you have turned to me
            and seemed to rock me tenderly
            like a child to sleep.

KING: Has it been so?
            I told them you should not have come.
            I told them.

ADELAISE: Told who?

KING: My counsellors.
            But, oh, they'd have you come,
            And now that you have—even to them—
            it seems less simple. Unless—unless,
            despite your beauty and youth, you
            see duty—see warmth as enough
            Are you content, my Queen? I will have it so.
            For never again will I try to subdue
            time or person to a plan.
            One must trust—Aye, on no lesser scale
            than the universal—one must trust—trust all.
            Are you content?
                            (*Sitting by her again.*)
            Oh, don't you weep—or we'll lose our way—
            and England be lost. For she needs this way
            through the dark woods lying ahead.

ADELAISE: And you yourself, what do you need?

KING: Me? I have no needs. I need nothing now.

ADELAISE: *I* am not so fortunate.

KING: No . . . (*Compassionately.*)
            You think you need love.
            Don't you?

ADELAISE: I don't know.
            I don't even know if Love is true.

KING: Oh no, it's not true. (*Looking into fire.*) But it is a
            fact—
            a compelling fact, which if truly pursued
            may lead two faithful people through
            the loveliest of all God's territory.

And it's not truly Heaven, as the foolish say,
but Hell is undoubtedly farthest away
when we are stalking close to that eager hind,
who's forever hunted, forever at bay,
but never fatally brought down. Aye . . .
                              (*Staring into fire.*)
many's the time both she and I
have stared in sweet ecstasy—eye holding eye
across that final untrodden ground,
over which all rush and where some say
divinity visits. Yet afterwards we
are always alone—no track—no true way
of denying the lie, that this dead thing
is the goddess at whom the hounds had sprung.
No . . . (*Rising and turning to her.*)
This is not that hunt.

                    In your majesty,
is it your will that you try with me
to give a heedless world this need—
which may be godly necessity?

ADELAISE (*rising and facing him tensely*):
You should not beg of me.
Are you not the King?

KING: Are you not the Queen?

ADELAISE: I was not summoned across the sea
as Queen—but as woman.

KING: I did not summon you.
Are you content? I will have it so.
Are you content?

ADELAISE (*in a sort of panic*):
This is a question you cannot ask of me.
I know no answer.

KING: Then what is your wish?

ADELAISE: You have taken me beyond all wishes now—
beyond will or desire, beyond . . . Oh . . . (*Weeping.*)
You should not have asked.
You should not have asked!

226

KING (*rising, with sword in hand*):

> That is not for you to say. It is no easy thing
> for the sun to beg warmth of the moon.
> As this sword has borrowed warmth from your fire
> I had hoped . . . But come to bed.
> Don't cry, my dear. Come to bed.

ADELAISE *buries her face in her hands.*

> Well . . . (*At a loss.*) I am tired—very tired.
> May I go to bed—to sleep? May I?

ADELAISE *bursts into uncontrollable sobbing.*

In compassion he touches her shoulder.

ADELAISE: No! ! ! . . . (*In an agonised cry.*)

Slowly the KING *turns and with his sword over his arm wearily goes towards the bed, leaving* ADELAISE *hunched and silent by the fire.*

As the music of DAVID THE HARPER'S *song plays in the distance all the glow of the fire is withdrawn from the scene, till it is dark.*

SCENE III

The sea, by the mouth of the Arun—a Spring morning.
Before rise of curtain there is the sound of the King's Horn.
On rise of curtain PARTICULO *comes in, listening.*
UNIVERSAL comes in and, coming up behind him,
taps him on the back. PARTICULO *turns nervously.*

UNIVERSAL: Ah, so it *is* you, Brother Particulo!

PARTICULO: It is what remains of me, after a winter's buffeting
by wind and sea.
But you grow fat inland, Brother Universal.

UNIVERSAL: Oh it's a virtuous paunch. It's the product of
praise.
I've made a mechanical lyre and sit all day

just turning the handle: to the glory of God,
and the Universal aggrandisement. But you—
are you still on these rocks, in that box of a cell?

PARTICULO: Yes, but I soon shan't be.
Look how the sea has eaten the land away
right up to my southern wall. (*Pointing.*)

UNIVERSAL: Hasn't it compensations—the music of the sea
so close to your pillow? Ah! . . .
the waves sparkle this morning; like chain mail, eh?
and every little link burnished to show
the old metal come up with the new. (*Breathing it
all in.*) Ah; . . .
Isn't Spring a miraculous thing.

PARTICULO (*dryly*): It puts Winter behind us.

UNIVERSAL: For all our sakes may the Lord some day
make you just a little lyrical. Goodday!

As the horn sounds nearer and UNIVERSAL *makes to go.*

PARTICULO: Wait, Brother Peter! What brings you down here?

UNIVERSAL (*casually*): Oh, personal politics—a word with the
Queen.
That green ship tied into the quay (*Pointing off.*)
is the King's ship. He's for Normandy.

PARTICULO: You're not sailing with the King?—are you?

UNIVERSAL: No. I'm turning my back upon the sea—
and forever. I turn hermit. It's time. It's true.
There's a forsaken cell I'll occupy
standing within the Queen's wood.

PARTICULO: And are you really retreating from the world?—
You! (*Amazed.*)

UNIVERSAL: To be honest—no, not from the world. It's going
with me.
Music is the only virtue in me.
I am retreating into my world of music:
from the centre of a dense wood I
shall raise constant praise to the changing sky.
And you don't approve?

PARTICULO: Did you expect me to?

UNIVERSAL: Allow me my occasional miracle. (*Looking off.*) Oho!
> *Horn off and close.*

There goes the whole regal caravan—
proceeding on foot, from warm saddle
to windy ship-board!

PARTICULO: Is that not the King's daughter by his first Queen?
—the good Maud-Matilda?

UNIVERSAL: Not " the good ". And she's bad for him.

PARTICULO: I am informed that her father the King will try—
while he is over in Normandy——

He whispers a confidence in UNIVERSAL'S *ear.*

UNIVERSAL: Maud-Matilda rule England? God forbid!
And why should she succeed him? Adelaise,
praise Heaven, will surely and soon
present him with a legitimate son.

PARTICULO: Really, one might already think that you
had left the castle for your dense wood.
The whole world knows by now that Adelaise——

He whispers again.

UNIVERSAL: Brother Particulo. (*Angrily turning on him.*) As one
of the world—
and not very distant from his Queen—
I should like you to know that *I* know no such thing
And may God who hates gossip catch up with you!
—*and* with Maud-Matilda. Look at her now!
That tongue should be forked. And it may be,
but it never stops long enough for one to see!
Look, she's said something hurtful to the Queen
and that poor lady turns this way. Come.

PARTICULO: But didn't you want a word with the Queen?

UNIVERSAL: In courtesy only.
It's all arranged. (*Moving off.*)
        My cell awaits me in Pyneham Wood . . .

PARTICULO *and* UNIVERSAL *go.*

ADELAISE *comes in, followed by* PETRONILLA.

PETRONILLA: One is not to listen to her with the ears—no?
—nor the mind—not the heart certainly.
My mistress, do you sail with the King?

ADELAISE *does not answer and* ALBINI *comes in.* PETRONILLA
withdraws.

ALBINI: My majesty . . . (*With intense concern.*)

ADELAISE: Gwylliam, I cannot talk with you now.

ALBINI: But they say you may sail.

ADELAISE: I *am* considering it. Go now.
                                          (*Turning away.*)

ALBINI (*urgently*): You know that my obedience is all to you.
But there is something I must say now—
and in disobedience of the King.

ADELAISE: The King requires fidelity.

ALBINI: And you? Did you know
that the King intends, while in Normandy,
to muster what support he can
for his daughter's succession to the throne? Did
                                                you?
And in doing so does he not brand you
in the eyes of the world as a woman who . . .

ADELAISE (*interrupting him*): My Lord Albini!—
if my husband withheld this information from me,
he did so to avoid a pain which you . . .

ALBINI (*interrupting*): . . . No, no!
I meant no such hurt. But, oh . . .

ADELAISE: Guard your tongue.
                                          Bishop Roger.

BISHOP ROGER *comes in.*

ALBINI (*openly*): The Bishop of Salisbury knows as well as I
that she rules her father. And if she has her way
we are sailing towards chaos!

ROGER: Aye, indeed, that is true.

ADELAISE (*with tense dignity*): Salisbury,
it has been agreed between my King and me
that affairs of State . . .

ALBINI (*his anger overcoming him*):
                          Tcha! Affairs of State!
It is simply an affair of state
that your most private sufferings should openly be...

ROGER: Albini! (*Silencing him.*)
                          You speak to the Queen.
I would now speak to her, alone;
and with more respect.

ALBINI: But not more love.

            ALBINI *withdraws.*

ROGER: The young are so passionately personal.
Yet you are young . . .
And what passion prompted him to say,
duty prompts me to repeat:
It would indeed be a disastrous thing,
if when our dearest King should die—
and may God long delay that tragedy—
it would be disastrous for England, and the world
     across the sea,
if that headstrong young woman should become
     Queen.

ADELAISE: Then you, my Lord Bishop, see a way
to avoiding this?

ROGER: Perhaps—if you do.

ADELAISE: My way is in faith but my hope is unsure,
Say what you have to say.   The tide will not wait.

ROGER: Should the King die the crown is not yours:
though, with the grace in you, would that it were so

ADELAISE: I'd not want to succeed my King.

ROGER: No.
Therefore *two* ways lie open to you:—
that the King should be given a son by you;
or that he should have you put away,
in favour of another who could. The latter we know
—and to your glory—the King will not allow.
So in fact there is only one way.

ADELAISE: To bear the King's son.

ROGER: To give the King a son;
or some fruit of your womb,
to stop him turning in despair
towards Maud-Matilda, as his heir.

ADELAISE (*facing him in anger*):
How am I to understand you,
when, being the King's confidant, you can speak
as if it were a matter of choice to me
to bear or not bear the King a son?

ROGER: To *give* the King a son, I did say.
(*Facing her squarely.*)
For, whatever the dear King's portion may be
—and I do not have his confidence now—
I think that it does lie with you
to give or not to give the King a son.

ADELAISE (*turning away*):
I . . . do not understand.

ROGER: Nor may you
understand what I now say
as other than frightening brutality;
yet it's far from brutal.
           Look around you.
On this prolific island it is Spring.
And in you God, in Nature, holds His sway.
Need we break Albini's heart? Need you sail away?
The King returns soon. No, sweet Majesty—
do not turn away from me,
as if I were the Devil. I assure you
that there's much in the sacred past
which would not seem sacred to you;
much purely holy not pure. Purity
is the true prerogative of the Divine,
and the false prerogative of Man.
Ours is utter devotion to Truth
and pure ends. We did not essay
from paradise pure. Will you sail away?

ADELAISE (*desperately*):
> The King has been made happy by me;
> the King requires my fidelity;
> the King will be made as he was because I
> have faith in my King and he in me.

ROGER:
> The King may never be the same again;
> the King in person craves fidelity;
> the King is human but the King is divine;
> and the Kingdom's King craves a son!
> Aye, and the King in person may know as I do
> the conflict in his hot heart. True—
> I would be the Devil were I simply to say,
> " Choose this! " or " that ". But I would be
> much less than Bishop of Salisbury,
> lover of my Land and the Conscience of my King,
> if I did not—with utmost fidelity—
> say now to your young majestic soul,
> " *There is your choice*";
> > > Our destiny—
> of England—of the world across the sea—
> rests now with you.
> > > Do you sail?

ADELAISE *makes no response.*

> Do you sail?

ADELAISE (*helplessly*): Who knows of this?
> Not the Earl of Albini?

ROGER: No. No.

ADELAISE: Not the King?

ROGER: I myself did not know.
> This was bred of the moment, and it shall die
> with the moment—if you choose it so,
> Do you sail with the King?

ADELAISE: He is coming. Delay.

ADELAISE *hurries away to avoid the* KING.

ROGER *intercepts the* KING *and his daughter by his first marriage,*
MAUD-MATILDA.

KING: Later. (*To* MAUD-MATILDA.) The Bishop wants my
ear.

MAUD-M.: But, father . . . father!
I insist that you listen to *me*.

KING: Oh, I should have christened you
Mad-Matilda. All right. Roger!
see that the crew has been examined.
Later . . .

MAUD-M. (*to* ROGER, *who hesitates*): Later.

ROGER *goes, reluctantly.*

KING: I must speak with the Queen too, you know.
What is it, my mad-cap?

MAUD-M.: Is she to come?
I mean the Queen—Adelaise. Does she sail too?

KING: Well, I have not insisted. She may.
I leave all insistence in the family to you.
She has come prepared to sail if necessary—
and I'm made happy by that.

MAUD-M.: And she's prepared to stay if necessary.
Are you made happy by that?
For it makes me furious. I cannot stand
a woman who will not make up her mind.

KING: And I cannot stand a young woman who
would always make up my mind for me.
Now, let the Queen alone.

MAUD-M.: But you wish her to come?

KING (*impatiently*):
I don't particularly want the sea
to come between us. Come.

MAUD-M.: You love her, don't you?

KING: Beyond all doubt. Come now.

MAUD-M.: And does she love you?
Is there any doubt in that?

KING: When we are on the ship and out at sea
        there will be both freedom and time to talk.

MAUD-M.:   But not if she sails with us.

KING (*turning angrily on her*):
        And that's for her—not for you—to say!
        And if your childish jealousy . . .!

MAUD-M.:   . . . No, no!
        I'm sorry. (*Soothing him.*) I'm sorry, peri.
        It wasn't just stupid jealousy.
        You know how I love you, and I must wish that you
        are loved, musn't I? I'm so afraid
        that she's even more of a natural nun
        than mother was.

KING: Little goat!
        she is, in every way but honesty,
        as unlike what your mother was as—
        as that blossom spending itself in the breeze
        is like waxen lilies by a grave
        aping perpetuity.

MAUD-M.:   Then she *must* be barren.

KING: Maud-Matilda! (*Almost speechless.*)
        There are times when I wish that Nature in you
        had not so damnably suddenly
        made up for your mother's dullness! Shut your
                          mouth!!
        This neither becomes taste nor dignity.

MAUD-M.:   Then she won't have you, and I see no dignity in
        that.

KING: By God's Death! Hold your vile tongue!
        Or I'll have it out!
        If there was any alternative to making you my heir
        you'd make me seize upon it now!

MAUD-M. (*coolly*):
        Which means that there isn't and it is as I say—
        there's no hope in her body.
        Well, why don't you deny it?

KING:　　　By Christ in His High Majesty!—
　　　　　I command you to keep silence until we are at sea!
　　　　　And may God in Nature work upon you
　　　　　to make you sea-sick and extend the silence.
　　　　　Silence! ! (*As she'd speak again.*)

The KING *goes off, leaving her pretty satisfied with what she has
made out of this interchange.*

ADELAISE *comes in.*

ADELAISE:　Why did the King go so abruptly?
　　　　　You must not distress your father. He is not well.

MAUD-M.:　It does not suit you to talk to me
　　　　　as if you were my mother. I
　　　　　have buried one husband, and have a second in
　　　　　　　　　　　　　　　　　　view;
　　　　　with sound hopes of being a mother myself.

ADELAISE:　　　　　　For your father's sake,
　　　　　it would not be good for me to despise you. Go.

ALBINI *comes in.*

　　　　　Go to your father.

MAUD-M.:　　　　　I go as I choose. (*Turning to go.*)
　　　　　My Lord Albini, persuade the Queen
　　　　　to stay in England. She would seem to be
　　　　　over-sensitive for Normandy, and me.

MAUD-MATILDA *goes.*

ALBINI:　　I could cut out that tongue.
　　　　　　　　　　　　What will you do?
　　　　　Adelaise—they are waiting. Will you sail?
　　　　　The King is aboard, searching ship.
　　　　　He will not come ashore again.
　　　　　Will you stay in England? Adelaise . . .

ADELAISE:　Gwylliam, I . . .

BISHOP ROGER *hurries in.*

ROGER:　　　　　　The King sends to know
　　　　　if you intend to sail, your Majesty?

ADELAISE *goes without a word.*

ALBINI (*as they both watch her go*):
          She's gone. She's going aboard with her woman.

ROGER: Aye.
          Then she thinks that the peaks of my mitre must be
          the Devil's horns.

ALBINI (*still watching the ship*): What did you say?

ROGER: I said, " God save the Queen! "

ALBINI: What? (*Eyes on ship.*) She's on board. She'll
          sail.

ROGER: The King raises his sceptre. Acknowledge him.

          As they acknowledge the signal, the Horn sounds off.

          What a spread of sail!
          With all its rippling little lions
          gone suddenly tense in the golden sun
          that sail is like a vestment spun
          for some giant hero. God speed the Green Ship
          back again.

ALBINI: She's gone.

ROGER: And what a strange and sad Spring day,
          when all of England's destiny
          stood poised in one person and seemed to be
          dependent on . . . adultery

ALBINI (*turning to him*):
          What do you mean?

ROGER: I mean " God save the Queen! "—
          from a much too fine fidelity.
          And us from chaos. Come. (*Putting his arm round*
                                        GWYLLIAM.)
          Nature, in all her banality,
          shamelessly holds to the old theme—and so do I,
                                        so do I—
          that " young love will find a way ".

                    As they go together.

                         237

ALBINI: Young love?

ROGER: Yes, *young* Albini.

ROGER goes and ALBINI, *with a last look out to sea, follows him almost eagerly.*

END OF ACT II

ACT III

Pyneham Wood—outside Peter Universal's cell—Summer—afternoon —hot.

Before rise of curtain Music is heard from a plaintive stringed instrument.

On rise of curtain PETER UNIVERSAL *is seen sitting in the sun, lazily turning the handle of his " Lyra pagana ", the original of the Hurdy-Gurdy. A resinous wheel turning against the gut makes the sound as he fingers out a tune on the keyboard.*

ALBINI *comes in, cautiously, and weary from travel.* PETER, *becoming aware of him, stops playing.*

PETER: Oh ... (*Looking up, embarrassed.*) My little "wooden lamb " has a strange " bleat ", eh?
I apologise for him; though the fault is in me.
I made him. (*Smiling.*)

ALBINI (*unsmiling*): Brother Peter, have you seen the Queen?

PETER: I'm no believer in apparitions, my Lord.
She's in Normandy.

ALBINI: No, Brother Universal.
She is home.

PETER: In England?

ALBINI: In Arundel.

PETER: Lord bless me! (*Rising.*)
And she promised me that as soon as she got home
she'd cross the valley and come to see
what I'd made of this place. Look at it now!
            (*Going in.*)
No, don't come in! My cell is littered with
                              instruments.

239

ALBINI: Instruments? Oh. (*Looking after him.*)
               How did you come by all these, Brother Universal?

PETER (*coming to the door with some instruments*):
               Loot of my journeyings. I collected them;
               a piece here, a piece there.
               No, not my little " wooden lamb ".

               (*As* ALBINI *picks it up.*)

               I made him myself from an original I saw
               at the School of St. Martial, Limoges.

ALBINI: Why " wooden lamb "?

PETER: Well, you see, (*apologetically*)
               in order to provide the very best gut,
               a little September lamb *did* agree
               to leave life early.
                                The tone, I'm afraid,
               is not worthy of the sacrifice.
               Again the fault's in me. Music is my weakness.
               My old Prior over at Boxgrove would say,
               " Music, my brethren, would seem to be
               Universal ". Ha! Yes . . .
               It wasn't really funny but for him they'd laugh.
               What brings you to the middle of Pyneham Wood?

ALBINI: We are on our way to Winchester.

PETER: By Arundel? With the King?

ALBINI: No, the King goes straight to Winchester
               with Maud-Matilda; from Windsor.

PETER: Oh, and what happened at Windsor?

ALBINI: The King had all the nobility swear
               allegiance to Maud-Matilda.

PETER: No. Then all's as it was?

ALBINI: And more hurtful still.
               So the Queen has come here and is walking alone—
               towards this wood. Wait, Brother.
               When she comes, I wish to speak with her—
               alone.

PETER (*uneasy*): My Lord Gwylliam, it may be
　　　　　that my time of life, the heat of this day,
　　　　　and the known temptations of solitude,
　　　　　make me see temptations where none may be.
　　　　　But, I'd have you know that my life is the Queen's
　　　　　—next to God.

ALBINI:　　　　　　　　And mine, Brother Peter.

PETER:　　And my allegiance is to the King.

ALBINI:　　You talk to the King's Cupbearer.

PETER:　　And who better has opportunity
　　　　　to offer the King a bitter cup?

ALBINI:　　　　　　　　　　You may trust me.

PETER:　　Then you may first trust me.
　　　　　Go back into the wood. Take your beast further in
　　　　　—for I can see him cropping where he'll be seen.
　　　　　And if the Queen—if she comes,
　　　　　should wish to see you,
　　　　　then I shall play a note or two
　　　　　on my " wooden lamb "—as a sign.
　　　　　Then come you out of the wood.

ALBINI:　　　　　　　　And if no music comes?

PETER:　　Then lead your dappled one quietly away
　　　　　and attend her at the castle, openly.

ALBINI:　　Why should I take orders from you?

PETER:　　No reason but Grace and the fact that I
　　　　　once took orders; and have learned to know
　　　　　when music's in order.

ALBINI:　　　　　　　　　I like you.
　　　　　I trust you.

PETER (*smiling*): That's in good order too.

　　AGATHA *and* ADELAISE *are heard laughing, approaching.*

　　ALBINI *slips away.*
　　　　　Woman's laughter! Women's voices. Ah . . .

　　　　　　　　(*Listening off.*)

how strangely good when it's grown so strange?

Eh, but go!

(*Turning.*) Oh, he's gone! Good, good.

PETER *hurries in to prepare for his visitors.*

ADELAISE *and* AGATHA *come in.*

ADELAISE: Ah . . . Agatha, I love . . .
with no qualification in the world at all—
I *love* the woods of England;
and this wood most.

AGATHA: And within the length of this wood do you know
what I have loved most, my lamb?
The echo of your laughter raftered away
up into the high pines.

ADELAISE: Listen!

AGATHA: There is someone in the cell.
He's at home.

ADELAISE: Then let us surprise him.

PETER: Oh!—but you do!

PETER *steps out of the cell.*

Welcome to my reliquary; (*Open-armed.*)
Here stands the relic!

AGATHA: Peter!

ADELAISE: Brother Peter!

As they embrace.

PETER: Oh, my sweet Majesty! *And* Agatha!

ADELAISE: Why? What's the matter with our dress?

As he looks at them so.

PETER: Was Woman as good as this? Oh! . . .
when He had more than finished Man,
then what a glory God began—
in Woman!

AGATHA: How " more than finished " Man?

PETER: The spare rib—the surplus bone.

242

ADELAISE (*laughing*):
　　　　And did God only make a beginning on us?

PETER:　　　Oh, but He's been at it ever since!—
　　　　and may He never leave off!
　　　　　　　　　Come in! Come in!

　　PETER starts ushering them into the cell.

　　　　It's weatherproof now, and the causeway . . .

AGATHA (*going*): . . . The causeway is like a Roman road.

PETER:　　　This Roman!

ADELAISE (*going*): And my path clear of all briar.

　　He follows ADELAISE *and* AGATHA *into the cell.*

　　STUFF trails in with PETRONILLA *in train.*

STUFF (*wearily, subsiding*): Oho! . . .

PETRONILLA: What you said?—to what I said?

STUFF:　　　I said " Oho! "—with a sigh.

PETRONILLA: " Oho " means nothing. It is no reply.

STUFF:　　　Don't ignore the meaning in the sigh.

PETRONILLA: This wood has seen better things between us.

STUFF:　　　Now don't be indelicate—nor maudlin.　(*As she
　　　　　　　　　　　　　　　　　　weeps.*)

PETRONILLA: Oh . . . you are cruel.

　　PETRONILLA goes into the cell, weeping.

　　　　Oho! What folly prompts me to postulate
　　　　cruel reality to a fiction of a girl.

　　The young HORNER comes diffidently in.

HORNER:　　I . . . I . . .

STUFF:　　　　　　　And what prompts you
　　　　to poke your germanic horn
　　　　into my Saxon silence? Eh? Speak up!

HORNER:　　I . . . I've come from the castle, where the King . . .

STUFF:　　　The King? (*Jumping up.*)
　　　　Is the King in the castle?

HORNER: By the causeway now. Yes. They do say
that on the road to Winchester his daughter and he
almost came to blows.

STUFF: Oh, why do they " do say " only " *almost* "!

HORNER: He's calling for you.

STUFF: He'll not call in vain.
Blow: " Quarry in View ".

    STUFF *goes off.*

    The young HORNER *obediently raises the Horn to his lips . . . then
lowers it again.*

HORNER (*shamefaced*): I've still to learn that call.
                  I . . . Master Stuff, will it do if . . . Master Stuff!

    HORNER *hurries after* STUFF.

    PETRONILLA *comes out with* AGATHA, *who sits.*

PETRONILLA: Oh, he's gone.

    PETER *comes out with* ADELAISE *who is holding the " wooden
lamb " and admiring it.*

ADELAISE: This instrument is quite strange to me.

PETER: Ah. (*Taking it from her.*) But *you* must not play it.

ADELAISE: Then you must play it to us. (*Sitting.*)
while we rest and prepare for our walk back.
Agatha, dearest, lend me your lap.
                      (*Lying back in it.*)
Ah, let's pretend we are back again
in the low garden in Louvain.
Sit, Petronilla.
                Play, We're waiting.
We all three love music, don't we?

PETRONILLA: I do.

AGATHA: I do.

ADELAISE: And I.

PETER: Yes, but so do I, and that
is four good reasons against *my* playing.

ADELAISE: Come, modesty!

PETER: But this instrument may have an unusual effect.
It is magical and dare not be played
unless not only he who plays
but the tune and he or, in this case, she
who listens is in harmony.

ADELAISE: You are very mysterious, Brother Peter.

PETER: And may have to remain so. But let us try
to tune " the lamb " to the company.
I must ask a few questions of your Majesty
before I dare play it—with effect. (*Looking off
behind their backs to where* ALBINI *is.*)

AGATHA: Don't answer him. It is a trick.

PETER: Let the Queen judge from the questions:
My lady, which is the higher thing?—
allegiance or trust.

ADELAISE: Allegiance or trust? Why, trust.

PETER: Why?

ADELAISE: The one—allegiance—is something we owe.
The other—trust—is something we give.
One ties the heart to the head, but trust
sends the heart searching.

PETER: This tunes a string. (*Tuning.*)

PETRONILLA: She speaks truth. My Stuff never . . .

AGATHA (*shutting* PETRONILLA *up*): . . . Sh!

PETER: My Lady, which is the better thing?—
compassion or love.

ADELAISE: Oh, Love.

PETER: Why?

ADELAISE: Compassion may bind by pity, but love
liberates, love sets free.

PETER: It tunes a string! but there are three.
My Lady, which is the greater thing?—
love of God or fear of him?

ADELAISE: Love.

PETER: And why?

ADELAISE: Love leaves God free to move as He wills.
     For, whatever fear His movement instills,
     to be moved as He moves is to be
     the instrument of all harmony.

PETER: Ah, this, My Lady, tunes all three.
            Yet,
     to cover an effect which I foresee;
         (*Noting* ALBINI *in forest.*)
     whose love do you covet most in the world?

AGATHA: Ah, don't answer that!

ADELAISE: In the world? Why,
     he who by loving I most would be
     reflecting God's love—in modesty.

PETER: Then let the instrument have effect.

    PETER *plays as over their heads he can see* ALBINI *approaching.*

    *The latter comes in and stands looking down on the unsuspecting
    Queen as the music concludes.*

ADELAISE: It plays strange music.

PETER: It does strange things.

PETRONILLA: Ooh! ! ! (*Suddenly seeing* ALBINI.)

ADELAISE: Gwylliam! (*Rising.*)
     But you were in Windsor.

ALBINI: And you were in Arundel.

PETER: And she was in Normandy; so you see
     the magic of this music! It transports one.

AGATHA: But what does this mean, Peter?

PETER: It means that I
     trust this young man to have something to say
     which is of importance and value to the Queen.
     And as he has trusted me, I trust him
     to respect the privacy of my cell.

ALBINI: Will you hear my message, my Majesty?

ADELAISE: Agatha, do not stir from here.

ADELAISE *goes in with* ALBINI *into the cell.* AGATHA *and* PETER *watch them go in and* PETRONILLA *slips away in search of* STUFF *again.*

AGATHA: Ah, don't they make a lovely pair!

PETER: A womanly observation. Remember the King.
             Come with me and I'll play to you
             where it is cool in under the trees.
             Agatha! (*As the latter is trying to overhear what's
             going on in the cell.*)
             Eavesdropping is a subtler sin
             than Eve's original.

PETER *goes.*

AGATHA *follows him and, as we hear the "Lyra pagana" begin to play again the Curtain falls for the following "fore-curtain" scene. . . .*

SCENE II

On a wood path—immediately after.

STUFF, *now again hot, weary and lost in thought, follows the* HORNER *in.*

HORNER (*stopping*): Master Stuff, (*diffidently*)
                      I was going to say . . .

STUFF: Mother of Magpies!—(*Looking off.*)—It's the King
             on his feet!

HORNER: That's what I was going to say.
                 The KING *comes in.*

KING: Aye, Fool, it's the pedestrian King.
             God's Death! It is warm. Let me lean on you.

As the KING *leans on* STUFF'S *shoulder and mops his brow.*

STUFF: Ah, Majesty should more often lean
             upon pure Folly.

KING: If it were pure.

STUFF (*feeling the weight of the* KING):
>   Might we rest the monarchical weight
>   upon that supposedly stout stump?

KING: Aye, dismiss that stump and let's sit on the other.
Who is he?

STUFF (*to* HORNER): Who are you, stump?

HORNER (*diffidently*): My . . . my father . . .

STUFF: He's his father.

KING: Then dismiss them both. I like the look of neither.
(*Laughing.*) Stuff, you lighten my heart and . . .
Well?

As the young HORNER *comes forward.*

HORNER: I . . . I was going to say . . .

KING: Well, come to the root of it, stump.

HORNER: My . . . my father blew your horn here.
He died and now I blow it for you.

KING: Your father? Is he dead? I'm sorry
young horn. I liked him. I don't dislike
you. But I do dislike your presence, boy.
It reminds me of my years. Call yourself
off. Go.

As the HORNER *hesitates, confused and then raises his horn.*

STUFF: He said go—not blow.

The HORNER *goes.* STUFF *sits at the* KING's *feet.*

>   Oho! (*Yawning.*)

KING: The horner is dead. The horn lives on.
What did you say?

STUFF: I said, " Oho "
—for on fairly good authority
I am assured it means nothing—and neither do I.

KING: It's a climb from the river. (*Looking off.*)
>   Who rebuilt the causeway?

STUFF: Universal.

KING: And who might Universal be?

STUFF:	A monk who is not particular.
KING:	And the zig-zag path to the edge of this wood?
STUFF:	Universal too.
KING:	And this broad path through it?
STUFF:	Universal.
KING:	Quite a Universal upheaval on the Queen's land, eh?
STUFF:	He has a cell in the heart of the wood. She's with him now.
KING:	Oh. (*Interested.*) A recluse?
STUFF:	Keeps himself to himself.
KING:	Like you? Does she favour him?
STUFF:	Mmmm . . . (*Provocatively.*)
KING:	What's he like?
STUFF:	Mmmm . . . substantial.
KING:	In Faith or figure, Fool?
STUFF:	Faith, fully in both—a bull of a man.
KING:	Oh. Of good stock?
STUFF:	Mmmm . . . A musician too.
KING:	Oh, a man of parts.
STUFF:	Mmmm . . . in parts.
KING:	Is he young?—attractive?
STUFF:	As attractive as the hog is to the sow; as young as Methuselah to the Ancient of Days.
KING:	Oh. Old and ugly?
STUFF:	By God's Death!—it would almost seem that you were disappointed? (*Looking closely at him.*)
KING:	Stuff, (*Looking away.*) Maud-Matilda will never understand England and the English. This is my land. And I love my land this side of the sea.
STUFF:	I love it this side of ecstasy. Look at our burbling river. There's joy.
KING:	Aye—running England's life-blood through the green valley—from chalk to clay;

STUFF: And growing salter all the way.

KING: But England's more than England. It is me,
and the one great deep fidelity
which centres on this symbol. Aye,
and I grow more symbolic every day—
less vital.

STUFF: Not by cubic capacity.

KING: Yes, laugh. But, Stuff, my boy,
you cannot laugh me out of final dread.
For I will soon die. Oh yes. And when I am dead
there will be a gap in affairs into which may flow
the whole wild sea. That's not to be so.
We must keep one faith, and that must be
like a river, with all faiths tributary;
all flowing at some calm point to that pool
where the waters pause and seem to be
unnatural, poised, and held in the lull
between roaring power and serenity;
between human lust and Heaven's will.

STUFF: And you are that deep mill-pool. Aye, true.

KING: Majesty, is the poised power between
the natural stream and the unnatural mill.
And it stands between all and the awful chill
of the moody, unruly, voracious sea.
There's no conception of Majesty
in Maud-Matilda. But Adelaise, she . . . (*stopping,
dreaming.*)

STUFF: She has the conception in her—in every way?
But you, my sceptre? Lost at sea?

KING: Aye, Stuff. But this ship must not go down.
(*Rousing himself.*)
What would make the Queen unfaithful to me?
Why, bells, why surprised?

STUFF: But you told me you loved her—

KING: —And I do.
And would through all infidelity.

STUFF: Love her—as a matter of forgiveness?

KING: As a matter of loving. Love asks no more
           than the occasion to love to capacity.
           What would make her unfaithful to me?

STUFF: Well, not the asking. More's the pity.

KING: No.
           What did you say?

STUFF: We're talking royal breeding, eh?

KING: We're talking breeding. But let it be
           like talking of delicate music, boy.

STUFF: Would the fidelities of this infidelity
           sanction taking when she'll not ask?

KING: No.

STUFF: Not even done with the greatest of delicacy?
           With all art and delicacy?

KING: No.

STUFF: Not even done within a dream—
           robbed of all that's personal;
           made Biblical; made sacred in
           the purest of folly and beyond all offence
           cast upon the great Non-Sense
           of care-less creation?

KING (*turning on him*): By God's Death!—
           whose cause are you pleading? Eh?

STUFF: Pax! Forgive! Don't strike the Fool! (*Rising.*)
           You said you'd never strike the Fool!

KING: I'd not have a little natural Fool
           grow up into my crown.

STUFF: No?
           It was folly to hope so. But a royal Fool!
           There might be a way to make Majesty universal.

KING: Yes. (*Rising also.*) I'd forgotten your Universal.
           Come, you're forgiven, Fool.
           I love you, and I love you to love her—
           short of folly.

STUFF: Oh, how can I
come short of that?

KING (*as they move on*): Lend me your arm.
           Have you any idea, my bells,
           how young Albini is disposed to the Queen?
           What shocks you there? (*As* STUFF *stops in his
tracks.*)
           His father was once taken for my twin.
           Oh, I know his eyes are on the Queen of France,
           but his heart—how does it affect my Queen?

STUFF: Will you accept my reply as mere matter of state?—
           as nothing to you or me personally?

KING: Why?

STUFF: He loves her.

KING: God's Death, so do all who see her!

STUFF: Ah, but he adores the ground she walks on.

KING: The ground's mine. That's royal trespass, eh?
                                   (*Lightly.*)
           Does she favour him? (*Uneasily.*) Need we be so
                                   solemn?

STUFF: Yes. Yes, she does.

KING: She does? Oh.
           And to what degree? The truth, Fool.

STUFF: To the farthest edge of fidelity.

KING: But not over it? Not over it!
           By God's Death, Stuff, not over it!

STUFF: No. Yet was not that the hope?
           But the hope had to hope for less jealousy.

KING: It's like the ivy holding up a tree
           long after the whole wood's dead. So ...
           She loves him. Is that so?
           She loves him? Is that so?
           Answer me! !

STUFF (*fearful of the consequences*):

>In her own youthful phrasing the phrase might be—
>when said to a mirror after supper . . . But oh,
>the phrase from her lips should mean nothing to you
>and the wise world, my . . .

KING: What phrase!
>What phrase?

STUFF: " I love you ".
>I mean she loves him.

KING: She loves him?

STUFF: No.

KING: But you said so!

STUFF: I said *she* said so.
>And there's a great difference, as you know.
>Oh, don't delegate meaning to innocence. Hold!
>Hold to your own. You know. You know!

KING: Lead me to this holy heart of her wood;
>I'm in a mood to make the Faith-full Queen
>less faithful. Who's that? Fetch her!

As PETRONILLA *comes in, gasps at seeing the* KING, *and turns to fly.*

STUFF *grabs her before she can escape.*

STUFF: She's fetched!

STUFF *brings* PETRONILLA *before the* KING.

PETRONILLA: But, Stuff, no! It is the Queen. Albini and . . .

KING: What did she say of the Queen? Woman, what did
>   you say?
>Woman, do you hear? What did you say?

STUFF: Come, his Majesty does you credit, my Pet,
>of calling you woman. What did you say?

PETRONILLA: I am faithful to my mistress the Queen. It is right.

STUFF: You are wrong. I think. Who is she with?

PETRONILLA: I am faithful.

KING: To Hell with Fidelity!
               It's a dangerous drug brought into my land
               by you and such foreigners. Walk!
               And keep silence, faithful, or (*Drawing his sword.*)
                                        by God's Death,
               I'll transfix you to a tree. Walk!
               I can hear the pine needles prick in the sun;
               let me hear their hot crackle all the way or . . .
               (*Stopping.*) What's that music? Lead. Lead on!

STUFF, PETRONILLA *and the* KING *go as the music of the next*
scene grows.

SCENE III

Outside Peter's cell—immediately after.

PETER *sits playing.* AGATHA *sits, dreamily by him.* STUFF *comes in*
from behind them as the KING, *sword in hand, comes in with*
PETRONILLA *following.*

AGATHA: Oh . . . (*About to cry out.*)

STUFF *claps his hand over her mouth.*
PETER *stops playing and in the silence the voices from inside the cell*
suddenly ring out, having no sound of music to compete with.

ADELAISE (*off*): Yes, Gwylliam, I know. I know!—

KING (*hushed*): Keep this from me.

Passing sword to STUFF, *as he advances.*

ALBINI (*off*):   And in this might not devotion to the King
                  be quite at odds with the Kingdom's need!
                  and perhaps his desires!

All attention is on the KING *as he stops in his advance.*

(*off*)   I love you as my own life. Does he?
                 Does he?

ADELAISE (*off*): Indeed he does.

ALBINI: Aye, but not in deed.

ADELAISE: Gwylliam!

               The KING *turns away.*

ALBINI: But what shall we do?

KING (*hoarsely, to* PETER): Play . . .

ALBINI: Long for his death?—when you know that I
              love him like a father, and for England's sake
              would have him live another century?

KING: Play.

               As PETER *plays, uncertainly.*

ALBINI: Adelaise, someone must suffer! But must *you*?

KING: Play!
              Give me my sword.

STUFF (*giving it*): Oh, my poor sceptre!

KING: Come, boy. Come, bells. (*Leaning on him.*)
              This is no place for us to be.

    *Turning on the others and almost with ferocity, speaking over the
music.*
              I was not here! This never happened to me!
              Speak of it and you'll hang upon that tree!
              Come, Stuff. Come, simple substance. Come.

    STUFF *helps the* KING *away as the music continues to a conclusion
and the others watch him go.*

    After a moment ALBINI *comes out of the cell.*

ALBINI: Who was that? Who was here?

PETER: The royal fool.

AGATHA (*quickly*): Stuff, the King's fool.
              He quarrelled with Petronilla. They're in love, you
              see.

ALBINI: Oh, I see. Aye, girl, it's a strain.

As PETRONILLA *breaks into genuine tears.*

          God bless you, Brother Peter. I'll rejoin my company
          and ride for Winchester. Not a word of this to the
          King.

PETER: And, (*delaying him*) for the sake of the honour of the
                                       innocent Queen,
          ride South, cross the river by the sea-ford,
          and don't let your arms be seen
          from up in the castle.

ALBINI: I'll ride within the surf till sundown;
          Aye, and maybe into the sea if there's a moon.
                                             (*Bitterly.*)
          Go to the Queen. She's in tears. But not for me.

                 ALBINI *goes.*

PETRONILLA: Oh, what will the poor King do?

AGATHA: Fool! What King?

PETRONILLA (*perplexed*): What King?

PETER: No King came here, Petronilla.

PETRONILLA: Oh . . .
          I am understanding. But it is hard for me.
          It is so hard for the . . .

AGATHA: Sh! . . .

As ADELAISE *appears coming from the cell. She is about to walk
in the direction taken by* STUFF *and the* KING *when the* HORNER
comes in.

HORNER: My Lady . . . I . . . was sent to say . . .
                          (*Thinking hard.*) . . . to say
          that the King called at the Castle. . . . Yes.
          But he has gone on his way, some time ago,
          towards Winchester. He borrowed your bay.
          And there was something else I had to say . . .
          (*Worried.*) . . . but I've forgotten it . . . I'm afraid I
          shall never be as good as my father.

          The HORNER *goes in distress.*

ADELAISE (*turning to* AGATHA): We'll walk further into the wood
today.

Peter, you must teach me to play—
but with different effect.

ADELAISE, AGATHA *and* PETRONILLA *go and* PETER *with his
little " wooden lamb " goes, full of doubt, into his cell.*

SCENE IV

The seashore—by the mouth of the Arun—some weeks later—Autumn.

The KING, *looking older and well wrapped up, comes in leaning on the
arm of* BISHOP ROGER.

ROGER (*talking as they come*):

Well, yes, your Majesty . . .
I do not pretend to approve of your going;
for England can ill spare the Sovereign now,
but there's your Red Ship. And a flat grey sea
lies ahead of her golden prow.
The wind's not so mild as gentle, eh?

KING:

Aye, an ageing wind—an Autumn wind?
Ah, well, my Bishop—my lock and my key—
my Keeper of England—eh?
my dear, dear old Roger—both you and I
are a bit towards the Autumnal too, eh?
(*Turning seaward.*)
But with or without approval I will cross that sea;
and contract the crown to this new-born hope.

ROGER:

All children start in hope. So,
even Maud-Matilda's may.
But my hope had rather been
that she'd worn her second husband down
even before the two had seen
the rudimentary amity
for procreation.

KING (*laughing wryly*): Come . . .
> you must not be bitter, even at her,
> on the day of my departure.

ROGER: No, but please God you do not rest
> your main hope of peace on your daughter's
> > offspring.
> For as long as she lives—and that may well be
> till her son is reduced to mere " Yes " and " No "—
> so long as she lives, he'll not rule—
> nor will you be much encouraged to live.

KING: Oh, this is all the greyness of the day.
> And my main hope is not Maud-Matilda's son;
> yet, see that the Queen—whom I leave with you—
> believes that it is. See she does. No,
> you're not to ask why. And see, also,
> that those around you believe that the poor Queen
> > and I
> have cause for new hope—in Nature. It's not so.
> But that is only for you to know.
> Give others hope.

ROGER: And I'm not to ask why?

KING: Not as I think you know it and are, towards me,
> compassionate. I go now because
> I lack the regal dignity
> to be quite inhuman. Do you see?
> Endurance, where the heart must stay,
> abhors heartache. Do you see?
> The authority I give you is England's need.
> Never speak of this again.
> The subject was Fidelity.
> They have a month, or so—or so.
> I have no wish that Albini should die
> thereafter.

ROGER (*searching for more certain mandate*): Thereafter?

KING: So, see that he is secret, you see.
> Pray you—for bitterness absolves me—
> pray you for a son. No, Albini's not to die.

His father is in Heaven. We had hoped to meet.
                                          (*Smiling.*)
And I have years of leniency
to recover from severity.
He's not to die for it.

ROGER: It would be the safer thing.
            But all clemency is of the King.
            And Oh, long live this, my present King—(*Going
                                          on his knees.*)
            for England's sake—for God's sake—for mine.
            Come back soon.

KING: Rise. I deserve no such tears.
            The day must keep calm. Stop the flow.
            Come, Roger. It's the ebb. The ship's trim.
            And Stuff—will you take care of him?
            He and I are rather fallen out—
            over the unspeakable thing.
            Make cause to call me back soon. You see?
            Albini! (*Calling off.*)
            (*To* ROGER.) See to the ship.
            I'll speak to him—and then to her,
            and say something to cut her away;
            for she may yet, like the miseltoe, cling.
            Then the tree's dead indeed—and the hope. Go.
            Yes, young Albini. I *did* call you.

                As ALBINI *comes forward and* ROGER *goes.*

ALBINI (*uncomfortably, as the* KING *looks at him in silence*):
            What is it, sir?

KING: Well . . . (*Looking long at him.*) . . .
            It was God made you attractive; and your father
                                          too.
            I've no cause to quarrel with either, eh?
            I have called you, Gwylliam, to say goodbye—
            Oh, as an old man's precaution on crossing the
                                          sea.
            I hope to be not more than a month away—
            a month or so . . .

S   259

ALBINI (*avoiding his eyes*): May God speed home your Majesty!
       Do you doubt my words, that you smile so?

KING: No, no. (*Searching for a way to say what he would.*)
       I think you mean what you say. I think you do.
       For like your father, who was a veritable twin to me
       you have been very faithful—too faithful, eh?
       For fidelity is folly stretched to that extent
       where " devotion to the King in person may be
       at odds with the kingdom's needs ", eh?
       And we—we must all—even I—
       serve the Kingdom's need. You see?

ALBINI (*uncertainly*): The Kingdom's need?

KING: *The Queen and you* . . .
       will be much in my thoughts. *The Queen and you,*
       are of an age and generation which I
       may not fully understand. *The Queen and you,*
       by your natural gifts may—more than I—
       influence posterity. (*Getting agitated.*)
       For you have a gift and so has she,
       to satisfy the Kingdom's need.
       You have that gift, but may the Lord curse you
       if you linger in it, or if you
       covet my majesty—that is of her;
       or betray my trust—that is of me.
       Well, there's a deal of salt water not in the sea
       on this grey day, Gwylliam my boy.
       Dry up your wide eyes, and know this:
       that we shall love you—*the Queen and I*—
       thereafter.
               Send the Queen to me . . .
                           No! . . .
               As he would kiss the KING'S *hand.*
       If I withhold my hand from your kiss,
       it is not lack of love. It is the excess.
       Send her to me.

ALBINI: Oh, believe, that in all things I serve you,
       my dear more than father . . . my . . .

KING (*violently*):
        but in one thing serve God alone!—or I! ! !... Ah!
        Swaying and holding his head.
        My head ...

ALBINI: Help! The King! (*Supporting him.*) The King!

ADELAISE *hurries in, followed by* ROGER *and others.*

ADELAISE: What is it?

ALBINI: He swayed and would have fallen down.

ADELAISE: Give me his arm.

KING: Adelaise! (*Calling out.*) Ah ... You are there.
        Your arm. I can walk. (*Impatiently.*) I can walk!
        Send these funereal faces away. Send these gaping
        fools away! Salisbury! Send them away.

ROGER (*herding them off*): Come, my friends.
        (*Turning to* KING.) Your ship stands ready.
        The tide's full.

KING: I know my tide. I know my time.

ROGER *goes, leaving* ADELAISE *and* HENRY *all alone.*

        Now, my love ... this farewell ...
        It is temporary ... temporary.

ADELAISE: You are not well.
        You must not sail now.

KING: Stuff and his nonsense! I must. I will.

ADELAISE: Then I shall sail with you.

KING: No—(*Alarmed.*)—that you must not.

ADELAISE: But why not? Surely you need my care?

KING: No, my Queen, (*Deliberately.*) that is where you err.
        Care and tenderness can, you see,
        quite cripple the heart. I must be strong.
        I must be about ... what was to be
        my son's business.
                     Care less for me.

ADELAISE: But Maud-Matilda cares not at all.

KING: Then I'll care for myself; and eat no fish. (*Smiling.*)

ADELAISE: No. I *cannot* stay here when you——

KING: Adelaise!—(*Silencing her.*)
               I have, I think, until today,
               commanded you in nothing. You will stay.

ADELAISE: But why?

KING: To avoid greater hurt. (*Then again deliberately.*)
                              I am to go
               to see the child: Maud-Matilda's boy.
               She says the child is like me;
               but I am sure I gave her no authority
               to call him by my name. That was to be
               for another.
                                        But, there, there!
               The fault is in me.

ADELAISE: And still the blame attaches to me;
               and the accusations—But when you are near——

KING: Near or far!—(*Passionately.*)—I'll cross the sea
               and cut into pieces the woman or man
               who calls you—(*Stopping himself.*)—

ADELAISE: Barren. (*Desolately.*) Yes—it could be.

KING: Oh, my love!
                    Almost forsaking his resolution.

ADELAISE: Don't—Don't leave me here. (*Clinging to him.*)
          ROGER *comes in at the back and* HENRY *sees him.*

KING: You must not cling to the dying tree;
               or all life will ebb, down and away
               and out at root. Trust the sea. (*Turning.*)
               Sound my horn!

ADELAISE (*weeping*): Don't forsake me!

KING (*tearing himself away*): Sound my horn; (*Going.*)
               Prepare to cast away!
                    The KING *goes.*
          (*Off.*): Sound my horn! . . .
                    Horn sounds off.

As ADELAISE *raises her head,* AGATHA *runs in and to her.*

As they both watch the ship go ALBINI *joins* ROGER.

They acknowledge a salute from the ship and turn to see if ADELAISE *will make any signal in response. She does not.*

STUFF *runs in and to* ADELAISE.

STUFF: He's gone without me, the royal fool!
          Why, what has he done to you?

ADELAISE *turns and goes, abruptly, followed by* AGATHA.

ROGER *and* ALBINI, *not knowing if they both share the same frightening confidence, go together.*

STUFF *stares forlornly out to sea.*

Oh, take care. Take care. And come back!

The horn at sea, distant.

ACT CURTAIN

ACT IV

Scene I

The King's Solar—Arundel—Winter—morning—bright—cold.

Some cold light fingering through the window hangings falls on the figure of
Adelaise, *asleep. She is like a stone figure on a tomb, the clothes cast
from her ; the King's great sword within reach.*

Agatha *comes from behind the screen with clothing for Adelaise, and
then with a bowl of fresh water.*

Agatha: Wake up, my pale one!

Agatha *draws the window-hangings to let light and air into the
room.*

Wake up! You've slept late.

Adelaise: Oh . . . (*Turning to light.*)
Oh, when it seems impossible to sink to sleep,
then sleep ebbs and, going, drowns me.
All through the night I lay awake
till I heard . . . yes, I heard the day break.

Agatha: *Saw* the day break.

Adelaise (*not stirring*): No.
It started with a caw and a caw
of single rooks; till the cawings grew
into one great mass of raucous sound.
I think, at that time, they must have been—
in the sight of the first rays of the sun—
like a feather-foliage to the trees:
like some dreadful Summer when all the leaves
grew in black, instead of green.
Then suddenly, hard on the ringing earth,
I heard—and they heard—hooves below;
and the mass of black sound rose up and grew,

264

till like surf on shingle, deafening me,
it roared, and rustled, and was sucked away,
out into the minor sounds of the day:
that ocean of little indicative sounds—
greenfinches grousing, cold cattle, the wind
fingering a leaf Autumn left behind,
and then . . . sleep . . . and then . . .

AGATHA (*briskly*): Then the bright day; Rise!
There's not a rook in the scrubbed sky—
except one for sorrow *and* two for joy,
flapping across the river flats.

> *Coming from the window and kissing her.*

And the hooves you heard, I dare say,
came from your ever-devoted Albini—
I mean—I hope—from his horse,
as he came in from the hunt. Rise.

ADELAISE: Does he not sleep either?

AGATHA: As for that I don't know.
But a wild boar died around break of day.
And it's as sweet a Winter morning moving toward Spring
as you ever saw in England.

ADELAISE: Or across the sea?

AGATHA (*choosing to ignore this*):
There's a sea of linen on your floor.
Rise I say.

ADELAISE: Let the covers lie.

AGATHA: Then, rise.

ADELAISE: No.

AGATHA: Adelaise! (*As though to a naughty child.*)
You cannot lie uncovered. You're like stone, child!

ADELAISE: Let me be.

AGATHA: Now, (*Sitting by her.*)
you listen to your old crow.
Was is not a strain enough to live as you did,
without living as a nun since he went away?

ADELAISE: A nun is a woman. I wish that I
were a felled tree.

AGATHA: Now *I* am angry!
It is downright wicked of you,
to lie there and brood so! Get up!
Here are your clothes all ready for you,
and there's warmth in the fire and . . . No!—not
                                another word!
Oh, why! Oh, why! (*Going to fire.*) will Petronilla,
always use your fire as her rubbish heap?

ADELAISE (*about to rise*):
Petronilla is not with you this morning.

AGATHA: No. Sick again.

ADELAISE (*stopping*): What makes her sick, Agatha?

AGATHA: Oh, it's no physical sickness that!
Dear Master Stuff will craze the poor girl
with poetic conceptions, and Poetry and she . . .
well perhaps it's as well,
or a simpler conception might make her . . . Oh . . .
(*Stopping and going to* ADELAISE.)
Forgive Agatha's foolish old tongue.

ADELAISE (*lying listlessly again*):
Do you also—do you also think . . .
that I am . . . barren?

AGATHA: I refuse to talk that nonsense with you.
Now get up. You can't lie there all day.
Don't you ever intend to rise.

ADELAISE (*with mounting emotion*): No.
I don't ever want to rise again, Agatha.
I never want to rise again.
I want to lie still in this stony room,
until all my limbs become
like the limbs of an effigy on a tomb
of some dead Queen—sterile, stone,
without passion . . .

AGATHA: No, no, my white one!

ADELAISE: Without passion! Ah . . . (*Breaking down.*) Christ
                                                in Majesty!
               —the passion that has lain in me!
               dammed up, encircled and kept from the sea
               of all my wild longings! Oh, Agatha,
               such longing—such longing in me!
               Were all the long trees which stretch away
               down to the Arun and on to the sea
               all my tall children, I would not then be . . .
               satisfied! (*Weeping.*)
               Oh, Christ in Thy Majesty—
               Help me! Help me!

AGATHA (*taking her in her arms like a child*):
               Oh, my poor baby! My poor royal lamb!

The door hangings open and STUFF *puts his head in.*

STUFF: Ladies!—the good Lord Gwylliam,
               so bad Christians call the man . . .

AGATHA (*screaming at him in anger*): Get out of here! ! !
               Get out, you Fool! ! ! ! . . .

STUFF (*awed*): Lord save us from the Leopard, I shall . . .
               Oh . . . (*Seeing* ADELAISE.) I shall . . .

                    STUFF *withdraws.*

AGATHA: Prying Fool!
               With the King away one would think that *he*
               was master of the castle. Now dry the royal eyes.
               There, there, now! There!
               These shoulders are like frozen snow.

                    As she slips clothes over her.

               Ah, my foolish one, Agatha understands.
               Agatha knows what's at the root of it all.
               And Agatha won't let the wicked King
               destroy her darling.

ADELAISE (*recovering*):   He's not wicked. But Oh,
               why did he go with that word on his lips?—

AGATHA: Barren? Pah! (*Fetching bowl of water.*)
Do you see these arms?—where you once lay?
These same arms will ache one day
with holding your son.

ADELAISE: I am ashamed. Wash my face. I am ashamed
of all this weakness.

AGATHA: If I were you,
I'd be ashamed of my strength up till now.
You should have seen Stuff's face. (*Laughing.*)

ADELAISE: He said something about Gwylliam.

AGATHA (*helping her with her toilet*): Did he? I don't know.
I was so furious. I could have bitten his head off.

ADELAISE: I think he thought you would.
(*Half laughing, half crying.*)
he withdrew it so quickly.
Oh, Agatha, what will I do?

AGATHA: Wash your face as if you meant to.

ADELAISE: Oh, no, Agatha, tell me what to do?

AGATHA: And you'll do it? Not a hope!

ADELAISE: But tell me all the same. Tell me.

AGATHA: My love, if I were you . . .

Timid knock at door.

. . . Oh, who is it now?
Oh, hurry, put this on. It must be your Gwylliam.
(*Calling.*) Wait, my Lord! Wait!

ADELAISE: But neither my hair nor . . .

AGATHA: Hush now.
You look just that amount déshabilée,
as to bring that whiff of night into day
that makes audience an intimacy
for the privileged only. Come in! Come in, my
lord!
. . . Oh . . . (*Dismayed.*)

As STUFF *comes in.*

STUFF: First anger—now dismay.
           But on neither occasion blame me,
           for the intrusion—blame Albini.
           He heard you weep and is beside himself—
           which is where he should be,
           he so enjoys his own company.

AGATHA: The Queen's in no mood for weak wit.

STUFF: The strength of my feelings are such that I
           must escape to weakness. I too heard you cry.
           And I felt the storm.

              As AGATHA *goes on with the Queen's toilet.*

                              Is all calm now?

ADELAISE (*turning to him*):
           You see my eyes dry.

STUFF: I see your eyes.
           If I could advise . . .

AGATHA: No. (*Shortly.*)

STUFF: Then I'll go below; and calm the hounds.

AGATHA: Why the hounds?

STUFF: Well, there's no use trying to calm him.
           He so paces to and fro that the hounds
           think he continues the hunt inside,
           and they stalk back and forth, so—
           like the leopards in the King's zoo
           at Woodstock.

              They laugh as he apes the hounds and ALBINI.

           Aye, laugh!—but there's more than doglike
                                       devotion in me.
           What's the news from where we're all at sea?
           What's the news of the King?

AGATHA: The Queen has no news.

STUFF: Let the Queen say,
           I watch all ships. The fisherfolk say
           " There goes sea-urchin. First I did see
           accrusted with bells! " What news last ship?

ADELAISE: With Maud-Matilda still.

AGATHA: Now go.

STUFF: My news is greener. It says that he
does the dangling upon his knee
with little relish—poor grandpa!
My news says he pines more each day,
in spending the night inventing delay
for next day's sailing.

ADELAISE: What do you want of me?

STUFF: Only my King, my majesty.
For he might never come back at all,
if there is no sufficient fool
to partner you in folly. I want my King.
Oh, I want my Queen too—with a worse want—
but that is forbade me. I want my King.

ADELAISE: This is a sad sort of cruelty.
What would you have me do?

AGATHA: He's a fool, don't ask him.

ADELAISE: Stuff, what should I do?

STUFF: Love with a little " l ".

ADELAISE (*sadly*):   Not even you
dare spell this King with a little " k ".

STUFF: Nor need you, so long as he
loves you with the larger " L ".

ADELAISE: But he doesn't.

STUFF: Oh, yes, he does! Shall I tell you,
how upon a certain Summer day . . .

AGATHA (*apprehensively*):   Stuff, no!

STUFF (*persisting*): How the King found his lady and her young
                                 love
in a cell in Pyneham Wood? And how he
turned and walked through Hell to pray
that heavenly business might send his way
a son and heir?

ADELAISE: No . . .

STUFF: Yes.

ADELAISE: And he walked away?
Then he did not care.

STUFF: On the contrary.
For he loved you, as he said to me,
" beyond all infidelity."
That day, he borrowed one little " l " from Hell
and in its white heat welded the two
to make the large " L " of his love. Adieu,
bring back our King, the only way.
                    STUFF *goes.*

AGATHA: You see . . .
even the King . . .

ADELAISE *turns away to the window.*

ADELAISE (*to self*): He loves me.

AGATHA: What did you say?

ADELAISE (*looking out*):
The air has a strange clarity.
I can see even to the sea today,
and the little white cell of Particulo,
like a white sail set against the grey.
Such a sweet lucidity
cannot last, can it?

AGATHA: No.
One must seize this sun.

                    Knock at door.

                    They both turn.

ADELAISE: Let him in.

                    AGATHA *lets in* ALBINI.

AGATHA (*as she goes*):
Bring her to break her fast soon;
she shows signs of hunger.

                    AGATHA *goes out.*

271

ADELAISE (*coming towards him*):
Good morning, Gwylliam. What is wrong?

ALBINI: Nothing. I could not stay below. But...(*Puzzled.*)
Stuff said you were in great distress.

ADELAISE: I was.

ALBINI: But now ... You seem so calm,
so happy?

ADELAISE: I am.
My father always gave me to understand
that being a woman entitled one
to sudden changes of mood and mind.
I am simply being a woman today.

ALBINI: Being a woman?—today?—simply?

ADELAISE (*turning from his scrutiny*):
Where shall we walk in my woods today?
Where shall we walk while we have this sun?

ALBINI: If, somewhere, like the sun, we may sink to earth
I'll walk to where he sets with you.

ADELAISE: He will not sink—nor, my lord, would I—
because of exhaustion. (*Smiling.*)

ALBINI (*amazed*):   Oh, my majesty!
Be more simple still.

ADELAISE: Where shall we walk?
The choice is yours today.

ALBINI: And the choice is quite open?

ADELAISE: Quite open.

ALBINI: To include all the Queen's territory?

ADELAISE: All of the Queen's territory.

ALBINI: Not excluding the forbidden wood?

ADELAISE: Not excluding Pyneham. No.

ALBINI: Nor the forbidden cell?

ADELAISE: Oh. (*Then recovering.*)
But the cell was only forbidden you
while I was a novice to music. Now—

so Peter my teacher says—
I may play, and not frighten the birds away.

ALBINI: Let it be Pyneham Wood. Do you agree?

ADELAISE: I do.

ALBINI: And in the cell you will play your music to me?
Do you agree?

ADELAISE: I do.

ALBINI: And that we go alone—except for the hounds?
Do you agree to that too?

ADELAISE: I do.

ALBINI (*almost unable to believe it*):
And do you agree that this sounds to the simple
                                   mind
like a wedding avowal?—Do you?

ADELAISE: I do.

ALBINI: Oh God! (*Risking all.*) Even to the slightest
degree, do you love me?

ADELAISE: I do.

He takes her in his arms.

ALBINI: Ah!—this heavenly simplicity!
And Oh, your eyes! My love, your eyes!
Oh, God in Heaven, let's go below
and seem as hungry as we may
the whole interminable length
of the shortest breakfast we can devise.

ADELAISE: But I am hungry. Why do you laugh?

ALBINI: The simplicity! I shall eat only that I
may drink to this simplicity! Come.
Let's not seem suspiciously distant. No.
Not so close neither. Oh . . .
the happy mean of true deceit!
It's so hard to strike! Come!

They go laughing.

And as the scene changes we hear the sound of the sea. It grows.

SCENE II

The sea by the mouth of the Arun—Afternoon of the same day—It is a grey day.

Before rise of curtain we hear the sound of the sea and then the sound of a goat bleating.

On rise of curtain STUFF *comes in, idly throwing pebbles and ruminating.*

STUFF (*turning to goat, off*):
> Sorry, brother ruminant.
> I said sorry, old goat! Far be it from me
> to mock an old he-goat tied by the sea
> to this sad landscape. Aye, scapegoat, Maaah!
> (*Turning away and throwing.*)

A cry of pain off " a stone's throw away ".
> What?
> What's this? Oho . . .

As PARTICULO *comes in rubbing his tonsured skull.*
> What!—penguins so far South?

Turning away to throw again.

PARTICULO: Will you cease throwing stones!

STUFF: I could stop. (*Throwing.*)

PARTICULO: I said, cease! !

STUFF: I said, " stop ". (*About to throw again.*)

PARTICULO: Stop! ! ! !

STUFF: Why?

PARTICULO: I was kneeling at prayer in my cell out there,
when this—this! (*Handling him pebble.*) struck me!

STUFF: Oh. (*Taking pebble.*)
There you have the advantage of me—
something in life has really struck you.
> Anyway—
why is your cell trespassing in our sea?

PARTICULO (*forlornly*): You might ask why the Winter sea
has risen and slowly washed away
all but the rock on which I stand!

STUFF: Yes, I might ask. But not today.
My devotion's to idleness, yet even she
works against me. I throw a pebble out to sea
and I hit an old goat. No, not you:
(*Looking off.*)
that pink-eyed mammal of the slit-eye
and the pale soft nose who so balefully
sniffs the air that he seems to smell
as far back into our history
as the original whiff of Original Sin,
preceding the act. Sit. Sit by me. (*Sitting.*)
Was Eden within scent or sound of the sea?
Or, like Universal, would the universal He
have to be content with an empty shell
and do as I do . . .? . . .

     Producing sea-shell and holding to ear.

                   . . . aurally deduce sea?

PARTICULO: Did you say that Universal's cell is empty?

STUFF: What? Eh? (*Absorbed in what he hears in shell.*)

PARTICULO: Why, is there something wrong with Brother
                         Peter? Eh?

STUFF: Eh? There's something very far wrong!
           Examining shell.

PARTICULO: With Brother Peter?

STUFF: What? No, with Nature!

PARTICULO: What? Why?

STUFF: We listen—
Listen! We hear no waves roar? Right?
For we see the sea as flat as—

    (*Taking the palm of* PARTICULO's *hand.*)

                No, (*Discarding it.*)
not as flat as the palm of your holy hand,

but as calm as lets that cormorant be
crudely mirrored, crudely flying over the sea.
But—I put this empty shell to—this " empty shell "

> (*Putting the shell to* PARTICULO's *ear.*)

and in your holy earhole what do you hear! Eh?

PARTICULO: I see.

STUFF: The new age of miracles is not so near
that ear-trumpets induce sight. You *hear*!
> (*Roaring at him.*)
You hear, Particulo! You hear the roar
of the treacherous ever-tempestuous sea!
And look at it! There's infidelity!
Not enough movement to seduce to sleep
a flea on a seagull! Oh hollow deceit! !

> (*About to hurl shell to ground.*)

PARTICULO: Stay! A sail. (*Pointing to sea.*)

STUFF (*looking*): A sail, turning in our way.
And by the power of oars—with fair power too.
There's a fair garland of foam dropped in the sea
about her bows.

PARTICULO: And did you say that Universal was not in his cell?

STUFF: Do they fear storm? No, not today.

PARTICULO: Oh, his cell is not vacated then?

STUFF: No.
Temporarily full of the sea.
While he's full of good food. That's a fast ship, eh?

PARTICULO: Not fasting either?

STUFF: No.

PARTICULO: To think what I suffer in the face of the sea
for the sake of a hardly attainable Grace,
while he eats and drinks disgracefully and . . .

STUFF (*interrupting*): That's a royal ship! (*Rising.*)
I'll meet it and try to milk it of news
like this other man's goat. Naah!

PARTICULO: It is a King's ship. Look at the prow.

STUFF: Lord God of the Fishes! What if it were he,
and all fell pat so perfectly—
to the day, to the hour, to the . . . Oh
it may be minutes. Particulo,
be a good monk, untie my mare.
She's tethered up by the quay—
No, I don't mean Petronilla. Let her be!
But for the sake of Grace and the Getaway,
be a good goat! (*Dashing off.*) Look out!

The goat bleats as STUFF *disappears.*

PARTICULO: To think that I should embrace the day
when a pagan King's heathen fool so orders me!
What?

Goat off.

Poor goat, the wind's growing cold.
Well, I'll go worship in my wet cell
till the sea washes over me.
For I feel at the end of my tether. What?

Goat off.

Yes, at the end of my tether, brother. Naaah!
Oh . . . it may be that this crack on the skull has . . .
Oh!
And while Peter gorges and . . . Oh! Oh dear!
(*Looking off.*)
The seagulls! The seagulls are into my cell!

PARTICULO *hobbles off.*

The goat bleats, and the sound of the sea fades and gives way to the music of the " Lyra pagana ".

277

SCENE III

Inside the cell in Pyneham Wood—the same afternoon.
Before rise of curtain music of " Lyra pagana ".
On rise of curtain ALBINI *lies by a wood fire, watching* ADELAISE, *who finishes playing the " wooden lamb "—" Lyra pagana " of the previous scenes.*

ADELAISE: Well, my lord? . . . (*And as he says nothing.*)
    Do you agree with my music master, that now
    I shall not scare the birds away?

ALBINI: Well, only little birds.

As she laughs.

    Yet, to me, it was utterly heavenly—
    I did not hear a single note.

ADELAISE: Oh!

ALBINI (*rising and going to her*): I lay,
    and watched your face. How could I be
    conscious in other than sight when I saw
    you, and you looking on me?

Taking the instrument from her and putting it aside.

    The greatest storm could have felled every tree
    in Pyneham Wood, until this cell lay
    amid creaking desolation, and I
    would not have heard one thunderous fall.
    I was drowned in the silence of your eyes.
          Why, what is wrong?

ADELAISE: You must not be so extravagant.
    This happiness is so simple to me—
    except in its acceptance. I do
    find that hard. Be patient. You turned the key?

ALBINI: The wind shakes the door.

ADELAISE: Why, is there a wind?

ALBINI: I hear it brushing the pinetops now.
    It's a sound that is borrowed from the sea.

ADELAISE: The fire was made. Where could Peter be?
            I wonder?

ALBINI: Wonder at nothing today.

ADELAISE: Gathering firewood, I suppose, don't you?

ALBINI: I suppose nothing. I know.

ADELAISE: That he's getting wood? But aren't you surprised
            at the delicacy of the food he has laid out?

ALBINI: No.

ADELAISE: Nor I. I always knew that Peter had a weakness
            for good food. Poor Peter, he professes to . . .
                                              (*Stopping.*)
            What's wrong?

ALBINI: Nothing. Oh, nothing's wrong.
            But I can't let poor Peter be slandered so.
            The food was for us. Yes.
            It was brought from the castle—by Agatha.
            Your music-master does not know it, but he
            is hostage to the Bishop's hospitality.
            Until sun-down he will not return;
            until sun-down, yet I might pray
            that snow would fall and make the way
            impassable for weeks.

ADELAISE: Gwylliam . . .

ALBINI: Yes.
            Surely, my love, you meant it so?

ADELAISE: But this is a consecrated place.

ALBINI: Surely there's consecration in this?

            As she looks up in wonder, he kisses her.

ADELAISE: May not someone come through the wood?

ALBINI: Into the wood and each tied to a neighbouring
                                                    tree
            sit twelve Irish hounds.
                        Yes. It was planned. It had to be.
            Are we not committed to deadly secrecy?
            It must be so.

                            279

ADELAISE: Then, Gwylliam, promise me,
that tomorrow, whatever then I may say,
tomorrow you must let me sail away.

ALBINI: Let you sail away?

ADELAISE: To the King—sail to Normandy.
And you must not try to persuade me to stay;
for if after this you plead with me
I may not be strong enough to go.
And I must. Promise me.

ALBINI: But tomorrow is only hours away.

ADELAISE: Once this circle of dogs is broken through
this will be an eternity away.
This is stolen out of Time. Promise me.

ALBINI: Sometimes you seem a witch, to me,
sometimes an angel. Or can it be
that you are both; and this complexity
is " simply being a woman ".

ADELAISE: Promise me!

ALBINI: I promise. Let me unbind your hair,
so it falls about you like the sea.
" Seaweed brown " I never told you
how I conjured your figure up out of the sea
and the King was . . .

ADELAISE (*stopping him*): . . . No!
We must lose the King now.
Tomorrow I shall remember the King.
For, tomorrow, remember, I sail away.

ALBINI: Today was tomorrow yesterday.
Did you foresee this?

*He embraces her before she can reply, and as the scene fades the
sound of the storm wind grows.*

ACT V

SCENE I

The Solar, the castle—sunset of the same day.

*Before rise of curtain the sound of the wind is heard. First gusts of the
storm wind are filling the room with smoke from the fire.*

On rise of curtain AGATHA *stands by the window ;* ROGER *paces the
room ;* STUFF *sits hunched by the fire.*

ROGER: Fool, can't you do something with that fire?
           We'll all be in tears for the wrong cause.
           Woman, it's that open window which blows
           all the smoke back about the room.

STUFF: I can't stop storm.

AGATHA: I can't reason with the wind.

ROGER: Yes, but the sun has gone in.
           There's not enough light to see them come.

AGATHA: I saw Peter go, lurching into the wood,
           his cloak like smoke about him;
           the wine and the wind confusing him.

ROGER: The threat of storm will bring them in
           long before he gets to them.
           And he knows nothing. He'll give them no word.
           What did you say? Have you seen them?

AGATHA (*still looking down and out*): No.
           There's no living movement—just the old sun
           narrowing down all his spread of wet gold,
           and slowly dragging his glory away
           behind the restless trees. But out to sea
           the storm is coming.

281

ROGER: And over the sea
          more than the natural storm will be
          approaching our shores. She would know—
          Maud-Matilda—much before we knew
          And now with her son . . . (*Coughing*.)
          Come from there, woman! What is it now?

AGATHA: There is someone, weeping, mounting the stair.

          They all turn and wait as PETRONILLA *comes in*.

STUFF: Oh. Only the Fool's folly.

ROGER (*to* AGATHA): Woman, did not I
          command you to tell no other?

AGATHA: I've not told her.

ROGER: Then why is she weeping?

STUFF: Oh, habit! Habit.

AGATHA: What are you weeping for, child?

PETRONILLA: He is so cruel. And I am so tired.
          I walk all the way back from the sea.
          because he rides off without me;
          and nobody seriously takes me
          when I ask to be mounted. (*Weeping*.)

STUFF: Oh, the tragic stumbling on comedy! Come . . .

PETRONILLA: Oh, why did I love a Fool so—
          it is so serious!

STUFF: Come, Pet, come sit by me.
          We'll be scorched by the same fire yet.
          I am sorry. I'm sorry for everything.
          Aye and for everyone—even for you.
          For the world I'm sorry. It may yet be
          the grief's universal. I'm sorry, sweet.

ROGER: Hush, Fool!

AGATHA: Hush, girl!

ROGER: Their hounds are in the Hall
          If they both come up—and after they know—

            I shall take Albini with me.
            The Queen—aye, the Queen of England—I'll leave
                                        with you.

            Rise, girl. Stuff, get up!

They all face the door hangings.

ADELAISE *slips in quietly, her hand held through the curtain by* ALBINI *as he takes his farewell.*

ALBINI (*off*):   Goodnight, my love.

ADELAISE: Goodbye, Gwylliam, dear.
            (*As she turns.*) Oh, this smoke! Agatha! (*Calling.*)
            Aga . . . Oh! . . .

As she suddenly sees the waiting figures around her.

ALBINI (*off*):   What is wrong?

ROGER: Call him in.
            ALBINI *comes in, before he can be called.*

ALBINI: What is it? Oh, the fire . . .

He stops and his hand whips to his dagger, then he sees who it is.

STUFF: Come in, the King's Cupbearer.

ADELAISE: You've been weeping, Stuff.

STUFF: The smoke. It quits the flame;
           when the flame quits.

ADELAISE (*frightened*): Agatha . . .

                   Going to her.

ALBINI (*tensely*): What does the Fool mean? Salisbury!

ROGER: Woman, see the Queen seated.

ADELAISE: No.
            For pity's sake tell me. What is wrong?

As he finds great difficulty in saying it.

            (*With great composure.*) Tell me the news of my King.

ROGER: My poor lady—my unfortunate Queen——
            The King is dead.

She stands, silent, motionless. The shock is delayed in effect.

> (*Nervously rambling on to cover the painful silence.*)
> in Normandy—a poisoning—
> by eating that fish which he knew
> must be fatal to him and . . .

ADELAISE (*with an agonised cry*): No! ! ! ! . . .

ADELAISE turns and flies blindly from the room.

AGATHA: Adelaise! Oh, my lamb!

PETRONILLA: Adelaise!

ROGER: Go after her, woman! Albini, stay!
              Albini! (*Restraining him.*) Go after her! (*To women.*)

PETRONILLA: Oh, my poor mistress the Queen!

AGATHA and PETRONILLA rush out after the Queen.

ALBINI (*sinking on a stool by the fire*):
              My God, Salisbury!—What have we done?

ROGER (*urgently*):
              What's done is in the past. There's so much to do.
              Fool, pour the Earl a cup of that mull.

STUFF (*rising*): There's no cup bitter enough for him—or me.

ROGER: Stuff! Where are you going, Fool?

STUFF: To drink the bitter sea.
              To drink the sea and walk across to him.
              I want my King! (*Weeping.*) I want my King!

                    STUFF *goes.*

ROGER: Poor Fool! Listen, Gwylliam:
              at first light I'll ride for Winchester.
              This you must do here. Listen, man!
              I am speaking as the King's Deputy.

ALBINI: Salisbury, for godsake have pity on me.
              I can hear nothing, see nothing, think nothing now.
              It's too sudden a descent.

ROGER: But you must. (*Pressing on.*)

      The sound of the wind growing.

Today's hopes are thrust straight into the past,
like trees in the path of a flood; all—
trunk, root, branch, hope of fruit—do you hear?
The future's on us like a flood-tide, man.
Peace died with him. There won't be one deer
alive in his forests by dawn's dawn.
Peace died with him; but as for her—
she has served England with all her soul.
It now is sufficient duty for you to see
that she sinks into this land's history
without stain. Very soon—Listen, man!—
you will marry.

ALBINI: Marry the Queen?

ROGER: Surely there's little dismay in that?
Marry, be fruitful, and prepare
for that England beyond this storm in which I,
no doubt, shall be broken. And God bless you!

        As he makes to go.

ALBINI: God help me rather.

ROGER (*angrily*):   What do you mean?
Did you not adore her?

ALBINI: Aye, and do.
But until the day I die,
she'll love the King, and him only.

As ROGER *looks at him perplexed,* AGATHA *rushes in.*

AGATHA: I cannot find the Queen! She can't be found.
She rushed through the Hall, but not a soul
has seen her in the bailey. Oh, my lord!
if she's thrown herself from the curtain wall!—
and all the world below like a dark sea—
lashing and lashing! Petronilla!

      As PETRONILLA *comes back in.*

PETRONILLA: Where is the Queen? Where is Stuff? Stuff!

As STUFF *rushes in.*

STUFF: The Queen's in the wood! In the storm!
The Queen's rushed out into the storm!
She ordered that fool to open the gate
and she's walked on out through the wet towers
towards the howling wood!
I was afraid to follow. It's the King's storm!

AGATHA: Oh, she'll perish, poor lamb, out there!

ALBINI: God's Death! Call the Horner!
Give me that cup.

He gulps the cup.

Call the hounds!
I'll drown that porter in his moat!
Unleash my hounds! (*Calling as he goes.*) Rouse the
hunt!
Rouse the hunters! Rouse the hunt!

ALBINI *goes.*

AGATHA *runs to the window, and the hangings billow over her.*

PETRONILLA *comforts* STUFF *and the room fills with smoke and
the lamps go out and the horn is heard off; and* ROGER *goes on his
knees in the dim firelight and smoke.*

ROGER: God in Thy High Majesty!—
through the chaos come upon this land
stir Thy ever-corrective hand
and drive us back upon Your way,
who tried to cleave a false path through
the dark wood! . . .

*Storm drowning all—Horn distant and persisting as the scene
changes.*

SCENE II

Inside the cell in Pyneham Wood—later the same night.

Before rise of curtain we can hear the music of the "Lyra pagana" played through the sounds of the storm.

On rise of curtain PETER *sits in the haze of smoke of his cell playing to keep his courage up. Suddenly he stops and listens fearfully.*

ADELAISE (*off and distant*):
>Peter! Peter Universal! Peter! . . .

PETER (*crossing himself*):
>Protector in Te sperantium Deus,
>sine Quo nihil est validum . . .

>>*He helps himself to a flask by the fire.*

>Come, my little " wooden lamb ",
>it's just the wailing of the wind, eh?
>Well, play the plaintive melody
>to all Nature's polyphony.

PETER *plays but stops again in awe as there is a knocking or scratching on the cell door.*

ADELAISE (*calling outside*):
>Peter! Peter!

PETER *stands terrified as there is the knocking again. He forces himself to go to the door.*

PETER: Protector in Te sperantium . . .

As he loosens the door it is thrust open by the wind.

ADELAISE *stands, drenched and torn and all but naked against the howling night.*

>Ah! ! . . . (PETER *cries out*)

ADELAISE (*as he cowers before this " apparition "*): Peter. Oh, Peter—(*In exhaustion.*)

287

PETER: Oh ... (*In wonder.*) ... my sweet Majesty ... Oh ...

Taking his cloak to her.

Wrap this round your poor body.

Closing door against storm.

Come to the fire. Come. Oh, my lady!

As he puts her by the fire and busies himself with wine there.

ADELAISE: The King is dead, and yet—

PETER: Sip some of this—It is warm spiced wine.
                What drove you through the howling wood to me?
                What did you say?

ADELAISE: The King is dead.

PETER: Jesu Christu! No. (*Awed.*)
                Then will chaos come.

ADELAISE: And I must leave this world, Peter.

PETER: We shall talk of that later—later—

ADELAISE: No.
                For they will set his hounds after me.
                Peter, listen. Near Alost, near Affligham,
                there is the convent to the monastery
                which my father endowed. I must go there.

PETER: My dear child such a thing is to be arrived at only
                in peace of mind;
                or when one has gone beyond one's task here;
                or when the vision has beckoned.

ADELAISE: It has beckoned me.
                Tonight I had a vision. Peter, do you hear?
                I had a vision. You must believe me!

PETER: Yes, yes. (*Soothing her like a sick child.*)

ADELAISE: But this was true!

PETER: Yes? (*Worried.*)
                What vision? Tell me. Where?

ADELAISE: Near here—outside—beneath your oak tree.
                You don't believe me.

PETER: But how can I, child?
Until you tell me. What vision?

ADELAISE: Then you will help me away?

PETER: What vision? Unburden your mind, child.

ADELAISE: Then you will help me to cross the sea?

PETER: What drove you from the castle at all?

ADELAISE: I don't know. I had to fly.

In the light of the fire all focus of attention falls on her face.

I just fled from the castle like a beast pursued;
no aim—no image of hope—was in my mind.
I wanted to fly, from myself. But oh the black
                                   wind!
—the black, dark wind that howled within the
                                   wood
was like enormous music to me. I ran.
It hurled my drenching body from tree to tree—
from trunk to streaming trunk. I could just see
the great grey beeches; and I felt the leaves
swirled about me, sucked from the whistling
                                   ground
and tossed to where the rooks in black despair
clung between hushed heaven and screaming air,
in all their brittle twig-world. I could hear
them adding all their cackle to the sound
of all that rushed between the sky and ground
and like flood-wrack brushed and battered me on.
And down and down that slippery slope of leaves
I went from groaning tree to tree until,
I fell across the fork of some twin trunk.
And there, in first exhaustion, unable to see,
I felt, in terror, the first beast breathe on me.

PETER: The first beast? (*Awed.*)
Through what nightmare world is this you have
                                   come?

What beast?

ADELAISE: At first I dared not know.
But through the leaves plastered over my hand,
my fingers felt up, found the horn, the hide,
for it was a panic-stricken hind.

PETER: A deer?

ADELAISE: It crushed my foot under its spurting hoof.
I cried with pain as it cried out with fear,
and shattered a horn against some mammoth trunk.
Then between the trees it reeled away
into the heaving dark and driving rain;
and on its splintered horns there flapped away
so much of my cloak that all the rain seemed then
to beat on my skin.

PETER: Poor child!

ADELAISE: I was lost. I was no longer I.
Yet in that utterly cruel impersonal wood
where all the trees were similar, it seemed to me
that I had a vision of this one great oak tree
which stands outside your cell.

PETER: Was this then the vision?

ADELAISE: No, no. No, I stumbled on.
And, somehow over the meadow flats I came—
through all that wilderness of slime and thorn
until I found the causeway.
                  You must believe me.

PETER: The causeway is under the flood, surely?

ADELAISE: Yes.
And as I walked out on to the flooded moss
and the slime from my feet was sloughed and washed
    away
downstream, seawards, there in the water I saw
these monstrous sea-bulls kept back from the sea
by the bar of the causeway.

PETER: Sea-bulls?

ADELAISE: Oh, each " bull "
was just the hump of the waves that seemed to be

butting and buffeting at the obstructing stones.
Each would tremble the stones then writhe and
                                 throw
the water back as foam-flecks. Then I saw
the great gap in the causeway. It seemed that I
must turn back. Yet as I stood still,
hesitating, one of the black waves gave
one monstrous butt; and a smooth chill wave
rose up my legs; all the soft moss moved;
the boulder beneath rolled over once, and I,
like Europa lost, was washed and swept away
on the black backs of the waves.

PETER: But the vision?

ADELAISE: Not yet. Not yet.
I reached the far bank and how long I lay I don't
                                 know,
But when I raised my eyes I could just see
the half-moon measuring all the speed of the sky
in flying cloud-wrack.
                  Rain stopped, and then a new
sound of the night came to my ears. There it is now!
The wind's whine, hushed and held and brushed
                                 away
in the minute millions of needles that toss and sway
among the pine-tops.
                  I entered this dark wood.
And though it was exhaustion made me crawl,
no otherwise could I have made my way
among the low, dead branches.
                       Crawling so,
I met the third beast.

PETER: Oh, child, and what was that?

ADELAISE: Perhaps it was a wolf—perhaps a bear—
I know that it had claws. It tried to tear
at my numb flesh, and so I cowered and grew
quite powerless to move. It sniffed at me.
And then it reared its muzzle up and it threw
a cry up into the face of the cruising moon

whose echoes died and died yet dying grew
other cries more distant, till about me
the whole wood howled!
> Then came the great wind,
and, in one cleansing gust, it seemed to blow
the whole wood clear of all the animal sound.
The beast was gone. I came upon clear ground.
And then it happened.

PETER: What happened?

ADELAISE: I met the King.

PETER: But . . . Yes, my child, which King?

ADELAISE: Why, Henry of England. I met my husband the
King.

PETER: Oh, my poor child!

ADELAISE: But this you must believe!—
that I met the King and that he spoke to me.
He spoke to me!

PETER: Yes, of course. What did he say?

ADELAISE: Soundlessly he came along the ride.
The wind was South and West and so it blew
soft clouds across the moon's face and these threw
a sort of moving moonmist which with him
moved, making his figure seem to swim
rather than walk. I clutched at a resinous tree;
even it moved; I felt that I must swoon.
But then he spoke with such serenity—
he spoke to me.

PETER: Yes? And what did he say?

ADELAISE: It was I spoke first, " I love you ". He simply
> smiled,
nodded his head and gently turned to say,
" We must make trust, then love will have its day "
" Where have you come from? " I cried and,
> " Where will you be? "

> " From him who rules the earth and rules the sky.
> I only rule the sea," he said, " where I
> must breed succession."
> > And then the music grew.

PETER: It would be I—playing my " wooden lamb ".

ADELAISE: Yet he was there. And as he went I called,
" What shall I do? " And again he sighed,
" Make trust." " But how? " I cried;
and faintly it came, " By bettering the sea.
Be both the tide and he who sails away."
What does that mean?
" Be both the seasons passing and the tree.
Make trust by trusting. Do not try to be
faithful without faith." That I see.

PETER: Much of this was in the words I sang:
much in the song; and I had taught it you.

ADELAISE (*with desperate insistence*):
But his final words were never in any song.
And *his* voice spoke them, *his* lips moved to say,
" Make trust, let love, keep faith,
> > and sail away."

PETER: Listen!

They both listen in silence.

ADELAISE: The hounds.

PETER: Yes, the hounds are in the wood.

ADELAISE (*rising excitedly*): Then they are coming for me.
You must help. You must believe me, Peter, they
would never believe. I must sail away.

PETER: Yes, it may be so.

ADELAISE: And you will help? You will help?

PETER: Yes, my child, perhaps it is best so.

ADELAISE: Why do you say it in that way? Oh . . .
You believe I am mad. They will all think so.
Peter, you're not to trick me. Peter, promise me!—
Promise me upon the cross at your breast . . .

PETER: Such oath's taken in distress . . .

ADELAISE: But I swear
                that I will not bind you to an evil thing.
                Peter! Peter! Am I not your Queen?

PETER (*frightened*): What must I do?

ADELAISE: Find a ship. Guide me straight away
                down to the Arun and through the woods to the
                sea.

PETER: But you are sick in body and mind and . . .

ADELAISE: Come.

PETER: And the sea will still be running . . .
                          Sound of horn at distance.

ADELAISE: Put out the lamp.

PETER (*doing so and looking round*): I can never return here.
                Oh, the fire! They'll find the fire.

ADELAISE: He will only find the fire he fed.

PETER: He?
                Oh, God guide us—for on this path to the sea
                I start as one who has already lost the way.

ADELAISE: It will soon be dawn. Come.

ADELAISE *and* PETER *go out into the beginnings of dawn as the
fire smoulders and fades and there is the sound of the King's Horn.*

SCENE III

The sea by the mouth of the Arun—Dawn of the same day—misty.
STUFF *and the* SHIPMASTER *come in.*

STUFF (*as they enter, talking*):
                But I have told you why!

SHIPMASTER: I am sorry, Fool, but I cannot sail.
                And I have told you why. (*Moving to go.*)

STUFF (*hanging on to him*):
>But I have money. I can pay.
>I can pay a full charter. Look!

SHIPMASTER (*turning on him*): Look, Fool,
>life's better terms of charter to me
>than any money. I say I won't sail!

STUFF: Has the storm made cowards of you all?

SHIPMASTER: With the sea against him any man's a fool
>who doesn't fear her.

STUFF: But it's calm now.

SHIPMASTER: Have you seen her? Have you seen the sea this
>morning?

STUFF: I've only seen scared seamen in a mist
>they don't care to have lifted. Look. Look up!
>The storm's blown over. Up above it's blue.

SHIPMASTER (*exasperated*):
>Aye, in the sky, on the land; but *not* on the sea!
>She takes longer to settle, and like me
>she's slow to rouse, but by heaven you—
>you limpet! Leave off, I say!
>>(*Throwing him off.*)
>No shipman in his sanity
>will sail on this tide. Would you drown?

STUFF: Aye, and I'll find one mad enough to know
>that drowning by sorrow's a worse overthrow
>than one wave's buffet and out!

>STUFF *goes and the* SHIPMASTER *calls after him.*

SHIPMASTER: Then out with you!
>and join that mad monk in his cell.
>He's all at sea and defying her too!—
>if he's survived the night—poor Particulo.

ADELAISE *comes in with* PETER *and hangs back in the mist as*
PETER *approaches the* SHIPMASTER.

>(*Turning.*) What? Peter Universal! (*Surprised.*)
>What are you doing down here?

PETER: Bless you, master Harold. Thank heaven it is you.
                For I have a very special favour to ask.

SHIPMASTER: And don't I owe it you? Remember? Eh?
                I'd have been seven years on the bottom of the sea
                when that over-holy pilgrim chose to see
                himself as God's steersman, if you hadn't . . .

PETER (*impatiently interrupting*): Yes, yes.
                But Master Harold I've something urgent to ask.

SHIPMASTER: Ask it. Who's the woman? A nun?

PETER: She has to cross to Normandy.
                It is a matter of great urgency.
                Can you give her ship?

SHIPMASTER: When?

PETER: Now.

SHIPMASTER: But you don't mean this tide?

PETER: I'm afraid I do.

SHIPMASTER: Can't be done, Peter.

PETER: Why not?

SHIPMASTER: Why, because I could not guarantee
                to clear the river's mouth. Look at the sea.
                Look, the mist's clearing.

PETER: Yes. I see.

SHIPMASTER: She's like a blown beast who'd savage me,
                or anyone else, who tries to sail her today.
                But tomorrow, Brother Peter . . .

                        PETER *turns away.*

                Peter, you understand, don't you?

PETER: Yes, I understand.

SHIPMASTER: Then, tell her tomorrow.

ADELAISE: No, Master of the ship—today—now.

                As she comes forward and he sees her face.

SHIPMASTER: Oh ... Brother Peter, why didn't you say?

ADELAISE: It must be now.

PETER: The risk is too great.

ADELAISE: For this it cannot be. We shall sail.

SHIPMASTER: But, my royal lady ...

ADELAISE: ... You must!

SHIPMASTER: But with all the river rains pouring into the sea
the mouth's a death-trap and on either side
it's whirlpools ...

ADELAISE: I will sail! And you will sail with me.
The King commands it!

SHIPMASTER: Brother Peter ... (*Turning for help to him.*)

ADELAISE (*quickly*):   Brother Peter too
is pledged to this.

After a dumb appeal to PETER

SHIPMASTER (*helplessly*):   Then, God help us.
Will you come to the quay? ·

ADELAISE: I shall follow.

SHIPMASTER: And how many go with you?

ADELAISE: Why, none.

SHIPMASTER: None? ... (*More troubled still.*)
I'll bring her close as I can to the quay.
You may have to leap.
Goodbye, Peter.

SHIPMASTER *goes.*

ADELAISE: Peter, goodbye.

PETER: Oh, my lady, my lady ...

As he falls on his knees kissing her hands.

STUFF *comes back in.*

STUFF: Monk!—get off your knees to Woman,
            and for the sake of manly majesty
            use your full holy authority
            to force these . . . (*Stopping.*)
            Universal! Peter . . . Ah . . .

                        Seeing to whom he kneels.

ADELAISE: Oh, Stuff, why have you come here now?

STUFF: But that, lady, is my question to you. Why?

ADELAISE: To sail away.

STUFF: To the King? (*Eagerly.*) To the dead
            King?
            Let me come too. They'll put out for you.

ADELAISE: But I don't sail to the King.

STUFF: Then where will you go?
            Adelaise! . . .

ADELAISE: To Affligham—
            to the convent of that monastery . . .

STUFF: No! ! !
            Oh not that, fool.

PETER: You speak to your Queen!

STUFF: I speak to a woman. I speak to her.
            And I speak with more love than Charity!
            Has she come from her dark wood only to be
            blinded by candlelight in the day?
            Would you escape from Love only to run
            into the ever-loving arms
            of the Ever Unattainable One?
                                No! !
            I'll not let you do that!
            Not now you know the love you know!

PETER: You sacreligious fool! Take your hands from the
                                                        Queen!

                PETER holds STUFF from the Queen.

                            298

STUFF: Let me go!

Sound of Horn distant.

Ah, the Hunt!
Better the Hunt than this! Stay!

PETER: If it is still your will, your Majesty, go.
The ship is by the quay. I'll hold him.

ADELAISE: Oh, Stuff, my dear one
(*Kissing him.*) Seek peace—in trust.

ADELAISE *turns and goes quickly.*

STUFF (*as they watch her go, off*):
Trust! says she—suspicious of Life.
Seek peace—and sows war in me!
Stay on the land, my love! (*Struggling.*)

Sound of Horn nearer.

She's leapt aboard. She'll sail away.
She's left the ground on which she'd grow
for a heaven of no fertility.
She's sailing away. Oh, Adelaise! . . . (*Weeping.*)

PETER (*letting him go*):
Yes—weep. You should be ashamed, Fool.

STUFF: You should be terrified, priest!
For you've sent her to false Heaven—
which is true Hell. She's cast away!

PETER (*going on his knees*):
God protect that ship!

STUFF: God protect that soul!

PETER (*as they both look anxiously off*):
What a turmoil where the river meets the sea.
Surely God will protect her!

STUFF: Why surely? Why?
Has it never crossed your holy mind
that these white horses might be His
that leap at the lip of that wicked ship?
Oh, foolish, frantic little craft

to try to escape His passion which we
may find as cruel as the cold sea.
They're in the mouth of the monster now! Look!
         Look, I say!
Above the spindle of a mast—
above the spindrift and the mist—
the White Ship celestial! See!

PETER: It is only the moon.

STUFF: Only? Ah . . .
don't underestimate the moon!—
hanging like a celestial scimitar
sent to cut through the mists of the sun!
The infidel moon!—Ah, fidelity!
Pray for the moon to stay her hand!

PETER: I pray to the morning star.
For there it shines and the ship is clear!
And there on the ship stands my Queen.

       (*Getting off his knees.*)

But why does she lean up into the shrouds so?
What is she doing?

STUFF: Watching the moon.
Holding a shroud she looks at the moon
like Aphrodite rising from . . . Oh! . . . (*Amazed.*)

    As they both look in awe.

She's in the sea! The Queen's in the sea!

    There is the sound of the Horn, close.

PETER: She'll drown!

STUFF: Then, Amen!
For God is merciful! Snatched from shame
she'll drown! She'll drown . . . She'll . . . No . . .
(*Aghast at the implied loss.*) Oh, no! ! . . .
Adelaise! Adelaise!

  STUFF *rushes off towards the sea, calling:*

         Adelaise! . . .

PETER: Stuff! Come out of the sea! You'll only drown too!
              Stuff! . . . Come back!

ALBINI comes in.

ALBINI: What was that ship? Who was that man? Monk!
              Peter Universal! Where is the Queen?
              Do you hear me? (*Seizing the weeping* PETER.)
              Where is the Queen?

PETER: God forgive me. In the sea!

ALBINI: In the sea.

ALBINI runs, appalled, towards the sea.

The young HORNER *comes in, and* PETER *turns into his arms, weeping.*

PETER: Oh, Boy, boy! The Queen is drowned!

HORNER: Don't cry, Brother Peter. When my father died.
              Oh—(*Stopping.*) Was the Queen on that ship?
              Look! They're making a human chain out into
              the sea. Come, brother. Give me your hand in
              mine. Come.

The HORNER *and* PETER *going off brush past the forlorn and storm-crazed* PARTICULO *who wanders in.*

PARTICULO (*slowly, pathetically*):
              Man is a strange animal—if he is so.
              But if so, woman is more so. Though
              that was no animal.

PETRONILLA comes in.

              What are you?

PETRONILLA: Holy man, have you seen my Stuff?

PARTICULO: I have seen the material woman—the substance
                                         thereof.
              And it is very strange—very strange.

PETRONILLA: I am not understanding.

PARTICULO: Perhaps none is.
not even the most familiar, eh?
But with such a sweet familiarity
she floated into my cell in the sea.
Ah, the stuff of life would seem to be
quite, quite beautiful—unfortunately.
For I consider myself dead. Is this the animal?

The SHIPMASTER *carries in the body of* STUFF.

SHIPMASTER: What? It's the Fool. He's dead.

                Laying him down and recovering his breath.

PETRONILLA: Oh . . .

SHIPMASTER: Have they found the Queen?

                The HORNER *comes in with* PETER.

HORNER: My Lord is bringing her across the rocks.
Is she drowned too?

PETRONILLA: Drowned! Oh no! . . .
Stuff! My Stuff! . . .

            PETRONILLA *weeps over* STUFF.

SHIPMASTER: Poor Fool, if she's saved,
then she was saved by him.
He pushed her from the surf into the cell;
and then I think that each little bell
filled up with water.
                        Let him rest, girl.
Stand aside, Horner.

            ALBINI *carries in* ADELAISE.

HORNER: Oh, My Lord, is she dead?

ALBINI: Run and bring my beast close to the shore!
Run!
                The HORNER *goes.*

SHIPMASTER: Why, will she live, sir?

PETER: Will she live?

302

ALBINI   She will not die.

Laying her down.

PETER: Then God be merciful! For I know that she is mad.

ALBINI: I think it is so.

PETER: Why? Did she speak to you? What did she say?

ALBINI: Nothing that made any sense to me,
              except, " He's dead."

SHIPMASTER: I suppose she meant the Fool.

PETER: She meant the King.
              He's dead, you know.

ALBINI: Yes—in body. But, in majesty——

The HORNER *comes back in.*

HORNER: Your squire is bringing the animal now.

ALBINI *lifts* ADELAISE *in his arms.*

ALBINI: Ride ahead. And have them see
              all the fires are lit in Arundel. (*With desperate
                                              tenderness.*)
              We'll need all the warmth in the world to thaw
              this . . . this . . . (*Looking down at her.*) Horner!
              Blow " The Kill ", as you go,
              to let all in the castle know
              that the hunt is ended.

The HORNER *goes.*

                              And bring the Fool.

ALBINI *carries off* ADELAISE.

The SHIPMASTER *takes up* STUFF *followed by the weeping*
PETRONILLA.

PETER (*seeing* PARTICULO *standing desolate*):
              Come, Brother Particulo. Come with me.
              And I'll find you some warmth away from the sea.

PARTICULO: Is that not the sun. Persistent, eh?
             Always will rise, whatever the day.
             Wilful. Warmth did you say?

                          Horn off.

             But why the horn? Oh, yes . . . I see . . . I see . . .

As the sun comes up PARTICULO *and* PETER *go off together and
the King's horn sounds into the distance.*

FINAL CURTAIN

For the Radio versions of the Three Plays
the casts were as follows:

THE OTHER HEART

CATHERINE DE VAUSELLES	Kathleen Michael
MARTHE	Joan Matheson
FAT MARGOT	Betty Bascomb
FRANÇOIS VILLON	Cyril Cusack
WILLIAM VILLON	John Turnbull
PHILIP SERMOISE	Laidman Browne
COLIN	Malcolm Hayes
RENÉ	Alastair Duncan
THE WOLF	Max Helpmann
SPANIEL	Bryan Bailey
NOAH	Clive Morton
GEMINI	James Hayter
1ST CARPENTER	Wallas Eaton
2ND CARPENTER	Ronald Sidney
CHEVALIER OF THE GUARD	Donald Gray
SERGEANT OF THE GUARD	Eric Lugg
4TH GUARD	John Vere
GAOLER	Manning Wilson

Music composed and directed by John Hotchkis

HÉLOÏSE

HÉLOÏSE	Pamela Brown
ABELARD	Robert Harris
FULBERT	Carleton Hobbs
THÉO	Allan McClelland
HUGO	Lyn Evans
ALBERIC	Howieson Culff
SUPIRO	Esme Percy
BERNARD	Laidman Browne
GEOFFREY	Harry Hutchinson
MADELEINE	Hattie Jacques

Other parts played by Malcom Hayes and
John Turnbull

Music composed by John Hotchkis.

ADELAISE

ADELAISE OF LOUVAIN	Claire Bloom
HENRY I OF ENGLAND	Clive Morton
STUFF, the King's Fool	Patrick Troughton
GWYLLIAM ALBINI, his cupbearer	Denis Cannan
ROGER, Bishop of Salisbury	Philip Leaver
LITTLE AGATHA, daughter of Adelaise	Ysanne Churchman
AGATHA	Grizelda Hervey
PETRONILLA	Jeanette Tregarthen
BROTHER UNIVERSAL	Peter Copley
BROTHER PARTICULO	Dodd Mehan
A SHIPMASTER	Stanley Groome
THE PORTER AT ARUNDEL	Ronald Sidney

Incidental music composed and directed by Norman Demuth.

The Plays produced by
E. J. KING BULL